BURN MY SHADOW

BURN MY SHADOW

by Tyler Knight

Barnacle \ Rare Bird
Los Angeles, Calif.

THIS IS A GENUINE BARNACLE BOOK

A Barnacle Book | Rare Bird Books
453 South Spring Street, Suite 302
Los Angeles, CA 90013
rarebirdbooks.com

FIRST TRADE PAPERBACK ORIGINAL EDITION

Set in Minion Pro
Printed in the United States

Author photo by Robert Sebree

10 9 8 7 6 5 4 3 2 1

Publisher's Cataloging-in-Publication data

Names: Knight, Tyler, author.
Title: Burn my shadow, a selective memory of an X-rated life / Tyler Knight.
Description: First Trade Paperback Original Edition | A Genuine Barnacle Book
| New York, NY; Los Angeles, CA: Rare Bird Books, 2016.
Identifiers: ISBN 978-1-942600-69-5
Subjects: LCSH Knight, Tyler | Motion picture actors and actresses—
United States—Biography. | Pornography—United States—Case studies.
| Pornographic films—History and criticism. BISAC BIOGRAPHY &
AUTOBIOGRAPHY / Entertainment & Performing Arts
Classification: LCC ML420 .K655 2016 | DDC 782.1/4092—dc23

If, then, to meanest mariners, and renegades and castaways, I shall hereafter ascribe high qualities, though dark; weave round them tragic graces; if even the most mournful, perchance the most abased, among them all, shall at times lift himself to the exalted mounts; if I shall touch that workman's arm with some ethereal light; if I shall spread a rainbow over his disastrous set of sun; then against all mortal critics bear me out in it, thou just Spirit of Equality, which hast spread one royal mantle of humanity over all my kind! Bear me out in it, thou great Democratic God! who didst not refuse to the swart convict Bunyan, the pale poetic pearl; Thou who didst clothe with doubly hammered leaves of finest gold, the stumped and paupered arm of old Cervantes; Thou who didst pick up Andrew Jackson from the pebbles; who didst hurl him upon a war horse; who didst thunder him higher than a throne! Thou who, in all thy mighty, earthly marchings, ever cullest Thy selectest champions from the kingly commons; bear me out in it, O God!

—Herman Melville

Moby Dick, **Chapter xxvi "Knights and Squires"**

CONTENTS

FOREWORD

THIS IS A MEMOIR. Anyone endeavoring to write their own narrative is, by definition, an unreliable narrator. Objectivity is impossible without the benefit of distance, and I'm no exception. When it was my intent to manipulate timelines, employ pseudonyms, and change details, it was in the interest of obscuring events and identities while still serving the story. When I did so unintentionally, well, shit happens. Anyone who takes issue with the veracity of this work is free to craft and publish their own account. (Good luck with that!)

My intent with this work is to show the human condition from a different point of view than most are accustomed to. Regardless of whether you're an aboriginal New Guinean, a vascular surgeon, or a line cook, we all know of joy, disappointment, hope. The human condition is the through line which unites all of our narratives and proves that we're all the same. This is the story of how the line runs through me.

—Tyler Knight

BUKKAKE

THE LINE OF MOPES wraps around the warehouse. The line moves. I take a step. These men are not the chiseled studs with forearm-length penises of the porn A-list. They will never get the call to work in a scene for even a mid-tier studio. This is the bukkake line.

I'm in line just like these mopes are, but I used to be a model. Even my shirt, the sample I wore on the runway that the designer let me keep, is proof that I'm different. Mopes lie. One mope brags about getting to fuck the girl for a solid minute before another mope tapped him on the shoulder to swap out. Another man describes performing in a one-on-one scene with a woman trapped by her own porn fame since her first movie, shot on actual film. "We had a connection!"

Mopes lying to each other about porn party invitations at nightclubs whose doormen would never let them past the velvet rope. The line moves. I take a step.

Directors for other bukkake movies and gang bang scenes rove up and down the line handing out business cards. One director poaches talent for a gang bang scene with an overdue pregnant woman. His scenes resemble a school of swarming piranhas stripping a cow to its bones. The scene will shoot close enough to Northridge Hospital in case the woman goes into labor.

The man in line in front of me disappears into the building. I follow.

Inside the processing room, production assistants tag and pack the mopes like cattle. As my eyes adjust to the dark, one of the production assistants foists a ballpoint and a talent release form into my face. I unfold my HIV test print out from a pocket and offer it to the PA, but he has already moved onto the next mope without as much as a glance at it. Next, I hold up my IDs next to my face, flanking my head on either side like mouse ears, and another PA takes a snapshot with a digital camera.

The line moves. I take a step.

I come to a closed door at the far end of the processing room where next PA commands everyone to be quiet in raspy whispers. Filming has started. Through the door, I hear it. Panting...snorting...a kennel of dogs? The door opens. I enter.

I take a step.

Bright and disorienting set lights scream across the room from every direction except the floor and everyone's breath hangs before them in the meat-locker crisp air, and the hairs on hirsute men's legs and forearms spring erect. In this main room, the line has collapsed into a gathering of man asses. They sag. Some cheeks pinch together, wide at the top and pointed at the bottom like inverted triangles. Others hang down, flapping against the backs of legs. Hair covers some. Sores dot another. I strip, find an unoccupied spot on the floor for my clothes and then join the crowd.

The other men also stand naked except for one distinction. They all wear shoes.

The mob packs in deep. Even standing on toes, and then hopping up and down in place, it's impossible to discern its center. The sounds echoing from the center of the crowd resemble a stadium of open-mouthed teens smacking chewing gum. Squishy penises slathered in lubricant and spittle are jerked off in unison. The sound echoes off the walls, punctuated by the moaning of the men at the center of the mob. The sound of…gargling, then coughing and gagging.

I take a step.

The current moves me closer to the front. Still, nothing visible except the other men who have now filled in close around me. The mob squeezes the mopes through its mass. Sentence fragments… A narcoleptic female voice slurring phone-sex platitudes: "…all over my tits…oh, yeah…"

Another woman's voice says, "I'm sooo horny, papi!"

I take a step.

The forest of mopes ahead thins, and the men in this rank try to stroke their penises up to an erection, spitting in hands for lube. The sour air—which has exited the lungs of strangers many times over—coats the back of my throat like secondhand smoke. I take a step.

The mob spits me out to its front. There they are. Two girls built like pagan fertility dolls, resting on their haunches, caked from head-to-toe in the multi-shaded come of every man who gave his offering before me. Drenched baby bibs tied around necks with large, cheerful loops. Faces covered. Hair pasted flat against their skulls. I can distinguish them only by their breast size. The studio lights above them heat the jizz on their foreheads, exciting convection currents of swirling globs of spunk. Both womens' breasts have space on the undersides where the semen has dried to a crust, crackling and flaking when skin expands or contracts.

Now, just a pair of mopes stand between me and the women. An amplified voice screeches through a megaphone, "You two! Snowball! Go! Go! Go!"

The two men take their steps.

A dripping slot parts just above the chin of the woman with the larger breasts. A mouth. She sucks the man in front of her while the woman with the smaller breasts sucks off another. Gooey hands grasp at the men's doughy asses for leverage as the girls shove their respective mope penises into their faces. The first man pumps into the face of the larger-breasted woman and, after moment, convulses, howls, and slathers his load into her mouth and onto her face. She swishes spooze around her mouth and teeth like Listerine. The second man shoots his load into the smaller breasted woman's mouth. Both women gargle their ejaculate in unison as the men step away and into the crowd, which reabsorbs them. The smaller breasted woman leans over and places her head in larger breasted woman's lap, and then opens her mouth like a hungry baby bird. Large Breasts then purses her lips. Come mixed with spittle, phlegm, and more come drips from Large Breasts' mouth in long strings and into Small Breasts' mouth. Small Breasts sits up and kisses Large Breasts. The women pass the gob back and forth into each others' mouths—the mixture growing like a snowball with each pass—all the while fingering themselves. The opaque liquid drizzles down their chins and onto their breasts and the floor.

Eyes, bloodshot and buried in slime, open and lock in on me. The ejaculate queens beckon me over.

The megaphone shrieks, "Go!"

I take a step.

When my foot lands it squishes deep into what feels like warm hair conditioner. My foot sinks and the gelatinous goo oozes hot between my toes. When I lift my foot the sticky floor doesn't want to let it go. Now I understand why the other mopes kept their shoes on.

I stand in front of the girls, penis in hand. Bereft of an erection. Large Breasts scoops spilled seed from the abattoir's kill floor and feeds it to Small Breasts, who sucks her friend's fingers dry. She smiles at me, blowing come bubbles. My stomach flips inside out. My breathing recedes to shallow gasps. My bones feel as though they're sucked out of my legs. I sway.

The megaphone shrieks, "Stop! Half-time show!"

The director's minions—dressed in what appear to be rain coats and fly-fishing boots?—cattle prod their way through the crowd carrying an industrial strength blow dryer. The appliance roars to life and the minions glaze the women's faces with the come like pottery. Fresh-broiled spunk wafts into my nasal cavity. I look around the crowd at the other mopes and see their eyes with nothing behind them. Heavy breathing. Moaning, and the *smack-smack-smack* sound of wet penises flogged in unison.

Hyperventilating, I turn around to leave and push through the crowd. Greasy penises brush against me as I pass.

With my pants in hand, the realization hits that I don't have enough for the bus fare to get myself out of the San Fernando Valley. I take a step. Back into the crowd.

The moaning mass of flesh wraps itself around me once again. I step, wait, and step again until the single-celled organism that is the crowd excretes me out to the front once more.

There is only one woman now. Small Breasts. She rests upside down on the back of her neck and shoulders. Legs apart, speculum prying her vagina open. The mope ahead of me drops his load down the chasm.

My turn.

A minion squirts watery lube into my hand from an industrial-sized drum. Eyes clinched shut, I think of that bank teller with the low-cut blouse who took my six-dollar deposit in loose change with a smile.

My eyes open. Her clamped-open vagina teems with mottled and bubbling spunk, occluded and overflowing. Penis clutched in hand, my eyes roll back and both knees give. I come to in time to break the fall by placing a hand on the floor and into the tide pool of semen.

A wall next to the pile of clothes supports my weight. Semen stuck between the webbing of my fingers tightens into a crust as it dries.

After kicking away a pair of skid-marked underwear to find my socks, I decide to leave them where they lay. I've got one pant leg on before stopping to look at the dried sperm crusting on my feet. I can't find my shirt. Scanning the back of the room, I finally spot it. A mope is using it as a jizz rag. I struggle to keep from weeping, managing just long enough to put on shoes.

As I'm leaving, a minion stops me.

"Don't forget your cash."

He hands me two twenties and a ten, and asks if I can come back next week.

THE WOODPILE

I SHAKE THE BOTTLE. A Viagra tumbles into my fist. I pop the pill and crush it between my molars. Works faster that way. Viagra, Valtrex, Valium…you fuck enough strangers, you're taking a blue pill with a "V" on it. For some performers, it's the trifecta.

Jack, the director, looks like a Hollywood screenwriter who hasn't sold a script since *Terms of Endearment*. We stand knee-to-knee in a makeup room the size of a parking space. This close, I taste the menthols on his breath. The fluorescent lights from the bank of vanity mirrors settle on our skin like a layer of soot.

He says, "You strike me as a man who understands the value of money."

He laughs and flops down onto the futon. A head taller than me when standing, he sinks between the fold of the mattress like a forgotten nickel. Jack stops laughing, looks at me and says, "We're going to have April call you a 'nigger' during the scene!"

"What?... No!"

Jack says, "I know what you're thinking, but it's not racist. It's porn!"

I hear a muffled woman's voice from the other side of the closed door: "Do what you're told, you purple-lipped beast! Obey me!" There is a loud smack and a man wails.

"Goodbye, Jack." I grab my shaving kit from the counter and turn for the door.

"Wait!" He springs to his feet. "Where are you going? I'm paying cash!"

"There is no way I'm letting anyone call me a nigger on camera."

He says, "There's a dozen guys I can call right now that'll do it for half what I'm paying you."

"So call them."

He sighs. "Okay, fine. We won't say 'nigger' in your scene, but how about—"

He pulls out a piece of paper from his shirt pocket and reads:

"—darkie…jigaboo…coon…uh, spade…spook?…jigaboo, ha-ha, I said that already—"

I take the doorknob and twist it.

"Wait!" He pulls a fold of one-hundred-dollar bills from his pocket, peels one off and holds out in the space between us. "I'm sorry."

I snatch the cash from his hand and shove it in my pocket.

The woman on the other side of the door says, "Oh my God! The stereotype is true—you don't eat pussy!"

Jack holds up a fist to give me a pound. "It's all good, playa!"

"Fuck off."

"Sure, sure, ha-ha..." he says. "Go ahead and fill out the paperwork, and I'll have a talk with her. There's only one scene up before yours—April with Jim Crowe, which shouldn't take long."

Jack takes my IDs and my HIV test, then opens door a to leave—

"GET BACK HERE AND FUCK MY WHITE PUSSY!"

Jack steps back in the room and slams the door shut behind him.

I hear her yelling from the set, "NIGGER!"

⇨ ⇨ ⇨

I FOLLOW JACK THROUGH the warehouse. He has long strides and I have to trot to keep up with him. He tosses sentences back to me over his shoulder as we talk.

We pass several set build-outs. A doctor's office with an examination table...a college dorm... He says, "I already spoke to her, and she promised not to say anything offensive—"

We pass an executive's office...a graffiti-covered wall with a waist-high glory hole... We stop at a jail set, where a wild-eyed and disheveled man who could be my cousin sits on the floor. He stands when he sees us.

A rape kit—the ubiquitous plastic box on porn sets that has lube, douche, enemas, condoms that never see the outside of a wrapper, and baby-wipes—sits on the floor. Jack picks it up and hands it to me. He pulls his fold of cash out and shoves some money into Jim's hands and says, "Okay, here you go."

Jim counts the money. He speaks. The rumbling timbre of his voice sends my adrenal screaming. He says, "It's a hundred dollars short."

Jack says, "Do you think you gave a performance worthy of your full rate? Because—"

"Yeah, man, I did my job! I mean…it was kinda hard to concentrate on the pop shot with her beatin' on me and all, but—"

"Immaterial. If a bukkake-line mope can come at will—"

Jim says, "My clothes are torn…ruined!"

"The budget for this movie is inflexible! Every extra dollar has to come from somewhere—"

I slide my hand into my pocket, where the C-note Jack gave me rests. I run my fingers over the paper's crisp texture and caress its folds. Then I stuff it down deeper.

"—and the location owner, who charges me by the hour, doesn't care why you struggled," Jack says. "And neither do I. Time. Is. *Money*—"

"Yeah, but—"

"—and right now, you're jeopardizing our business relationship by wasting more of it!"

Jim's shoulders slump. He shuffles through the door. He never bothers to put his wad of cash in his pocket, so he drops a bill as he walks past us. Jack picks it up and pockets it.

"Ha-ha-ha…"

⇨⇨⇨

APRIL SITS ON A schoolteacher's desk, holding an eraser. Her legs dangle and swing over the edge. She looks like she dove into her mommy's makeup box and then got bored with the game of dress-up and stopped somewhere in the lingerie drawer. The kid looks up at me with big Disney princess eyes and fairy tale blonde hair, smiles, and opens her legs. The bald folds of her pussy peek through the sheer fabric of the panties.

She says, "Hello, mister."

A blackboard looms behind the desk. Columns of chalk-scribbled writing say:

"I will not say nigger in this classroom."

She hops off the desk, and skips to the board. Her butt wiggles as she erases "nigger" from each sentence.

My jaw clenches. I look at Jack. Jack looks at me through the camera's viewfinder. The camera's greedy lens sucks my image through it and splashes my pixilated ghost across his face in pale blue light.

I open my mouth to speak, but her hand tugs my chin so that my face is square with hers. She wraps her arms around my waist and pulls herself into me. We kiss.

⇨ ⇨ ⇨

MELANIE STOPS KISSING ME and the girls laugh and laugh… Eileen slides my backpack off my shoulders… All of us are in the house next door to Eileen's house… Eileen had told me that she had something that she wants to show me so I followed her, Melanie, and Krista into the house… The house, still under construction, has open walls and I wish I wore my jacket and my hat because there's no wall on one side… Just some wood… The floor is cement… I'm sitting on it now… It's cold… Krista says, "It's my turn!" but Eileen pushes Krista out her out of the way because Eileen is a lot bigger than Krista. She is bigger than I am, too.

Eileen says, "Now we're gonna play 'Show us yours and we'll show you ours.'"

"What do I hafta show?"

The girls giggle and laugh and Eileen says, "Your penis."

"What's a 'penis'?"

"Stand up."

I stand up.

"This." She unzips my pants and pulls them down and then she pulls my underwear down, too. She grabs my thing. "This is a penis."

The other girls don't giggle. The clouds hide the sun enough that I can look at it without hurting my eyes, and I can see everyone's breath floating like clouds, but my face feels very hot.

Eileen tells the other girls to pull their pants down but Melanie doesn't. She leaves. Krista doesn't pull her pants down either so Eileen grabs her, but she runs away, too.

Eileen lifts up her skirt. No underwear.

I know I'm not supposed to look but I can't help it… She has hair… A lot of hair.

"Have you ever seen a pussy before?"

I nod.

"Come here."

My thing kinda hurts and I look down and I see that it's standing straight up.

Eileen says, "Wanna touch mine?"

I look over at the front door of the house, nervous about getting in trouble. I shake my head no and Eileen gets mad and pulls her skirt down again…

Footsteps. Krista's mom walks in the house and Eileen starts crying and runs away past her. My pants are still down at my ankles; I try to pull them up. My stomach drops.

She stops in front of me and I strain my neck to see her face… Krista's mom looks kinda like Cinderella… She has yellow hair like Krista and all the daddies in the neighborhood talk real sweet to her. Her perfume smells nice.

SLAP!

My eyes fill with water and I see her all blurry.

She says, "You dirty pervert! I knew something like this would happen the moment you niggers moved in. I'm telling Krista's father, then I'm going to the police so we can get rid of you!"

I still feel her hand on my cheek after they leave.

I hate living out in the country. I hate my new school and the kids. I walk past my house and hide behind a station wagon... The lights are off in the house and my dad's car is gone. It starts to rain. My clothes stick to me and I shiver, so I keep going. I know where I can hide.

Robert answers the door and we walk to his backyard and he opens the woodshed. I sit down on a pile of firewood. It smells like Christmas. Sometimes Robert sits next to me at lunchtime when nobody else will.

I tell him what happened, and what Krista's mom called me and he tells me what a pervert is. We eat some cake.

He asks if sometimes don't I wish was white like everybody else. Like in a cartoon, I feel a safe, tied to my heart and falling off of a cliff... I say, "Yeah."

Somebody bangs on the shed's door.

My dad yells, "Get your ass out here, boy!"

⇨⇨⇨

I OPEN THE BATHROOM door. Jack is there.

"Great job," he says. "April had to go but she wanted to tell you she had fun. We're going to add you to our male talent rotation. What are you doing next Thursday?"

I grab my towel from the shower door and pick up my shaving kit. The money earned from today is already earmarked for bills and it's not going to be enough, but, as Sun Tsu says: "When dealing from a position of weakness, feign strength."

I say, "I'd have to look at my schedule."

We don't speak as we walk through the warehouse. When we get to the front door, Jack hands me my money. Unlike Jim's crumpled wad, he hands me my cash in crisp, neat bills. I count it. It's all there.

I push the door open, pause, and turn to Jack. I say, "How many guys let you call them a nigger?"

He looks down at me and laughs. "All of them."

METTLE

THE BAG SLIDES HEAVY off my shoulder so I heft it back to its place and continue walking through the dark. A dot ahead of me burns red, the night wraps around it. The next time it flares, it's closer; the sweet scent of the kush reaches me a full pace before the man's features fill in around the blunt between his lips.

I recognize him from the smut rags. For years, he's been famous for keeping his spotless shoes on while fucking porn starlets. He wears chains that rattle and slap against his chest with pride as we approach each other on the driveway. I remind myself to pause and chat so I can maintain the subterfuge.

He smiles, but in Los Angeles a smile amongst competitors is never what it means. That's how it works in this business. As a new guy I take what foothold I can get. When someone can't get his dick hard, I get the call that starts with, "How soon can you get here?" He leaves, I take over. A pile of cash gets pushed my way and my *fuck you* stack grows a little bit bigger. I nearly have enough to pay the move-in cost for that apartment—two more scenes will get me there. I could use some of the cash stuffed in my pocket for a room tonight, but I save every cent. Discipline. If my old man taught me one thing it's discipline. Still ringing in my eardrums.

Note to all the other male talent out there: I'm not your friend and if you see me walking up the driveway, you've fucked up. Sure, I joke around with you and laugh at the appropriate moments, confide my throwaway secrets and pretend to listen to yours, but I don't give a damn about you. I want you to fail. I pray to God you blow a scene because, at this early stage in my career, your failure is food filling my gut. I'm sick of not having money, of being homeless. I have zero problems elbowing you out of the way so I can have cash for a place to stay another night.

I see how the upper echelon guys live. They roll up in their flashy cars, brag about the civilian girls that send X-rated Myspace messages or pictures with their pussies spread open. The most famous male talents gets stopped in airports by guys who would offer their girlfriends to be like them. And some do. The top male talent live like gangsta rappers and rock stars. They get piles of cash, upwards of twenty thou a month. For *fucking.*

A grungy, pretty-boy porn star, who thinks Linkin Park's "Crawling" is an anthem, not a warning, took me aside on a set last week to spin tales of Bacchanal parties in Vegas during the *ATM* awards; signing autographs during the day, then diving into a mountain of coke and cunt while the vacationers were long asleep. He told me how he stood with his pants at his ankles while clutching his award, back against the floor-to-ceiling glass window at a height that will kill a man long before he hits the ground, while twins played spit-and-swap on his cock; the lights of the Vegas Strip bursting thermite-neon at his back below.

He says, "If anybody hasta replace me, I'm glad it's you."

This guy, like everyone else, sees me as harmless. A bumbling Colombo type. This allows me to operate with impunity. Sun Tsu would be proud. Gangsta crosses his arms. I mirror him by crossing my arms.

"And when you get to be my level," he says, "soma these bitches gonna fuck wit you. Normally I regulate on a ho, but this was my third scene today an that's why I struggled—"

Right. Whatever makes you feel better.

Gangsta offers me a hit of his blunt. A police cruiser passes nearby so I slink into a shadow, and crush the red embers between my toe and the driveway. Gangsta slows his speech to a drawl and his posture to a slouch. So do I.

He talks and talks. The kush seeps its thick, sticky fingers into my skull, massaging my brain.

He looks down at his fresh-from-the-box shoes that cost more than the average American worker's wages for a week. Fucking *shoes.*

I look down at my shoes. Their uppers look okay but there's cardboard between the inserts and the soles.

"Hey, Travis—"

"Tyler."

"Taylor, come down to the street. Lemme show you the DVD player I put in my car—"

I don't believe this! Motherfucker is stalling. He's trying to cock block me from succeeding even though it's too late for him.

"Some other time," I say. "If I don't get inside and let them know I'm here, they'll just call somebody else." I excuse myself and continue up the driveway.

"Did you see my car is sittin' on DUBs?" he hollers at my back. I don't slow down.

Shit, a phone call and a taxi ride ago I was sitting at a twenty-four-hour Internet cafe where I was going to spend the night, stealing shut-eye by the minutes. Now I'm walking up the driveway to a single-level ranch style house in Panorama City.

I enter the house without knocking. There's talking going on in the back of the house. When I reach for my cell phone to turn the ringer off I see that I missed a call from the director of tomorrow's scene. Assuming today's and tomorrow's scenes go well, I'll have the money I need to get a place of my own. I'll call him back later.

The voices lead me to the kitchen. Food-caked dishes that clog the sink look like they've been there since man first learned to cook with fire. Red cups of stale malt liquor litter the table.

Everybody smokes. The director, the assistant, and the girl, a naked goth chick: all elbows and knees, lips painted red, matching lipstick smudge around the filter of a cigarette on slow burn, dangling between her bony fingers. She sneers, revealing the teeth of a medieval Englishwoman. Meth. The other male talent, I'm told, is on set in the living room. The director's assistant hands me paperwork, takes my IDs, and photographs them.

The director explains the scene.

"Ever done a double penetration before?" he asks.

Nope.

"Once."

The assistant hands my IDs back to me.

"How did it go?"

A cockroach scurries across the wall behind the director's shoulder. I answer the human roach who is going to pay me.

"Okay, I guess…" I say, "the proximity of another dude's balls as he digs in a girl's ass while I'm fucking her pussy isn't my favorite thing to do, but fuck it, it's money, so whatever… As long as there's no sword fighting involved, I'm cool."

The director walks away. Conversation over.

The girl and I play I'll-show-you-mine-if-you-show-me-yours with our STD tests. The other male talent's test sits on the table.

After we show each other our homework, I shoulder my bag and excuse myself to the bathroom so I can freshen up and return the missed call.

⇨ ⇨ ⇨

THERE IS A SINGLE, bare light bulb above, layered with dust, radiating my skin jaundice yellow in its sickly light. Dark and fuzzy spores of mold speckle the walls.

A Smurf-patterned shower curtain hangs outside the tub, sagging on two rings, caked-on soap scum at its tattered bottom.

The tub itself is a primordial tide pool. A corpse could be dissolving in the bottom of the murk for all I know. Calcium deposits on the shower head probably focus the flow into an industrial water-jet beam that can cut steel.

Not going to wash my balls in that thing. May as well return the call.

He answers on the first ring. "Yeah, look man, I'm sorry but I can't use you tomorrow."

I take a breath before speaking. I don't say the first four things to come to mind. "Why?"

There is a pause. "You know I like you and I think you're gonna do well in the business—"

"Get to the point."

"Nadia decided she doesn't want to do interracial."

I suppress a laugh though nothing is funny. I've never heard the term before. Even though it's self-explanatory, I still want him to come out and say it. "What the fuck is 'interracial'?"

"Look, you're black—"

"Really?"

"—so she won't work with you."

I want to set the bag down, but a glance at the mildew-infested floor makes me think the better of it.

I say, "This is ridiculous. Nadia is Asian and there are exactly zero Asian male porn stars… Zero. Every scene she does is interracial, ipso facto."

"That's not the point."

"I've fucked models from all over the world. My race was *never* an issue with women until I got into this business—"

He says, "Photographic evidence."

"'Photographic evidence'? What am I, a fucking yeti?" I reach into the bag, still on my shoulder, and pull out my toiletry kit. "That's the problem, you people believe everybody outside the porn bubble thinks like you do, and you assume that most—"

"Look, I don't make the rules, man—it's whatever the girls and the studio want."

This month's *ATM* magazine has a full-page, one-sheet advertisement of Nadia doing some apocalyptic shit on camera.

I say, "So the act of getting chain ass-fucked by ten guys—all of them coming inside her while dunking her head in a toilet, then blowing shit-and-come bubbles out of her asshole on camera—is okay with the parents at home, as long as it's not nigger cock. Is this correct?"

"Hey man,—"

"Did it ever cross you mind to—gee, I dunno—cast a black girl for a change? Or perhaps one of the four trillion other girls, most of them way hotter than her, who have no 'moral dilemma' doing an interracial porn scene?"

"Well, heh, her morality has a price… She will do the scene, but I'd have to pay her extra money to work with you. It's not in my budget, but if you agree, we can pay her the extra money out of your chec—"

I click the cell shut.

Tyler, the mope.

I take my time brushing my teeth. The routine of grooming before a scene relaxes me. A little. I picture my new girlfriend, Amanda. Then I focus on my objective: money. With tomorrow's scene now canceled I can't afford to fuck up today's scene so I reach into my toiletry kit for my in-case-of-emergency Viagra and put it in my mouth.

I chew the pill. It powders between my molars, tart and citrusy in my mouth, with a twinge like licking a nine-volt battery that fires up my salivary glands. My tongue pries loose the caked-on deposit from my molars. No water. I swallow.

⇨ ⇨ ⇨

IT'S BEEN A LONG time since I've had a good night's sleep, and it's catching up with me. I should be okay once the scene starts, though. I stand off-camera.

Goth Girl and Lance, the other male talent, screw on a sofa with a matted surface that would jump to life under a black light. The sofa looks like you could get pregnant by sitting on it. Lance looks like he just came from a Motel 6 coke binge with Gary Busey.

The scheme is to restart the scene from where they stopped filming with the gangsta-porn star I'm replacing. The footage of him will be edited out as if he never existed. The director is filming three minutes of run-time of the other two before I enter the scene so the editor's job will be easier. I sit on the carpet.

A silent, over-the-shoulder wave from the director is my sixty-second warning: Get ready.

I sit on the carpet and slide off my slacks. I'm halfway through the second leg when I'm on the verge of nodding off, and I lose my sense of time. The motion of the director's hand waving me onto the set pulls me back. I stifle a yawn and kick the pants away, stand, and stumble into the sex with the deftness of a reanimated corpse.

Lance and Goth Girl clear my spot on the sofa. I collapse on the couch. The Viagra has kicked in and Pfizer's finest sloshes through my system. Goth Girl straddles me, spits on her hand, and drips strings of sparkling saliva onto my cock. She rubs my head on her slit and slides herself down on me.

Insertion.

Goth Girl exhales, spraying an aerosol of hot spittle on my cheek. Sour meth-breath. One of my hands grabs her hip, the other coils a fist-full of drenched hair. She coos. I grip. My fingernails find their purchase into her scalp and I yank her head back with a snap and hammer up into her.

Lance towers over us standing on the couch, and shoves his prick into the girl's mouth.

Bouncing.

Sweaty tits slapping together in my face.

Lance dismounts the couch and backhand strokes his dick as though his aim is to rip it off, then positions himself behind the girl.

Double penetration time.

Because I'm on the bottom, my job's to anchor. I stop thrusting into the girl and I pull her down onto me so that her tits squish flush upon my sweat-slicked chest. I'm still in her vagina, her asshole is angled and ready for Lance to penetrate.

He spreads her cheeks, pushes at her sphincter—it gives with a *thuk*—and he's into her rectum. The added weight of him and the girl on top of me steals my breath and sags the sofa like the piss-sponge of a mattress I sometimes sleep on in the flop house. Her vagina tightens as he penetrates and there's a sensation on the underside of my vagina-sheathed dick, like my penis is a tube of toothpaste and Lance's cock is forcing my mass upwards to the nozzle of my head. I steal sips of air. The standard amount of footage needed per sex position: three minutes. I count down.

2:57.

He starts slow. When Lance finds his angle and rhythm I join the action and fuck the girl, also. My enthusiasm for this is no greater than if we mashed both dicks together and rolled on a single condom. The two-finger width of girl-flesh and taint between us is compressed to the point of being moot. Each gliding pass of his dick pumping in her asshole feels as though I'm getting worked by a hardwood massage roller. With an imagination like mine, shutting my eyes to escape this moment and into my mind would be worse, so I stare at a greasy smudge on the wall.

The assistant director stoops low and gets in close with the C-light, broiling my balls. The heat sizzles right up to the edge of discomfort, crosses into pain, then backs off to tolerable and stops as he moves in and backs out with the light to find his range.

2:42.

Lance looks over the girl's shoulder…and is searching for eye contact…with me? He's determined to marry our eyes. My head's range of motion is restricted; wherever I turn he's always in my field of vision. His gaze sears into the side of my face.

My eyes and his eyes dart, climb, and dive in a dogfight for the ages. I evade. He chases. All the while, both of us fucking away at the girl between us.

2:09.

Lance's jaw slackens and his tongue looks like it's breaded in flour and it's draped out the corner of his mouth.

He crashes against Goth Girl's ass in waves. I hold fast. If she moves, one or both of us pops out of our respective meat-holes.

Vaginas are good… It's just me and her…alone.

Lance is not looking at me as much as his eyes seem to focus at a point deep inside of my skull. My clenched jaw grinds my molars to dust.

I am alone with this girl. Fucking…just like God intended! Right?

1:43.

It's not Goth Girl's job to fuck; it's to receive. My arms coil around her waist, my hands fix into a wrestler's Gable grip. The pace quickens. Dueling pistons in alternate in-and-out action. I can't see the director, he's crouched down somewhere feeding his hungry camera lens.

I need a focal point, like: Goth Girl's pussy feels good with the added tightness of something in her asshole at the same time…

1:30.

Lance gets lazy with maintaining the optimal angle that both avoids ball-to-ball contact and maintains the camera's ideal sight-line. I feel the first hint of scrotal heat. The proximity, juxtaposed with the super snug cooze milking my dick, is conflicting. Lance hammers harder and moans. Goth girl is slipping and I double my grip. The hair of his balls tickles the base of my dick where my cock and sac meet. My natural reflex is to cringe. My flinch and Lance's anal ramming pops me out of the vagina.

I say, "Can I get a minute? I need to get my edge back."

Partly because the words are spoken on a third of a breath, partly because I'm flustered, this comes out as a whisper. I'm insta-pissed at myself for sounding so fucking weak.

The director says, "Fine, but we need to get an additional thirty seconds of runtime for the editors because you verbally asked to stop."

"As opposed to what? Semaphore?"

"Yes, actually. If you need a break, signal when the camera isn't on you."

"Noted." I say to the flesh pile on top of me, "Get off me. I can't breathe!"

It's now that I notice the room is fetid.

I say to the director, "Why an extra *thirty* seconds?" He says, "Because now I have to look at where we left off through the viewfinder and cue it back a good ten seconds to overlap your voice. On top of that, I have to give the editor some extra footage to work with so he has a margin of error."

"Oh."

"When we start again," he says. "You guys have to give me the same pace so that it matches."

I step out from under the set lights that are triangulated on the couch. As soon as I do my sweat dries cool on my back.

I say, "Lance, chill out with that shit."

"I don't know what you're talkin' about, man."

"The staring into my eyes and the ball-on-ball shit! Not cool."

Lance scoffs. "If that bothers you, then you shouldn't be doing porn."

"Incidental rubbing is to be expected, but you were *into* it."

"Hey," Lance says to the director, "his negativity is messing with my chakras."

"Did you just tell on me like a little bitch?"

"Let it go," the director says. "Both of you." The chopper lingers. "Everyone shut up while I record room tone for audio." I'm standing next to a coffee table that's been pushed aside to make room for the lights. An ice-cooler sits on the floor next to the table. It's filled with ice, sodas, and waters. Next to cooler is the rape kit. I grab the lube from it and stroke my dick back up.

I take a Tyler moment with an icy cold water bottle on the back of my neck. My breathing slows to normal.

Money… "Room tone done. Whenever you're ready."

"Okay," I say as I walk back on the hot side of the lights, "let's get this fucker done."

2:00.

Same position. I hold Goth Girl steady. Lance lowers and enters her once again, except this time something is different. It's much hotter on the backside of my dick and far tighter inside her, too. This new compression is right on my sensitive spot. My eyes roll half-lidded back in my head and I'm rounding the corner from inhaling to exhaling my own primal emote of pleasure, then I feel the slither of the back-stroke, and in an instant, understanding flashes by me.

No, he can't be in the same hole—"I'LL KILL YOU, MOTHERFUCKER!"

Lance says, "Why you gettin' all hostile 'n' stuff, man? It was an accident."

I don't bother with my socks and underwear, pulling on only my pants and shoes.

"Let him go," the director says to Lance. "Are you two available tomorrow so we can finish this?"

Shirt now on, I heft my bag over my shoulder and leave the room. I go through the kitchen to the table with the red plastic cups. With a sweep of an arm I clear the table, splashing the wall with booze and I walk out under the starless night sky of the city. And I walk.

The residential neighborhood gives way to a street with shopping centers. I reach for my phone.

Amanda answers after a few rings. She knows what I do for money. Our relationship is simple. She never asks the details, so I'm never compelled to lie. It works. For now.

"Hey."

"Hey."

It's hard to breathe, my eyes water and my vision blurs and I tilt my head back as headlights from a passing cars find my face, hang there, and move on.

⇨ ⇨ ⇨

THE GYM NEVER CLOSES. It's pay-by-the-day and for a couple of bucks I can lift weights, take a shower, reread my worn copy of Sartre's *No Exit* or nap in the sauna. Nobody fucks with me.

Towel slung around my waist, I walk over to the locker, unlock it, and pull out my pre-paid cell phone. Time to get to business.

"Good morning. DVD Gangstas. How may I reject your call?"

"Excuse me?"

"How may I direct your call, sir?"

My voice echoes off the tiled walls. "This is Tyler. Wanda, please."

"Oh, she walking in right now. This is Tyler...?" she asks.

Finally. Okay, get right to the point and don't take no for an answer. I sit on the locker room bench.

"Knight. Tyler Knight. Remind her that I was referred by Gino Colbert."

"Hold please."

The girl does not bother with placing her hand over the receiver. The intent is for me to hear everything.

"Wanda," the receptionist says, "Tyler Knight is on the line for you. Again."

There's a sigh. A second woman's voice says, "Tell him I'm in a meeting."

Fuck this! I hang up before the receptionist can spin some bullshit. I reach inside the bag and swap the towel for clothes, pull out a VHS cassette, dump the bag into the locker then slap my padlock on it. I give the lock a couple sharp tugs and head out of the men's room into the gym proper.

⇨⇨⇨

DVD Gangstas' warehouse is not the first time I've ever seen a porn studio. I used to live two doors down from the high-end studio VELVET Video camouflaged as an arts and crafts company. It was tucked deep into a residential neighborhood of single-family homes in Van Nuys, and I was never the wiser. If you ever drive through LA's Porn Valley, you can play the game Porn Studio, Not A Porn Studio. They range from the garish edifice wrapped in neon to the innocuous warehouses hidden away in business parks.

DVD Gangstas' office building falls into the latter category. They are *the* studio in the high-end ethnic porn niche. One successful scene for them can ignite the booster rockets of my career.

⇨ ⇨ ⇨

"I'M SORRY," THE RECEPTIONIST says, "but Wanda doesn't receive visits from male talent. Especially unannounced."

By the way she crosses her arms throws glances at the door to the inner office, I'm concerned that she pushed a silent alarm and anti-mope goons will bust in at any moment. A boy band is singing a tune of teen love on the radio behind her command station.

"Calling on the phone to set up an appointment wasn't very effective so here I am. Can you at least tell her I'm here?"

"I'm quite sure she won't care."

"A good friend of Wanda's referred me. Isn't there someone here I can see?"

I watch her look at the tape in my hand, then I feel her eyes probing me. "Sure," she says. "Why not?" She picks up the phone and presses a button. "Stan, come to the reception area, please." She replaces the phone back on its receiver.

"Stan is our contract director. He's absolutely brilliant. A genius, really."

I sit on the edge of a replica Barcelona chair. "Thank you."

"Nothing personal, I'm doing my job," she says.

"I understand."

After a while, the door bursts open. A white kid wearing a visor backward and upside down on his head, a T-shirt down to his knees, pants hanging off his ass, and bright blue sneakers limps out like he's shit in his pants.

He says, "What's crack-a-lackin', my nigga?" He bends his arm like a chicken wing and extends his elbow.

I walk over to him. "Uh…hi?"

His elbow is still pointed at me and I figure it out. I bump elbows with him.

I say, "I'm Tyler Knight. I'm looking to get on your roster of male talent. I brought this." I hold up the video tape.

"What's that?"

"A recording."

"Of?"

"Me, fucking."

He says, "Who's the girl in the scene?"

Who cares?

"I forget."

Stan snatches the tape from my hand. "This is a professional scene? Not some bullshit with you setting a camera on a tripod and fucking a chickenhead from around the way?"

"Of course."

"A'ight, coo', coo'. Let me check this shit out. Chill out here, I'ma be right back." He slithers back through the door he came from.

I pace, sit, and pace some more. Stan returns, waving the tape.

He says, "That was some bullshit with you setting a camera on a tripod and fucking a chickenhead from around the way."

"Yeah," I say, "how 'bout that?"

He looks at the VHS tape and laughs. "It's the twenty-first century, nigga!"

"Look," I say. "Just give me a shot, man!"

"Get a talent info sheet from the receptionist and fill it out." He turns for the door, opens it, and I get a glimpse of a cubicle bullpen filled and buzzing with workers.

"So I'll call you to see if you have anything going on?"

"Nah, man," Stan says, "I'ma holler at your ass if I need you, player."

The door closes behind him cutting off the noise of worker activity. I stand there a moment, looking at the door. When I turn around to the receptionist's podium there is a clipboard and pen. I fill the form out and leave the building.

I fucking blew it.

⇨ ⇨ ⇨

WHEN I RETURN TO the gym, the management finally tells me I'm no longer welcome, so I take a final shower, grab my bag, and leave.

Sitting on the Hollywood Library steps, I call porn studios that advertise in the trade magazines like *ATM*. When I'm tired of getting yelled at or hung up on, I stop calling.

⇨ ⇨ ⇨

TONIGHT I'LL SLEEP ON the train. The Blue Line is cool if it's raining or if there's nowhere else to go. The chairs are metal sheets folded at ninety degrees and covered with low-pile fabric designed to resist wear and stains rather than provide comfort. They are absolutely not designed to be used longer than the forty-minute ride from Downtown Los Angeles to Long Beach. Because I have a monthly pass, I have unlimited rides. The plan is to stay on it all night as it makes its continuous loop back and forth.

I don't really sleep on the train in the truest sense because it glides right through the kill zone of South LA. What I do resembles torpor. Hungry wolves enter and exit the train cars at each stop, hunting the weak, stupid, and alone. I'm alone. God help you if you are caught unable to defend yourself because nobody else will.

It's dark and today bleeds into tomorrow as the train rumbles onto a towering overpass. Outside the train window, South Central LA sprawls below. The day's events replay in my mind until it tires out. My eyes shift focus from my profile reflected in the glass, to the rows of yellow streetlights beyond. The ghetto appears peaceful from this high up, but then, so would Fallujah. Occasional greens and reds regulate the non-existent traffic.

The landscape is aglow with buildings burning orange, stretching to the horizon. Black columns of smoke put a lid on the boiling pot and choke out the stars. The homes and the businesses blaze once again with hope as kindling. I can't hear the wailing—human or siren—this high up and from behind the train's glass, but I don't need to. Pain is universal.

The minstrel show plays itself out for me in my rolling balcony seat. Blacks and Latinos, the Koreans with the rifles on rooftops; all races play their parts to the critical acclaim of the media and its spectatorship. Cops keep everything inside. Contained.

My long-suppressed emotions surrounding race are stoked to a flame. Raised in suburbia but grappling with the implications of this urban conflict, I grew up in both worlds yet fit into neither. It is at once familiar and foreign. I want to get off at the next stop and go down there but if I did, what would I do? Would my hands choose to mend or rend?

⇨⇨⇨

THE TRAIN DOORS SNAP open and a kid with French braids pokes his head through. He scans the car, eyes passing over me as he evaluates his odds, then stalks off to the next car.

The train rolls. My cell rings.

"Yeah."

"Yo, TK, this is Stan at DVD Gangstas. Somebody just canceled on me. You wanna work tomorrow, nigga?"

⇨⇨⇨

THE SUN EVAPORATES THE dew on the car windows and starts to work on the fog, but it does fuck-all to the frost in my mind. Bag over my shoulder, I trudge up the steep residential neighborhood toward the set.

I hear a *thwump-boom-thwump* of bass as I approach the front stairs of the hillside McMansion.

I open the door, and 50 Cent's "In da Club" throttles my face. Stan enters the foyer, affecting a stooped-over pose and clutching his crotch through his baggy jeans like he's about to pass a kidney stone. He shuffles toward me, one hand holding his pants up by his cock. He lifts the other arm, bends it at the elbow, and points his elbow at me. We bump elbows.

The effects of sleep deprivation start again. I glance at his "Fuck You, I'm Batman" T-shirt… The Life Saver-colored letters rearrange themselves into, "Fuck You, Black Man!"

"Thanks for the call last night, Stan."

"No sweat, my man. Did I wake you?"

"Nope, I was in bed playing Xbox," I lie, "it's all good."

"Coo', coo'. The girl's in the bathroom cleanin' out her booty. Julio St. Lox is in the kitchen where the paperwork is at."

I've only owned one TV for a month in my entire adult life. I've never watched much porn, but even I know who Julio is. The man is a legend.

Stan continues, "It'll be you an' him with Lana Pierce. I'ma take the pretty-girl stills for the box cover when she done cleaning up and changing before her makeup gets all fucked-up from fuckin', and we can get crack-a-lakin'."

"Sounds good."

There is the distinct rumbling bass of two black men talking coming from deep in the house, punctuated by the staccato laugh of a young woman.

Stan says to me, "You done anal before, right?"

Never, you freaky bastard. That shit's nasty. But I need the cash.

"Yep."

"A'ight, coo'. Lemme handle some bidness an' I'll come get you in a hot minute."

I'm wondering what kind of people rent a home like this out to let strangers fuck on their furniture just as Stan says, "This is Ray Golden's house...he directs for Red Assholes Films but we gotta wrap this shit up before his kids get home from school."

He peels off to another part of the house and I continue straight into the kitchen.

Julio sits at the table sipping on a Hennessey. He passes a blunt to another instantly recognizable man wearing his trademark baseball cap, Mr. Darkus.

Darkus has a brunette girl sitting on his lap. She looks like she should be going door-to-door selling cookies. She's wearing a neon fishnet top and squirming on Darkus's lap. His cock is out and she's stroking it. I recognize her from the trade magazine as Assley Screw, the reigning Female Performer of the Year.

Julio sees me, and Assley and Darkus turn to where he's looking. The boys are all pussy-and-rainbows smiles.

The girl releases the cock, hops off Darkus's lap, points her elbow at me and says, "Hi, I'm Assley."

She's sincere. I sense a kind soul without the slightest hint of jadedness or artifice in her at all...not at all what I'd expect.

I offer my hand to shake, but then I remember where her hand was a moment ago and it's right about now that I gain an appreciation for the porn handshake. I say hello and return the elbow bump.

She says, "Okay, I have to get to my next scene so I'll see you guys later. It was great working with you again, Darkus." She slips on some flip-flops, snatches some keys from the table and drags a travel bag by the handle like an airline stewardess. The guys introduce themselves, and when I hear myself say, "I'm Tyler," in my nasal mid-Atlantic accent, I immediately want a do-over. My idle hands need to do something to keep busy so I snag a diet Red Bull from the ice chest on the floor and join them at the table and they resume their conversation about phat Brazilian ass. I don't talk. I nod and listen as they dish. "So-and-so girl is a freak," and "Those crazy white boys that shoot their dicks up with needles to get hard," and "Did you film in Prague yet this year?" and "Yo, Rex is working day and night. He clocked twenty gees last month. Nigga be straight ballin'!"

My brain is shutting down from lack of sleep, but I don't want to miss a single anecdote. My head's on a slow swivel from Julio to Darkus as I read their lips; the lip movement seems to come a full second before the words hit my eardrums. I let their baritone voices lull me into their world: an exotic lifestyle of travel, flash cars, bitches and money. I reflect on my world: an exotic lifestyle of running after busses and washing my scrotum with paper towels in a McDonald's bathroom sink.

Stan slithers into the kitchen holding a video camera. "Yo, we good to go, niggas. Let's do this!"

When everyone clears out of the kitchen I pull a Viagra out of my pocket and chew it. Darkus says goodbye and how it was nice to meet me and, unlike most people in LA, I believe *he* means it. None of the upper-level talent are anything like I expected.

Julio and I follow Stan back to the foyer. He motions me to stop and we hang back a few paces.

Stan continues to the base of the steps. Stan says, "A'ight, so I'ma talk to Lana and we gonna go up the stairs and into the bedroom. TK, just hang back and do how Julio do, and you'll be straight."

"Okay."

Julio unbuttons his shirt and slides off his pants and stands in his underwear. I undress as well. Stan turns on his video camera and points it at Lana on the steps. They talk.

"Tell us your name."

"I'm Lana Pierce."

"And where you from, Lana?"

She sits, and the shorts strain against the puff of her pussy. "I'm from Canada."

"Tell us why you're here today?"

"I love it hard, deep, and black in my ass..." she says. "...I'm here to fuck."

Naked, I rock back and forth on my heels and toes. My hands clasp, unclasp, and then search for pockets that don't exist on my side. Two scenes more...enough money for own spot.

I fold my arms.

Stan says, "Stand up and let us see that fat white ass, boo."

Lana is on her hands and knees, bent over with her ass aimed at the camera and she looks over her shoulder. She pulls her booty shorts to the side, plunges a finger in her with a *sklisssh*, pulls it out, and shows the camera. It sparkles! Julio spits in his hand and strokes his elephant cock. My hands cup over my softie in an attempt to hide it.

Fuck, he's already hard and I'm still soft! What the hell is taking the Viagra so long? I can't blow this.

Stan says, "We got two stiff black cocks for you today."

Lana moans as she frigs her wetness with three fingers now. She says, "Hurry up with that black cock! I'm a big girl, I need more cock than the average woman!" She rips the fishnets so that her muff is unobstructed.

Stan says, "Here you go, girl!" and hands her a vibrator. She turns it on.

The vibrator roars to life. Julio has pre-come. Lana's pussy glistens. Stan goes in for a close-up as Lana attacks her clit. My cock hangs cold and inert. I want to flee.

Julio speaks to me in a whisper, "First time doing anal?"

"Um…yeah."

He backhand strokes his cock. The vibrator is a muffled howl when it's plunged into the cooze. It rattles like a can of bees on the out stroke.

I should have taken the pill earlier… Julio smiles. "Relax, it will happen. Use your eyes. Hear her breath. Work with your body."

Lana coos and places the sex toy on her quivering folds that ripple and dance. The aroma of her pheromones invades my nostrils.

Please, God…this has to happen… Stan says, "Let's go upstairs to the bedroom. I'm sure we can find you some black cock."

Lana clicks off the vibrator, stands, and walks up the stairs. Hips swing, the fishnets threaten to snap under the strain, and ass cheeks wiggle as she climbs the stairs. I feel a twinge. My cock climbs to room temperature. The Viagra kicks in.

Stan follows her up the steps, the camera's lens a tongue-length from her wonderful fleshy backside. Stan waves from over his shoulder without looking up from the viewfinder as he walks. Julio and I follow them up the stairs. My skin stretches tight.

Lana kneels doggy style on the bed. Stan backs away from the action and blends into the wallpaper like a goddamn ninja. Julio rubs his cock on her lips and her tongue flickers on the head. Then he stuffs his cock in her mouth.

Slurping.

I take a lung full of air and climb onto the bed and position myself behind her and with one hand, then I grab her by a hip that's already slick with a sheen of perspiration. Her flesh gives fractionally in my grasp and pushes back against my fingers. My other hand is just able to wrangle my dick. The skin on my dick feels like it's separating like a wet paper bag. My tip rubs on her pussy lips to scoop up some juice for lubrication.

I push past her lips; she gives a sharp inhalation. Synapses overload. My mind snaps alert!

⇨ ⇨ ⇨

JULIO AND I PLAY "fuck, fuck, pass" with Lana. We've both taken our turns going biblical on her with savage impunity for the vaginal sex positions. There are only two anal sex positions in this scene and he's already done the first one on Lana. It's my turn.

Julio slides off the bed and steps off camera to clean his dick with a baby wipe from the rape kit. Lana rolls over onto her belly, props up on her elbows and rests her head in her hands.

Pussy drunk when I step off the bed to grab a bottle of lube from the rape kit, it's with all the grace of a newborn fawn discovering its legs. I hold the bottle of lube over Lana's ass cheeks but do not squeeze it. Gravity does its work. The clear and sparkling oil oozes from the nozzle with the velocity of rolling tree sap. When the cold lube hits her skin she emotes a squeal pinched off by a cough, and the lube piles upon itself before breaking surface tension and spreading out under its own weight. I write my name on her ass the way a kid would decorate a pancake with syrup. My heart pulses in the tip of my cock.

I drop the bottle. With my shaft, I slather the lube on her cheeks, then on her asshole with my tip…the goo warms with the friction… Next, I take the excess fuck oil on my hands and massage it into Lana's cheeks… Kneading. Needing.

I take a Tyler moment to enjoy my handiwork.

The primo pussy scent hangs in the air. It's inebriating. I inhale deep.

A slap from my hand makes her flesh jiggle and glint golden under the lights.

Lana coughs and lies on her side, inviting me to lie behind her like a spoon.

How does a girl that looks like this end up getting her ass bored out by two strangers…in porn?

Right before I insert into her anus I notice something odd. That voice that usually screams in my head when I'm unsure, afraid, or trying something new…is silent. I wait for something to go wrong, like locusts to come crashing through the bedroom window. Nothing happens. Sometimes things do work out for me, I guess.

My tip pushes past her O-ring and she grips me tight and I take my first hit of ass. Ever. Not sure what I should have expected… It's like pussy, but…tighter. But only at the entrance. Not bad, not great. Just…different. While fucking away, I forget I'm partaking in the sodomy arts and I say how great her pussy feels, out loud so the camera can hear, by mistake. My first anal position speeds by without incident and is over faster than it took Stan to film her crawling up the stairs.

Stan says, "A'ight, we gonna take the stills of the sex now, then do them pop shots."

I forgot the bastard was even in the room.

Julio takes command and says, "Let's work backwards—last anal position with Tyler, then mine, then wipe our dicks off for vag and BJ so we can fuck pussy to pop. Easier."

Stan says, "Coo', coo'. TK, just stay in the ass since you all up in it right now."

"OK."

Stan snaps stills of me spooning Lana's asshole.

The three of us go through all the positions for stills. Julio knows when to pump to keep his erection going between shots and when to freeze for the picture. He changes up fuck faces, hitting each pose sharp. I take notes.

Stan says, "A'ight, who gonna nut first?"

Lana coughs.

Julio says, "Let Tyler go first. I can pop at will."

"Yeah, I know how you get down, Julio," Stan says, "TK, we gonna clear off the set so you can fuck to pop without a bunch of niggas starin' at you 'n' shit. Holla when you feelin it, but give a nigga thirty seconds so I got time to turn the camera back on, a'ight?"

"Yeah, sure."

Even though Lana and I have been slam-fucking for the entire scene, now we may as well be first cousins sitting in church. We sit side by side on the bed, both of us staring straight ahead and out the window, looking but not seeing the city sprawling below.

She's the girl I picked up at the club to fuck and when I wake up she's still there in the morning and we've got nothing to say to each other. My alter ego turned off with the camera and I've got nothing to hide behind. Right now, I'm not Tyler Knight, just Erik, and being Erik without pretending to be somebody else has always been hit-or-miss with the ladies. No one is more amazed than I am for the high-quality actress and model pussy I've scored in spite of myself.

Lana makes the first move by stroking my cock. "I guess we better hurry, they're paying location fees by the hour."

"Yeah."

I lean over to kiss her but she turns her head. Smooth! Real smooth, Erik.

She says, "We should keep it professional. Besides, I have a cold."

I take her by the chin and turn her head toward mine. She smiles at me…really smiles at me, and I lose the power of speech. I'm fucking doomed.

"You're beautiful," she says to me, not much more than a whisper.

She looks into me and I into her… I swallow and I feel a fire gliding down my throat and into my gut like a shot of aged rye. We kiss.

I manage a "thank you."

She strokes my cock as I finger her clit, which swells under my touch.

I say, "What the hell are you doing here?"

She smiles. "Same as you."

Lana lies on her back and pulls me on top of her… Kissing… Our faces pull away…eyes sync. I enter her.

Within a few strokes our pace speeds to a blur and I wrap a handful of her sweat-drenched, honey-flavored locks in my fist. My other hand cups under her ass. Our pubic bones slam together, over and over. Her lips part, framing teeth like slick alabaster. Eyes exchange what actual words would ruin. Connected. Our mouths touch again and stay that way, shattering the last vestige of the pretense porn stars construct to keep it professional.

Biology pulls a "Surprise, motherfucker!" on me.

FUCK!

Lana's face screws into a questioning look. "Did you just come in me?"

"No!"

I look away, and this time it's her taking me by my chin. "Tyler?"

"Yeah... I'm really sorry."

She furrows her brow. I feel like the time I got caught stealing sunglasses at the mall and security called my mom. Lana says, "Why did you lie?"

"I dunno."

She chuckles. "It's okay," she says. "I'm on birth control."

I say, "I'm still screwed, though. No way I can give a pop shot now."

"Relax, you're still hard. Call Stan back in, and when we set up the pop shot I'll drop to my knees you'll pretend you're coming in my mouth. Leave the rest to me."

"Thanks."

⇨ ⇨ ⇨

I STROKE MY DICK. Lana kneels in front of me. Julio hangs off to the side. Stan rolls camera. I give a wail like I'm having the best orgasm ever felt by man or beast then I shove my cock in Lana's mouth. When I pull out, she lets spittle dribble from the side of her mouth…and fuck me if it doesn't look like come! She smiles at me with her eyes and I do my best to keep from laughing. When I step back Julio steps forward to deliver his load.

"Cut, we got it," says Stan.

Lana and I exchange complicit grins.

The three of us pose for the pop shot stills, and I hold a freeze-frame pose. I do my best to put on my my-face-is-contorted-in-the-thralls-of-ecstasy look but it comes across as my I'm-taking-a-shit-but-the-log-is-too-big-for-my-asshole face. Apparently this is good enough because Stan says, "Stills done," and leaves to go downstairs. Julio follows him, Lana goes to take a shower. I sit on the bed, evaluating.

A place of my own.

A yawn pushes past my lips as I come down from the vagina high and I lay back.

⇨ ⇨ ⇨

"How do you think that went, Gee?"

I open my eyes.

Okay, he's not looking for honesty. Don't say shit about the pop shot.

"Well, Stan. I think it went well."

He sits on the bed beside me. I'm still naked. I slide over to make more space between us.

"Yeah," he says, "I was sure you'd find a way to fuck up, so I threw you in the scene with another guy that I knew could handle bidness in case you failed."

I nod. "Sure."

He says, "Didn't know if you could do it. I had to protect the studio's money. The pop shot was tricky—"

Fuck.

"—next time tell a nigga if you gonna nut in a ho's mouth— but I caught it on tape. You did your thang though, homey. You did it."

He offers his elbow. "Give a nigga a pound!"

We bump elbows.

"You can pick up your check in a couple of days from da office."

He gets up, walks out the door, and tosses, "I'ma have Wanda holla at you!" over his shoulder.

Lana comes out of the shower. The booty-shorts-and-fishnets whore uniform is gone. She's back in her denim gardening bonnet and cargo shorts. She covers her mouth, coughs, and walks over to me.

"I'm Lisa."

She extends her hand, I take it.

"Nice to meet you, Lisa. I'm Erik." I kiss her hand.

We smile.

"You're going to go very, very far in this business, Erik."

⇨ ⇨ ⇨

"Tyler?"

"Yeah?"

"This is Wanda calling from DVD Gangstas."

Wanda! I sit up, "Hello, Wanda! Nice to finally talk to you! How's it hanging?"

Jesus, "How's it hanging?" You schmuck!

She says, "Your check is ready. The receptionist has it at her desk. Also, Stan said you didn't blow it the other day, so I'm letting 2Cock go and giving you his slot in the male talent rotation. Expect a call from our directors Dana and Alfred Divine tonight. You're working for them tomorrow."

She hangs up.

"Thank you."

Amanda, now awake, sits up, too. Her bed is small. Contact from someone with no ulterior motives is rare in my life. I never told her I'm sleeping in twenty-four-hour Internet cafes or the train. But I don't have to. One look at my rumpled clothes and matted hair and you know my story. Every once in a while I crash at her place, but not too often so I don't feel like I'm taking advantage of her kindness. What the hell does she see in me? I can't figure her out.

We speak in Spanish.

"Who was that, Papi?"

I smile. "DVD Gangstas," I say. "I'm in the male talent rotation."

⇨⇨⇨

THE SHOWER IS SET to magma. Hospital tag on my wrist. I cough, shake, and cough some more. Droplets plink against the basin around me. I move into the denser, humid air and turn to face the nozzle. My hands brace against the wall, straddling the showerhead. Head bent down, I hack my lungs inside out in back-arching fits and my throat feels like I've gargled shurikens.

Eventually, but not today. Amanda sleeps. Her mouth naturally inclines up at the corners, hinting at a smile…like she knows something I don't. She probably does.

She's let me spend nights at her spot since I came down with this fever. Her idea. One day of sleeping at her place carried over to a few days. This is the first chance I have to sleep in a bed for a few days in a row, but I have to camp on the couch instead lest I make her ill. I still haven't unpacked that bag because…the fuck if I know why, really?

The fever wouldn't break on its own after a few days so last night she put my ass in a taxi for the ER.

⇨ ⇨ ⇨

No INSURANCE. I WAIT amongst the knifed, the burned, and the left for dead who have changed their mind about dying and crawled into the ER waiting room. People are seen, and afterward, some of them leave. Some don't. My name's called over the PA.

⇨ ⇨ ⇨

I'M PULLING MY UNDERWEAR back on underneath the gown to salvage some dignity when she zips in like a hummingbird. Clear skin. Firm calves. Bags under eyes. How old is she? She says, "Take your underwear off."

"Can you put on some Barry White first?"

The doctor shakes her head.

She got the reference… She's older than she looks.

She turns her back, dashes to a counter, and hovers there long enough to snap on latex gloves, then takes her stethoscope off of her neck and quick-steps toward me.

I need all my strength to climb onto the table. While in motion, there's a sliver of a time where I may not make it up to the top on my own power, but I don't let on. I sit. Though I don't have an erection, I'm still pitching a mini-tent because I'm full commando under the gown. If I fold my hands in my lap, will that call unwanted attention to it?

She puts the business end of the scope on my chest, listens. "Take deep breaths."

I clear a lingering tickle in my throat. "You know, this gown isn't my color. I'm a winter."

She glances at my pile of rubbish I wore to the hospital lumped on the chair. "I seriously doubt it matters. Stop talking. Breathe."

Doc puts a disposable thermometer strip under my tongue, and steps out of the room. When she returns, she carries a goddamn lawn dart sealed in plastic... A syringe! She places it on the counter.

She reads my temperature and tosses the strip in the trash then she takes a swab of my throat.

"How long have you been feeling ill?"

"I dunno, two days?... Three?"

"And you're just now coming in?"

"Yep."

I can't stop looking at the syringe. It's massive enough to have its own gravitational pull. She places her hands on her hips, arms akimbo, and says, "That's stupid, you have a fever of a hundred and three. I'll be back with the results of this culture." She leaves again.

Chicks dig me.

I consider putting my underwear back on, but I doubt I'd make it back onto the table by myself.

No fucking way am I staying overnight and missing tomorrow's scene... Almost have enough cash saved up.

I swing my legs, the paper rustles.

The doctor comes back into the room, pushing a stainless steel cart. The top of the cart has all kinds of shit on it.

"So, what's up, Doc? Will I live?"

"Not if it's up to you."

I read her face for a sign of jest. Stoic.

"What do I have?" I ask.

"Strep. Bacterial pneumonia." She snatches the syringe off the cart. She says, "Hop off the table, lift up your gown, and bend over."

"But Doc, we just met, ha-ha-ha."

"I don't have time for games. There are many other people needing care."

I say, "Aren't you supposed to distract me with a sock puppet?"

"Please. Act like an adult."

"This is gonna suck."

"Good. Next time you'll seek medical care sooner."

"What happened to 'Do no further harm?'"

She swabs my ass cheek. "Stop moving."

"Can't you just give me a pill?"

She sighs. "Let me do my job!"

I say, "I know, but—"

Doc says, "Relax your buttocks!"

"I'm trying."

Okay, think of something else:

On my back, looking up. Argyle, knee-socked legs straddling my head. Amanda standing over me in a skirt. White cotton panties. Cooing in Spanish. She sits... I feel Doc wiping the injection site, slapping on a Band-Aid and then some tape.

"Get dressed."

I walk over to the chair and balance myself against it as I pull on my boxer-briefs.

She writes something on a pad of paper with brisk strokes of the pen. She says, "The hospital pharmacy is closed for an hour so I'm writing you a 'script. Fill it, and take all the medication until it's finished even if you feel better...and stay in bed."

She furrows her brow as she gives me orders. Under other circumstances I'd love to oblige, but fuck staying in bed and losing my slot in DVD Gangsta's male talent rotation.

I say, "Listen, Doc, I'm not normally such a smart a—"

"Apology accepted. We all have our defense mechanisms." She pushes the cart to the door. "Are there any questions before I see the next patient?"

"Yeah, can I get a lollipop?"

The corners of her eyes crinkle as she gives a hint of a smile, but it's gone before it develops at her lips.

She says, "You can get out."

⇨ ⇨ ⇨

THE NEXT MORNING I stuff my wallet and key in my pocket, kiss sleeping Amanda's forehead, and go out the door.

I *should* be in bed like Doc said. I've got some reservations about going to work and possibly making my costar sick, but it's a zero-sum business and I'm far from home free. So I'm gonna get that paper. Either it's me or the next guy who wants my slot. Fuck the next guy. Besides, short of a dirty STD test result or oozing lesions, many studios will film you, sick or not. And there have been cases of directors and talent fudging STD tests, as well as directors filming blatant Herpes-afflicted crotches from their "good" sides instead of canceling a scene.

The first time you see burst-open Herpes pustules oozing from someone's genitals, you are never the same. I saw my first two Herp victims on one set during a five-on-one gang bang scene. One of the other mopes had some sores on his dick head. It looked like his bookie held a Zippo lighter to it until it bubbled and popped. The mope passed his sores off as "razor bumps" from shaving, and nobody, not one person, protested.

But the girl. She had the porn affliction trifecta: Staph on her ass that she claimed was a spider bite; opaque, Gonorrhea-induced discharge seeping from her crotch that reeked of something digested alive inside her vagina (you're only required to an STD test once a month these days, so you can carry STDs for weeks between tests), and Herpes that looked as though the girl shaved her pussy with a sand blaster. There is no testing for Herpes in porn.

Why in the name of fuck would you show up on set like that with the intention of having your diseases immortalized on film for thousands of people to see? Another mope, without a second thought, went down on her.

It's still dark outside when I leave for the set, but my call time is early and I don't want to risk being late because I miss a bus. That shit won't fly in LA. (The caught riding a bus part, not being late. Everybody is late in LA.)

⇨⇨⇨

AFTER SEVERAL BUS CHANGES I get to the barrio where the set is located. An abandoned hospital. Vic Vermont, the cage fighter turned porn star, stands by the door, watching my approach.

I say, "Are you with the DVD Gangstas shoot?"

He points into the dark mouth of the building. "No, I'm shooting for Red Assholes films. There's a lot of different shoots going on here today. The Gangstas crew is on the third floor."

I look up at the building. Each floor sprawls the length of a football field. "Thanks, I'll find it."

I enter. Each step I takes greater effort than the one preceding it.

⇨⇨⇨

DANA DIVINE GREETS ME. "Tyler, I've heard good things about you!"

"Really?"

She gives me a hug. "You're burning up, are you okay, honey?"

"I'm fine."

"Yeah, Stan said you did well for him," she says, "and the number of black male talent worth a damn can fit into my SUV, so I'm excited to have you here. Speaking of good men, have you met Jack Hammer?"

She points to a dreadlocked kid bursting out of his black wifebeater with a Punisher skull on it. I need to get on creatine.

He offers me his hand but I counter with my elbow. He looks at the elbow for a moment, shrugs, and bumps it with his. Dana takes my copy of my HIV test and my IDs.

Dana says, "Alfred is shooting camera. I handle the ancillary issues. We've got two scenes before yours. I told him to push your call time back a few hours," she shakes her head, "but he never listens to me."

My body trembles. My eyelids feel weighted.

I say, "You got a place I can lie down while I wait?"

"Yeah, there are some old hospital cots around the corner but I can't speak to their cleanliness."

"That's okay. Don't care."

"I'll come get you when we're ready for you."

The cot. I curl up. Shaking. Eyes shut.

⇨⇨⇨

EYES OPEN. HAIR SOAKED.

Dana says, "Welcome back to the living."

I stir. Moan.

Dana says, "How much longer? Well, Alfred is shooting Jack Hammer's scene right now so it won't be too much longer."

Dana, smiley. Crinkly foil triangles.

She says, "I saved you some pizza. I wrapped them for you."

I moan again.

"Oh…okay. Well, it'll be here if you change your mind later."

Eyes shut.

⇨ ⇨ ⇨

I AWAKEN FEELING A bit better but still weak. My tongue is dry. Light filters through the dusty windows at the same angle as when I arrived, but when I look outside the sun is setting instead of rising. Different cars are outside. I set out in search of water. All the same items of video equipment lay wait in the staging area where I met Dana and Jack Hammer but nobody is there. Silent. I snatch a water from the ice chest and explore the hospital. Peeling paint. Office furniture and documents piled into corners. Medical equipment from the mid-century. Freddy Krueger would love it here.

Voices.

I stalk down the hall, down a flight of stairs, following them to their source.

"…or hold my cock steady."

"Why can't you do this yourself? Don't be such a pussy."

I peek in an abandoned examining room. Two guys. One with his eyes shut and his pants down. The other, fully dressed, but kneeling and aiming a syringe at the side of the first guys dick.

Walk away, Erik.

Too late. Needle Boy looks up. He says, "Hey, you. C'mere and gimmie a hand with this."

"No."

"No?"

"No."

Cock Boy's eyes are still squeezed shut.

I say, "You guys getting high or something?"

Needle Boy has a Boston accent. He says, "Nah, were caving."

"What's 'caving'?"

"Caverject. I'm shooting his dick up to get him hard for my scene, yah know?" He clarifies, "I'm the director." He turns back to the cock.

This time, Cock Boy speaks. "Look, if you're not gonna help then don't distract him, okay? Please, just leave!"

"Whatever."

"Thank you!"

⇨⇨⇨

I RETURN TO THE staging area. Fucking sounds from porn ghosts echo from various shoots occurring throughout the building.

Dana returns. So do my shakes.

Dana says, "Hey sweetie, we're ready. Follow me to the basement."

⇨⇨⇨

THE BASEMENT, WHICH REEKS of standing water and sewage, could be a set from a first-person shooter zombie game. Industrial and damp. Pipes and valves jutting from the walls, and puddles welling on the concrete floor. Nothing obvious to fuck on… For that matter, where's the girl? Dana and I stop next to a ladder.

A man twists his way through the labyrinth of pipes as he approaches, swelling his lats like a cobra. I'm tempted to start a bodybuilding pose-down duel.

He says to me, "Wanda said you were taller."

"I'm six foot seven when I stand on my cock."

He stares.

Dana says, "Tyler, Alfred. Alfred, this is Tyler."

I say, "Howdy," and offer my elbow. Nothing.

He says, "I already shot the girl's part of the intro leading up to the sex. I'm going to shoot yours now."

"Okay, but I left my vibrator at home."

More stares.

Dana says, "Why don't you explain the scene to Tyler."

"Yeah…right. Remember the video for Duran Duran's "Hungry Like The Wolf," where the girl is crawling through the sludge in the jungle? That will be you. You'll start over there…"

He points to a console of switches and levers on the other side of the basement.

"…then you make your way through the maze of pipes on your hands and knees—and this is very important—like there is a deep need inside of you, but you don't know what it is."

"What is it that I need?"

Stares.

"So anyway, you'll make your way through here and up this ladder…"

With my eyes, I follow the ladder up until my head is at a 180-degree angle with the floor. I feel unseen presence peering down at me.

"…to the top of this boiler tank where the girl is waiting for you. When you get there she'll judo flip you over like in the video—be careful, there's no railing—and she'll attack the cock.

I cleaned off the dead roaches and most of rat shit, and I even laid out a blanket so it's cool."

He stares again.

I start to tell him what I think of him and his plan when Dana says, "Wanda says you called her every day for weeks until you got on the male talent roster. Alfred, remember how much you worked for DVD Gangstas back when you were just starting out?"

⇨ ⇨ ⇨

THE DETRITUS-STREWN FLOOR CHAFES my knees raw. God knows what pathogens from the floor are invading my body through the countless takes crawling on cement.

My shaking now comes and goes in fits. On the ladder, I have to stop climbing twice on the way up to gather strength. The "set" is a platform no bigger than the hood of a Prius, high enough from the basement floor to have its own microclimate. Gasping, I crawl onto it and flop down to the girl. Her hair piles on top of itself in several tiers, resembling at once a beehive hairdo and a wedding cake, acrylic nails at a length that makes closing her fist impossible, and shoes with heels long enough to punch clear through a cinderblock... How the hell did she get up the ladder?

Alfred clings to the ladder, camera in one hand with its red dot blinking.

"Action!" Girl flips me, snatches my cock... Does things to me. Position after endless position... Finally, doggy. On my knees again, trying not to wince on camera... Maneuvering behind the girl. She backs up. I back up. We fuck. She backs up to adjust herself. I back up. My knee finds—nothing.

Dana screams.

"He's okay, Ranishia snagged him before he went over," Alfred says. "Thank God. I still need to get the pop shot from him."

⇨⇨⇨

"Don't stress, Tyler," Dana says. "You're sick. How you got hard again is beyond me."

We're back at the staging area. This scene put me over for what I need to get my own place but I have to smooth shit over with the Divines because Wanda will ask for a performance report on how I did today. I'm not giving up my slot in the rotation without a fight.

"Thanks, Dana. I'm not one to quit."

Alfred says, "Yeah, well, you still took too long to pop and time is money. It's *your* fault this production lagged and we went way overtime today. I'm docking your pay to compensate for location fees."

Cocksucker! I could point out his fucked-up time management skills, but that would be a Pyrrhic Victory. Even after the partial theft of my money, I'll still have enough for move-in costs.

⇨⇨⇨

Amanda wakes me. She speaks to me in Spanish. "I filled your prescription. Sit up…come on, sit up… Open your mouth."

She puts a pill in my mouth, then holds a paper towel under my chin as she pours a few sips of water into my mouth from a cup of water. It's still dark outside but I don't remember how I got back. Where's the bag? My old shoes?

"I gave you the top two drawers," she says, "and washed what was worth keeping."

My copy of Sartre's *No Exit* stacked atop of Celine's *Journey to the End of the Night* on her dresser... Well, our dresser now, I guess. What's to become of this? How wise is it to live together before you know what the other person's like at that point in a relationship where everyone stops being polite?

She says, "*Tú eres el mío.*"

For the first time in my life I feel the power of a woman's unconditional love.

Amanda mounts me. Her pussy is hot.

I drift.

⇨ ⇨ ⇨

THE OPENING BARS OF Radiohead's "High And Dry" nudge me awake. Sunlight. My stomach twists and grinds, crying out to me to put something in it.

The song's bass drum repeats itself. I grab my cellphone off of the dresser and open it, ending the ringtone.

"Hello."

"Yo nigga, this is Stan."

"Hey."

"So I'ma come right to it," he says, "Wanda got your performance report from the Divines this morning."

"Yeah? That was fast."

They're gonna dump me... Great, I fail at porn! Well at least I have Amanda, and now the move-in money can last us until I get a job telemarketing or something.

"TK," Stan says, "We'd like to make you DVD Gangstas' first ever male contract star. You gonna blow up nigga!"

I hang up, and I do not move. The tears want to come.

I let them.

THE RISE OF THE MECH-PEENS

TODAY I'M TO HAVE my genitals molded for mass production. I gaze out of the passenger-side window of Stan's SUV, paying as much attention to my fellow Angelenos as they pay to me. Everyone playing hurry-up-and-wait at the 101/405 freeway interchange. Stan's been on the phone since we left the studio, playing verbal grab-ass with a porn starlet who is the "it" girl of the moment. We snake our way through the freeway on the way to the Premiere Exotic Novelties, Inc. (PENI) factory.

I'm not sure how I feel about latex facsimiles of my cock sold and distributed across the Earth…each with a half-life of 7,794 years. Seven millennia from now archeologists could excavate our ruins and brush debris away to discover my rubber phallus in situ wedged inside a female skeleton's pelvis, and extrapolate what life must have been like at the dawn of the twenty-first century. Shit, the most thought I've given to the still nebulous process of casting my cock was the mention of a fluffer girl to keep me hard…what will she look like…

We turn onto a major boulevard where the single-family ranch homes and the pink-stucco apartment buildings dissolve to warehouses and business parks.

"I dunno why they picked *you* for a sex toy." Stan's off the phone, scraping his SUV between two parked compacts. "You ain't packin like Lance or them other niggas."

Stan knows how to put a gimp in my swagger with the skill of an ex-wife.

He's right…this is insanity! I'm making a fool of myself! I'm gonna make a run for it as soon as we stop.

I don't. Instead, I stand in the parking lot evaluating the PENI complex. No sign to distinguish it from its neighboring office buildings and warehouses. Could be an auto-supply firm. Could be a covert DARPA weapons test lab.

At the door, I close my eyes and listen to the sound of passing traffic while I put my stoic mask on. I enter.

⇨⇨⇨

THE EXECUTIVE IS ALREADY waiting for us when we enter, standing square to face the door.

She introduces herself to me. "I'm. Jen." She hands us visitor's badges. "This. way."

⇨⇨⇨

THE CONFERENCE ROOM. ANOTHER female executive in a well-crafted suit who resembles my mother sits poised on the edge of the conference table. She stands as we enter. In the center of the table is a glass-encased dildo. Its latex skin is sliced open and pinned back to expose skeletonized robo-guts. Spread out in front of the executive is a stack of documents.

"I'm Roberta! It is just such a *joy* to finally meet you!"

Christ, did she say "finally"? No one at PENI knew I existed a week ago.

I say, "Hi," then I sit.

Roberta, with perfect enunciation, explains the engineering and design of the cock in front of me with enthusiasm. I'm not listening as much as I'm letting an occasional phrase find its way into my ear.

"—like the next generation, teste-shaped motor housed in the scrotum!" she says. "The heart and soul of your signature vibrating phallus—"

Did she just use the word "teste" in a sentence?

"—because we want only the best. *No expense* will be spared for your product line!"

Riiight.

Stan whips out his video camera and films the meeting's proceedings.

Jen slides a document and a pen over to me. "If. You. Sign. Your. Name. Right. Here. With. This. Pen. You. Can. Have. Your. Next. Check." Since Jen laid eyes on me, she has been speaking at me in monosyllabic words. It's as though she expects me to break out an English-to-Ebonics dictionary from my back pocket and mouth out syllables as I work through a response. "Oh-kay," I say. I hold the pen in front of my face and ponder it with a grimace as if I've never seen one before.

Jen blows out her cheeks with a sigh and says, "Please!"

I skim and sign. In a coordinated effort, Jen snatches the document and Roberta slides a check across the table my way.

Next, I watch them good-cop-bad-cop me through an explanation of the toy-making procedure. But I'm not listening. I stare at the mechanized penis centerpiece...

A faint red glow pulses from the "teste" inside the robotic dildo's surrogate scrotum.

The Future...

Eardrum-bursting bangs of concussive bombs exploding in the distance quake the ground; the crunching of concrete crumbling underfoot. Closer still, mechanized servos whine. Crackling fire stoked with burning flesh, the nutty stench invades my nostrils. I raise a tattered sleeve to my face. It filters the soot but not the misery.

Gunfire...

I snatch the glass of water and kill half of it in a single chug before the ice slaps against my upper lip.

I slam the glass down and reach over to tap the dildo's head and say, "Is this thing...on?"

Laughter all around the room. Jen says, "What. Else. Would. You. Like. To. Know?"

I dig my crumpled STD test out of my pocket and smooth it out onto the table with the enthusiasm of a kid showing a report card full of As.

"Yeah," I say, "When do I get to meet my fluffer?"

Jen and Roberta glance at each other, passing information in the unspoken exchange.

"The...what?" asks Roberta. Her demeanor shifts, now mirroring her coworker, Jen.

"Fluffer!" I say. "You know…the girl you guys are supplying to, uh…keep me going through the long molding and casting process?"

"There will be no fluffer." Roberta says the word fluffer the way you would say "gonorrhea."

"Look," I point to the dong. "I'm not a machine—"

Despite how it makes me feel to ask a woman who could be my mother to fetch a girl to suck me off, I hold my ground.

"—you can't possibly expect me to obtain, let alone maintain an erection surrounded by factory workers as you've described in the process."

Stan joins in, offering his council. "You're a professional. You should have no problem." Roberta steeples her fingers. "I'm confident we can accommodate your needs with some lubrication and a magazine for the first molding. When we get to the body cast—"

"Body *what*?"

"Yes," she continues, "the body cast. You did bother to read the contract, right?" She punctuates her verbal bitch slap by stabbing a finger at the stack of papers in front of Jen.

"Of course. I read the entire document."

"Very well, then," she says. "As I was saying, when we get to the body cast portion of your commitment," she punches each syllable of the word, 'commitment', "you will be provided with your fluffer. Are these acceptable terms?"

What the fuck! She's acting all indignant as if I asked her to personally toss my salad…I mean, we're sitting at a table in a sex toy company, not a prime table at Le Cirque. Her job is to make dicks! *DICKS!*

I say, "Fine."

"Very well," Roberta says.

She gathers the papers, places them in an attaché case and heads for the door. As she walks, she hugs the wall away from me as if she thinks I'll touch her.

She says, "Good day," to no one in particular.

This fluffer better be good.

Jen says, "Come. With. Me." We leave for the production floor.

⇨⇨⇨

PENI'S FACTORY IS THE sound of a radio stuck between stations. The drone of machinery spritzed with Spanish. White noise of Southern California industry. Workstations stretch across the floor. Workers mill about the second-tier loggia bringing supplies down to the floor below. Industry in this particular factory is sewing vinyl pubes on "Vanessa Velvet's Vice-like Vagina," rumpling rubber foreskins, and attaching "nubbed-for-your-pleasure anal-tract A" to "sphincter B."

The Artisan's workstation is situated on the periphery of the action, unique from the others in that it's cast in shadow. A child-sized man is hunched over in deep concentration, jeweler's loupe squinted tight in his eye, he peers through the opening of the halo-lamp at his work. The master finishes his task before setting his brush down and placing the loupe in its worn leather case. He stands.

Eyes cast down, he moves toward us through the station as if remembering where he buried land mines. The lights beating upon his narrow shoulders diminish him before my eyes like a chip of ice dropped in a cup of hot tea. He stops, eyes scan from face to face until settling on mine. He stares as if burning every detail to his retina.

Jen introduces us, says she'll be back when it's time to do the body cast, and leaves. Stan stays.

The craftsman hands me a magazine and some Vaseline and tells me to go behind a curtain hanging at the end of his station and to let him know when I'm ready. Stan looks like he's going to follow me but the murder in my eyes stops him cold.

It's a leg fetish magazine. Not my third choice but it gets the job done. When I emerge I follow the man to the factory floor, not breaking stride as I stroke to keep the erection going.

I'm instructed to lie on the table. I do. The craftsman hands me a Plexiglas tube which I place over my stiffy. He has a bucket of gummy, viscous solution he's whisking with a painter's stir-stick. He then pours the material through the open end of the tube and onto my genitals. The sensation feels as though I'm buried in cold, wet mud. He tells me it is extremely important to hold the tube still so that my penis does not move while the solution sets. As the mixture dries, I feel its weight. There is a tightening sensation around my dick, like a fist clinching deliberate and slow. The feeling is transitory, going from the periphery of perception to a very fleeting stage of "Hey, this shit ain't half bad" to the discomfort of a shoe a full size too small. Just as it starts to strangle, the craftsman says it's set. He gives the tube a tug and my dick comes out with a hushed *schtooop*. Stan gets a close up of this.

First mold done, I'm instructed to roll on my belly. More workers rush in with buckets and get to work while the craftsman barks orders. Cloth soaked in Plaster of Paris is then layered on my back from my lower lats, across my ass, and to mid-hamstring. It feels the same as wet washcloths. This takes considerably longer than the dick-in-a-tube mold to dry.

Bottom half done, the cast is removed and I'm rotated onto my back by the assistants with the efficiency of a NASCAR pit crew.

Yeah, there is no fucking way I could get and stay hard without help for the front part of the casting… I can't believe these people would even make this a point of contention… It's win-fucking-win if they get the best cast possible from me, right?

The craftsman tells me he is going to fetch Jen, who will then get my fluffer.

The fluffer is here? That was fast… I'll bet they had her on the way the entire time. Christ, what the fuck was all the hemming and hawing about? I'm tired of these fucking games.

The crew starts plastering the non-vitals while I'm counting my money from the check in my pocket.

It's fluffer time. Jen peeks her head in the station, grins, then goes out to the factory floor and shouts a command in Spanish. The factory workers stop working, and through the shadows a woman of a certain age who is wider than she is tall waddles forward, wiping her hands on her apron.

Fuck my life.

Jen, heels clicking, trots over to a group of less battle-hardened factory girls, spreads her arms like a horse whisperer, and corrals them into a tight group. Jen isolates one girl and rustles her over.

The Girl she retrieves is a dark-haired, sun-toasted chica. She looks like she walked off a Mexican soap opera set. Parchment-thin jeans are shrink-wrapped over her camel toe. Her T-shirt, hanging there on aspirin-hard nipples, is begging for a super soaker gun.

The Woman. A low-to-the-ground, Weeble Wobble–shaped specimen with half-empty water canvases for tits and features sandblasted by seasons of desert wind. She could have ridden with Pancho Villa.

I say to Jen, "What the fuck, man! I asked for a fluffer and you give me a used-up worker with skin flaps for tits, and some sponge brain, tight pants girl?"

"I speak English," says The Girl.

Oops.

"Sorry."

"You should be," The Girl says.

Jen snickers and leaves. The more seasoned of the two ladies, without any more comment than flashing her Jack o' lantern smile, scoops a three-fingered gob of Vaseline from the container, and it's NAFTA on my cock. The Girl does not seem to be experienced. She's resorted to interpretive dance which is supposed to pass for a slow tease, mixed with cheerleading the old woman in a dial-a-date voice. While I'm on a roll, I say something sensitive like:

"Stop talking, pull your pants down and show me your ass."

Did either of these women have any idea that this day would come when they filled out their job applications? I seem to be the only one who's hung up on this situation, because both of the women take to their duties of giving me, some strange dude, my jollies without complaint? Because some skinny bitch in a suit told them to. Just like that.

Another fulfilling day at work. You never know what adventures you face on the job working for the man in the US of A...cleaning toilets or stroking fat negro cock. But hey, God bless America, right?

Doesn't take much to get me hard again 'cause that's just the kind of buck-toothed pervert I am. When I'm erect the women back away from the cock and the crew rushes in and does their thing.

While the crew works, I cup a handful of young-girl ass and ask two questions. "How old are you? Swell. After this is over, you want to go somewhere and fuck?"

Why the fuck not? She's already handled the package, right?

The crew has gone, taking the casts, with them. The Girl and The Woman stay.

Somebody forgot to tell The Woman the job is over because she pounces on the dick. The mastery of her hands is unsettling. Each twisting downward stroke sends sparks shooting through my shaft, sending my jaw slack. She strokes me way past the point of pleasure. The place where any normal man would have long since surrendered control and just released but I hang on where it's uncomfortable. I still have this hang up about what's going on in my head but this moment, I am hers. No on-screen alter-ego bravado bullshit. I'm just me, and I've got nowhere to hide. She double-fists me, the slick, wet *schliiip* of her hands dripping with Vaseline goo is warm with the friction. Maestra reads the conflict written all over my face.

"Shhhh. *Cálmate*," she purrs. Her voice and the rhythm of her hands lulls.

My body relaxes one muscle at a time, melting into her slicked hand. The tug-of-war for Oedipus's ghost is lost, I let go. She slays me. I empty into her hands with all the guilt of eating meat on Lent.

She wipes her hands on her apron and rubs a hand through my hair. Her voice is soft. It takes me a moment to realize The Girl has vanished. Like a freshly-turned-thirty Hollywood ingénue, you don't notice she's faded off the lips of conversation until she's long gone.

I'm back in the Artisan's station. He's gone for the day. My clothes lie folded on a table with a copy of the receipt I signed on top. Next to the table is a gift basket full of PENI merchandise.

ORGY

I OPEN THE DOOR and enter the reception area of Elusive Scoundrels, the studio owned by Alpha Man.

Coming from outside, my eyes need a moment to adjust to the lower light. I hear the voices before the faces fill in. Asian girls of every shape, skin tone, color, and size lounge around some sofas. One dark-skinned girl with waist-length black hair is dressed in a bright floral print dress and a crown of flowers on her head. Some girls are dressed in sweats, some in designer fashion. All are evaluating their options.

Today's scene is an orgy. For these events, girls typically have a limitation to the number of boys they will fuck within the scene…unless more money is offered. Among these girls are a handful of black men who are fighting for position. Though the pussy is guaranteed, boys preen and seduce; each one doing his best to show why he's the most desirable mate.

Someone notices me standing at the door and the seduction, pathos, and negotiating stops. A score of eyeballs burn into a singular point. Me. Some girls smile. Others play coy but their body language betrays them. The Flower Girl flat-out stares at me, mouth open and googly-eyed. The other men grumble, suck their teeth and sigh. One man takes his preening rituals up a few notches and struts between me and the girls, talking loud. In his Borealis-blue track suit, he resembles a chortling peacock on the make. The girls ignore him.

Alpha Man bursts into the reception area from the office proper to coordinate who will be working with whom, and how many partners each girl will work with. The girls point to me. All of them. Obviously, all girls on me cannot possibly work out for an orgy. Negotiations, barters, begging, and ultimatums ensue from all parties as I hide in a corner making myself invisible.

For the disruption my presence is causing, Alpha Man is probably contemplating choking me out and dumping my groggy ass in his warehouse while they drive to the location without me. He shoots me a look that can cut steel.

After a while, this studio's male contract porn star, Mitch Adams, strides in from the warehouse. He's a master negotiator, and because of this I have never been so happy to see another male talent. He cuts the tension by selling the virtues of the other men in the room to the girls. Guys sitting on the sidelines like fifth graders picked last for kick ball are now popular. All is forgiven as Mitch coordinates a flowchart of sex partners to everyone's satisfaction.

⇨⇨⇨

I'M STANDING IN THE eye of the Orgy. Wet sounds of sixty-nines and blow jobs all around me. On my little sex island, Alicia Lee and Belinda Rose are both on their knees slurping away on my cock as if to establish who's the best cocksucker in Christendom, and I'm dying, trying not to come. If you come too soon, you will be fired on the spot and your reputation as a professional male talent will be ruined. My eyes rove the room in an attempt to divert my attention from what is happening to me.

Everything looks surreal under the bright Keno Flo lights, washing reality in a garish, cartoon flavoring. Colors are punched up. Edges sharpened. Sweat glistens. One Asian girl double fists another guy's whale cock as it flips to-and-fro in her hands. It's an X-rated hentai cartoon with a girl wrestling a tentacle!

Below me, the swap-sucking continues. One girl is gracious enough to hold my dick in place while the other girl assaults it. Belinda then stands to kiss me leaving Alicia on her knees to attend to my dick, solo. Lazy arms draped across my shoulders. Me cupping a firm, young ass. I drift in the moment.

I guide Belinda down to the floor and fuck her where she lies. I cover her with my body, turning myself into a man-blanket, only to be chided by Jackson, a camera man, that "I can't see shit! Open up for the camera."

"*SWITCH!*" screams Alpha Man from behind another camera.

The game of musical cocks begins. The girls all make dashes crisscrossing the room to their next fuck partners like door busters on Black Friday. I see a Korean girl, Lena, who insisted on sticking with only two guys, including me, look at me with pleading eyes from across the blur of bodies sprinting across the space between us. Before I can react, a tiny hand with alarming strength tugs at my arm, dragging me away. I give Lena an I'm sorry shrug as I am pushed down into the sofa. I'm looking up at a pair of eyes peeking out at me from behind a cascade of sweat-drenched hair. The familiar warmth of snug vagina encircles my penis. I sit there while she bounces up and down on my dick, getting off several times. A few girls nearby our spot in the orgy stop to watch as this kid flows from orgasm to orgasm.

"You go girl! Get you some!" cheers one of the other girls. Occasionally, I actually fuck her back, but the reason I'm conservative with the fucking is the girl has a death-grip pussy. If I fuck her back and I pop, I'm done for.

Moans, more akin to a zombie invasion than a fuck-fest, fill the air from all corners of the room, punctuated with staccato squeals. The girl on top of me humps away. This kid is killing me. Everything in me is telling me to come in her but I fight it. I divert my focus… It's really hot under these lights… I'm sweating. Wet slapping sounds of bodies crashing into each other surround me.

My balls twitch in preparations to unload. Not yet!

"*SWITCH!*"

Thank you, Jesus!

Before I can move, another girl lowers her hot muff onto my dick. Mercifully, she is not anywhere near as snug. Another coupling occupies a spot on the sofas next to us mirroring the same cowgirl position. Two pistons, side by side, in hypnotic up and down action. Keeping myself busy, I grab a breast dangling in front of me. Damn…fake. I suppress the desire to laugh as I recall an earlier conversation between two girls in the Alpha Man's waiting room:

"Wow, your tits look amazing. Are they real?"

"*Of course they're real!!*"

"*SWITCH!*" Still on my back, this time stretched across the same sofa. Two different girls. Random Girl Number One smothers me with her ass on my face. She and Random Girl

Number Two lick my cock in tandem as beautiful curtains framing bubble gum pink dangle in front of my nose. I lick. Can't see who is doing what, but you can feel that they have two distinct fellating styles. A tongue up and down one side of my shaft, while lips encircle the head.

"Sonoavabitch!" from somewhere across the tempest. Somebody has come too soon. There is always one. Arguing erupts.

"I'm okay! Gimmie a minute to recover!"

"Get the fuck off of my set, you goddamn mope!"

Better him than me.

"*SWITCH!*"

The fucking flowchart order is fucked to hell, so this time it's Tyler's choice. I want Alicia. A rival turns to my quarry. Fuck. *That.* I sprint, balls flapping and cock swinging, across the room and tackle a giggling Alicia Lee! I bend her over.

We lock together doggy style. She is shit talking. Taunting me while we sprint-fuck at the upper limits of my Viagra'd-up heart.

"Fuck me, damn it!"

"I am!"

My lungs burn as they fight to keep up the exchange of stale air for fresh.

"Harder! Fuck me like you mean it! C'mon, give it to me! Give-me-your-cock!"

The smell, once only on the periphery of my consciousness, now takes its place front and center of my senses. A unique bouquet of pheromones, assholes, balls, sweat, and pussy, all stirred up and baked under the Kino Flo lights. Inebriated by the musk of animal lust, I want to beat my chest and howl.

The Tourette's-afflicted Alicia says, "Yeah motherfucker, that's my spot—no don't slow down, you idiot! Ugh, you suck at fucking!"

Alicia flexes her Kegels. She aims to pop me, and she will if I am not vigilant. We've been locked together into this position for several rotations now, ignoring the calls for "Switch!" Same nerves on my dick being stimulated over, and over. Her pussy heats to the friction.

She coos, "There, there, it's okay."

Somebody calls, "*SWITCH!*"

Alicia, talking shit, does not give me the option of zoning my mind out. Each time I'm on the brink, I attempt to compartmentalize my environment and what is happening to me. Each time, she finds me and drags me back to the orgy. No escape.

I'm a professional… I cannot let this girl make me pop too soon… I made it this far!

The hormones and chemicals soaking my brain mix lust and fear. Fear that if she does pop me I will be humiliated like the mope that got fired earlier. Reputation in this business is everything, and a fuck up this early in my career will cost me my livelihood or, at best, send me back to the bukkake line. I make an error of looking down… A heart-shaped ass wrapped in golden skin. Sweat beads skip and bounce, pooling in a reservoir on her lower back… A tan line-shaped "T"; the top of the T spreads out across her hips and the stem plunges down into the crevasse… My hands gripped around her hips. Fingers digging into her flesh. My eyes lose focus and my balls twinge.

Dear God, I'm gonna co—"*CUT!*"

Teetering on the edge of bliss, I withdraw myself from Alicia with great care, but she reaches back and claws my side, fighting for my dick like a snarling hyena on a bone. I'm free.

Pop shot time.

The girls all kneel side by side. The men file behind one another to one-by-one jerk off into the starlets' faces.

And that would be me, last in line, standing in front of the kneeling, drenched women. Torqueing my dick. Unable to come. This is almost funny.

The pop shots are all timed. Timed in the sense that the director's dream is to get every pop shot off within seconds of each other. Timed also in the sense that I know they are running out of tape. This pressure is not conducive to getting off. It is cruel, having to save my one shot for when it is most convenient for someone else. I know there is nothing erotic about stroking off to girls drenched in other men's come. So I choose to not see them. I shut my eyes.

Stroke-stroke-stroke-stroke… Sounds of snowballing—come swapping between the girls—enter my ears. I've learned from experience with a bukkake that I have to keep my eyes shut at all costs.

I stand over the last girl who is drenched in come, almost ready to glaze her face with my load. If coming too soon is the worst, then coming last in an orgy is a close second. I go into my mind and conjure up images of Alicia, doggy.

Stroke-stroke-stroke… An unseen girl says to another girl, "Mm mmm. Lemme lick that come off your chin!"

Shut the fuck up!

Stroke-stroke-stroke…

Swishing sounds.

Almost there—Stroke-stroke…

Cum gargling.

I find my groove and release my load.

Two hours of non-stop fucking.

I hate pussy.

As soon as my pop, the last pop, is delivered, Alpha takes his hand-held camera and asks the girls to rate each guy and how he fucked her. The mini feuds that I was oblivious to during the orgy surface. Some men rate a two out of ten. The kid that came too soon gets a zero. Mitch, whom all the girls love gets an average score of a nine. I get an eight. Can't please everybody.

⇨ ⇨ ⇨

THE HOUSE SEEMS EMPTY. Talent has headed to Alpha's Elusive Scoundrels office to get the paychecks. I find an empty bedroom and attempt something I've always wanted to try. It has been said that Ron Jeremy could suck his own dick. Using a wall for support, I flip my legs over my head. I stick out my tongue.

Damn! Just a half inch more—just then, the lights come on with a *flick!*

The bedroom floods with light, and from my upside down point of view I see porn stars that still have some fucking left in them enter. Other naked people whom I had no idea were in the room scurry about like roaches.

And then there's me. Asshole in the air. Trying to suck my own cock.

SOMETHING'S ROTTEN IN CHATSWORTH

I'M HOPPED UP ON Viagra tossing an Asian girl back and forth with Malik like we're Joe Montana and Jerry fucking Rice. Chemically enhanced, my skull is crunchy cereal caught in a vice from the Inquisition and I've got a tone in my ears from my own private emergency broadcast station, wailing just for me.

"Cut," says Jackson. "We got enough vag, let's get the anal."

Great, ass-spelunking. I've never been a fan of the Sodomy Arts. When you see me digging in a girl's asshole, it's all about the money.

"Are you clean?" I ask the girl.

The female talent's preparation for an anal sex scene begins a day before she sets foot on set. This is when she stops eating. In a perfect situation, the girl has the discipline to fast for the entire day. If on the day of her scene there are pages of dialogue to shoot, the girl may still have to wait around for an additional half day before the filming of the sex actually starts. Dialogue is always filmed before the sex scene to preserve the girl's hair and makeup.

Food catering, aka craft service, offers temptations. Because of expediency, craft service is almost always some kind of fast food. Mexican. Or Chinese. Often there's Starbucks delivered to set, which could restore her food depleted energy levels. Today is no different.

Right before filming the anal sex, the girl takes an enema bottle and a box of baby wipes to clean out whatever residual matter may still be lurking inside her colon. The amount of food material remaining depends on the individual's digestive system. And her discipline. The starlet alternates between the enema and warm water. When she's confident she's clean, she chews a couple of Imodium tablets which slow her bowels.

Our girl says, "Yeah, but lemme clean up a little bit more," and goes off set to the bathroom, taking a box of baby wipes from the rape kit with her.

With no girl on the bed, I'm self-conscious lying next to another dude while we both stroke our cocks to keep our motors running in feminine absence. I stand up.

Jackson, the director sits on the foot of the bed and says, "You been doing an a'ight job for Elusive Scoundrels, dog. You really stepped up these past couple of months."

DVD Gangstas reneged on my performing contract without paying me a cent, so I've moved on, shooting for any studio that'll use me as a hired gun. Business is spiraling down the toilet industry-wide thanks to Internet piracy and torrent sites, and to a lesser degree, the economy. The Elusive Scoundrels are taking care of me on a per-scene basis, and they shoot me a lot. I perform well, I'm insulated from economic pain.

"Thanks, man," I say. "I always give it my best."

Malik is the new "it" kid. He's on his back stroking his cock, using two hands but it's really a job for three. His dick is a baby's arm holding an apple. Malik busts a freestyle rap.

"So," I say, "I figure since I have a normal-sized dick I'll warm the girl up with me doing the first anal position."

"Nah, nigga," says Malik. "Lemme tap that ass first while I'm still hard. You got a smaller dick so you don't need as much to keep you going."

Pulling the size card... Nice.

"Whatever."

I've popped two one-hundred milligram Viagras in the past hour. This is many times the doctor-recommended dose. When I was a rookie, a chip of a pill could get me up. But after so many scenes, there are diminishing returns. Even at best, Viagra only helps me for an hour, two at the most, before it works against me. Where's this girl? This is fucking with my Viagra timing... let's go!

"Okay, back! Let's fuck!" she says, as she bounds onto the bed and into Malik's arms. They fall down together in their own little laughing pile of youth, and I'm as welcome as a speck of rat shit in your vanilla ice cream.

"Let's shoot this fucking thing," I say, and the kids stop their grab-assing.

"Action!" shouts Jackson, and back into the melee I go. I'm lying on my back, my dick in her mouth while Malik widens the gauge of her asshole with his dick. The blowjob sucks, and in this case this not a good thing. Malik is a battering ram and each impact either scrapes my dick against her teeth or knocks it out of her mouth entirely. I'm getting blown by a blender's hungry blades on puree. I feel the drug's window of efficacy closing and that's a motherfucker because my heart wants to leap the fuck out of my mouth and I'm getting a serious case of Viagra-numbed dick.

Malik is going DEFCON 4, slamming into the gates of her ass as though he's a barbarian laying siege to Constantinople.

"Switch," says Jackson.

Malik stops the assault and I position myself behind the girl's ass. Her sphincter is open, red and raw. Her gaping O-ring is damn near blown out, offering a clear shot of her textured, pink innards that seem to tumble on to infinity. On her rim, flecks of fecal matter that have the consistency of gruel and the color of bread gone bad. An unholy stench of slaughtered cows suspended in a vat of mayonnaise left to turn in the desert leaps out of her exposed cavity and slaps my face like a dame in a Bogart movie. The worst part of this is, the Viagra-and-exasperation cocktail has left me short of breath. And my mouth is open.

I snap my mouth shut and vacuum seal my lips, but the phantom taste still lingers on my palate.

Jackson peeks over the top of the camera's viewfinder. "Go ahead, nigga. Fuck ass. I'm rolling camera."

"I need a minute," I say.

Malik and the girl, giddy with porn-induced psychosis, continue their sport fucking while I kneel next to them with my cold cock in hand. Normally if my dick goes down I just have to look at a girl's ass and I'm dealt back in the hand, but I'm taking a bad beat on the river because sewer cheeks has eliminated my last out. Looking at her ass is not an option.

I'm rubbing a brittle, dry-rotted eraser passing for my dick with the business end of her ass, seen through my peripheral vision, aimed at me. I get off the bed and go into my mind.

Within the time it takes to microwave a bag of popcorn, an eternity in pornoland when timed location fees tick away like a taximeter, I manage to conjure up some shit from my mental wank bank to get me going.

I'm fucking the girl's ass, not looking down, mouth closed and taking sips of air from my nose because smell is the lesser of two evils.

Jackson positions himself behind me, holding the camera next to my head and shooting over my shoulder and down for the point-of-view/you-are-there shot. His dragon breath blows hot on my neck.

He whispers, "Gimmie some in-and-outs."

What he wants is for me to pull my dick out of the girl's asshole entirely so he can zoom in and shoot the gape. Every bit of common sense in me screams, *Don't do it!* Even if I was in a "normal" scene it's a challenge because I'm fast becoming erection-impaired, and I can't get the sloshing tempest I'm stirring up inside the girl's bowels out of my head.

I extract my penis and Jackson's stubbly face over my shoulder is making us some kind of fucked-up two-headed porn chimera and I'm cresting the apex of a roller coaster looking down.

I shove my cock back into her asshole and get a few strokes when Jackson whispers voice-of-God style into my ear, "Do it again."

My heart goes supernova and my field of vision diminishes to a speck. Could be from the adrenaline dump, could be from the side effects of the Viagra. Who the fuck cares? What difference does it make at this point? Again, I back my dick out of the asshole and—the barrel clicks on empty.

I look down. Her sphincter puckers and protrudes like a toothless old man's lips with a mouthful of Skoal. There is some seepage.

My dick freefalls. I stroke three or four times, not looking at the flecks of fecal matter on my shrinking shaft. I could point the leakage out to Jackson so the girl can clean up, but it's camouflaged into my skin and the last thing I want to do is stop the camera. I won't ever get back anything resembling an erection if we delay. I don't want to quit but my options are grim. So, I rub the shit flakes into my dick, using it as lube. A python plays grab, twist, and pull with my guts, and there's an acrid bite of bile in my mouth that singes the back of my throat.

I settle my gut and enter her asshole once again. This time I have to death-grip the base of my shaft like a carnival balloon to milk enough blood flow for penetration. Once again, fucking away with my flat-lined dick, not penetrating past the sphincter, and I'm so soft Stan does not have to tell me to pull out. She shits my pathetic nub of a cock out, and I concede defeat.

I'm still behind the girl in the line of fire when it happens. The aperture of her asshole snaps open and convulses and puckers like a heaving cat struggling with a hairball and her hole is a water cannon. Well, fecal cannon to be accurate.

She Gatling-guns feces, cabbage chunks, lo mien broccoli bits, sesame-sprinkled shit, and kung-pao crap (all held together by a matrix of translucent, Starbucks-steeped globs) onto me. Jackson uses me as a human shield.

It's *The Running of the Bowels*. Malik leaps off the bed and across the room as the girl scats on me. Nothing unshielded in her asshole's line of fire will ever be the same. Starting from the nexus of her dripping sphincter and radiating outward is a wet, sloppy, Cone of Death.

I hyperventilate, which, considering the circumstances, I may as well be huffing a colostomy bag. The fetid air is seasoned with intestinal spices; its taste coats thick and heavy on the back of my throat.

"Okay, cut!" Jackson says. Not a drop on his white track suit. "You need a minute, my man?"

I take a moment to control my breathing, but I can't. I say, "No, I do not need a 'minute'. It's a wrap for me, I'm done for the day."

"But you gotta finish. This is only the first anal position for you, and you gotta fuck her ass to pop."

Fuck her ass to pop... Is he fucking insane?

The mattress has dookie islands bobbing in a lake of molten shit. Fits of dry heaving overwhelm me, and I nearly blow chunks, adding to the geography with a puke archipelago. My penis curls up and out of the way for safe storage like a butterfly's proboscis.

"Jackson," I say, "I can't imagine anything that will get me hard again, let alone be able to fuck her ass to get off for a pop shot!"

He inspects his camera lens for flyaway spew, peels off what looks like a corn flake glued in place by yogurt, then sets his camera down. "Don't be a punk, man. You're a professional, take a Viagra or something."

My heart is no longer beating. It's vibrating so fast it glows in my chest like E-fucking-T.

"If you don't finish the scene," he says, "it's gonna jeopardize our business relationship."

Malik snatches the girl and throws her on the floor and fucks away.

Many seasoned porn whores develop an ability to check out at will. The girl, on her back, has unlit vacancy signs where her eyes once were. She reminds me of the lizard I saw on the Discovery Channel that flips onto its back and plays dead until danger passes. Hard to tell if she's even breathing. Apparently, this was as good for her as it was for me.

I say to Jackson, "What are you insinuating?"

Jackson says, "I think it's clear. This studio is putting cash money on your black ass."

He looks at Malik, masturbating with the girl's live body. I imagine a bit of her soul escaping from her slacked-open mouth with each savage thrust.

"I don't have to tell you it's competitive out there. There's a gang of niggas that want your slot, and they all got bigger dicks than you."

My pulse thrums in my eardrums and my mouth feels as though it's full of hot sand. I want to say something but when I pass my tongue over my cracked lips it snags like a cotton ball dragged over sandpaper. My skin should be drenched with sweat but it's dry. A clear sign for the onset of heat exhaustion. The ice chest by the door beckons to me. It has a lid, so its contents shouldn't be contaminated. I grab my clothes and stumble to the ice chest and rip it open…no ice…a half-empty Snapple and a room temperature can of Colt 45.

I make it down the hall to the bathroom and into the shower, and turn the knob to cold. You can almost hear the spray of water sizzle and pop off my skin. I lift my head and open my mouth.

RUY LOPEZ

IT'S AFTER THE SCENE and the director left and the pimp took his girl home. I'm wandering through the halls of the building, The Entertanium, in search of the bathroom so I can take a shower. When I enter the bathroom, a realization hits me... This building was the location where my porn career started, even before the bukkake. This is the bathroom where I almost fucked it up. And this is the story of how I met the woman without whom's love you'd be piecing my story together through an oculus sliding across a Ouija board.

The tech bubble had burst and company failures have reached critical mass as threats of Y2K loom. I'm in the cafeteria of my part-time day job picking over a sandwich I can't afford from the in-house Subway, contemplating job prospects because the firm announced phased layoffs. This job, in the telecommunications industry for one of the Baby Bells, was supposed to supplement my income between seasons while modeling was slow.

My first booker when I started modeling, Nick, at LA Models (who at the time represented a stable of supermodels), dropped me for not booking enough gigs. I visited Hero Men's Model Management/Fontaine through an open call. None of the other bookers sitting around the giant round booking desk showed interest in me, but Miguel stood up, stepped forward, and took me in.

Over the next decade Miguel took me with him from blue-chip agency to agency, so when the day came that he asked me to follow him to a nascent boutique shop, I didn't hesitate. When I stopped in to say my goodbyes, one of the other bookers at the agency warned me that Kurt, the guy whom Miguel was going to work for, was a notorious coke whore who couldn't be trusted. I thanked her for her concern and reminded her that the only reason the agency represented me was because Miguel brought me in. She sighed, pulled my Zed cards from the wall, and handed them to me.

At the smaller agency, I was no longer the third black male model in the depth chart so I booked more gigs: A local designer's fashion week show, a black hair care product, department stores, and *Women's Forum*, an Australian magazine that I was assured nobody would ever see. That first month things were going well. Another month came and went without checks in my mailbox for any of the work, and my rent was almost a month overdue. I called Miguel to ask about my checks, and he told me to come into the office to pick them up whenever I wanted. The next day I went to the agency, and pushed the door open to a cleaned-out office with impressions in the carpet from where the booking desk used to be. It turned out that right after my phone call with

Miguel, Kurt fired him then absconded with all of the models' money earned from bookings over the previous month.

So, after my modeling career died, this part-time day job became my only source of income. One day, when exiting the library, this guy runs up to me, introduces himself as Gino Colbert, and hands me a business card.

"Have you ever considered making films?" he asked.

"What kind of films?"

"I think you know."

"Ha-ha, no thanks, dude. I'm straight."

"It's cool. I've got connections on the straight side. You're a handsome guy, but you're not going to look like that forever. Why not earn decent money while you can?"

After a week of burning a hole through his card with my eyes, I called. Then I was on my first set for VCA, failing through a sex scene with Chloe, their contract starlet. The set was dressed like a restaurant and filled with background extras staring at my limp penis. All I had to do was get hard, but with two dozen people in the room it was impossible. At that point in my life I'd only been naked before my mom, a handful of girls, and God, and this magical blue pill was just a rumor. So I stroked my nub of a penis buried so deep into my pelvis it could have been mistaken for a retractable claw. The silence was broken only when men balancing twenty-pound Betamax cameras slung over their shoulders sighed in contempt.

The director, Veronica Hart, called "Cut!"—handed me a stack of nude magazines and told me to step off set to get myself hard. "Come back when you're ready," she said.

I took a magazine, *JUGGS*, with me to the bathroom, sat in the shower stall, stroked myself up to an erection…but came in my hand! Now I just wanted to escape rather than return to set and face the wrath of the crew. I considered getting a running start and diving through the second-story window, but my pants were still on set, and it's only cute running around downtown LA in a shirt with no pants if you're Winnie-the-Pooh.

The other contact Gino gave me was at DVD Gangstas, but they weren't returning my calls. Word of new talent failure spreads fast in Porn Valley.

The day before, I came home from work to a Three-Day Notice to Pay Rent or Quit tapped to my apartment door. The only job listing in *LA Weekly* which I could get hired right away was a call for men to perform with their favorite porn starlets in a bukkake...whatever a bukkake is. After looking up "bukkake" on the Internet, I allowed myself a moment to melt the fuck down. Then I wiped my eyes, tore the ad out of the paper, and started packing essentials into a sea bag.

A girl enters the cafeteria. A sheen of perspiration on her skin. Glossy like a fashion magazine. High heels click. White linen shorts thin enough to almost see through as she walks past my table. She sits down with some other girls. The woman is Helen of Troy. When she walks past my table again, I look down into my mutilated turkey and Swiss... The clicking of heels on linoleum stops.

"Infermo mental, pervertido sexual!"

"Hi...I, uh...sorry, I don't speak Spanish."

"You understood what I said."

"Who the hell starts a conversation with someone they've never met by calling them a...a pervert?"

"A girl sick of you staring at her ass every day for months. This is the last week before the company shuts down. Were you ever going to say something, or just creep on me?"

"I uh. I..."

"Good. I'm giving you a do over. Get up, come back, and introduce yourself properly."

"L'esprit de l'escalier?"

"This is America. English, please?"

We laugh together.

"We're already talking."

"I'm a traditional girl. Now come back and introduce yourself like a man. Come on, get up!"

"But, people are watching—"

"Let's go, pervert. Stalk is cheap, baby!"

"Sorry. I guess I'm all stalk no action… Besides, you've heard it all before."

"I have. You choked. I already left. You let me go, so there's no pressure. This is so you don't beat yourself up on the long bus ride home."

"Alright. Fine."

Get up and return.

"Hi, I—"

"Fuck off, creep."

Laughter.

"Aww, Pobrecito. I'm Amanda. Sit."

"Erik."

"Erik, nice to meet you."

Smiles.

"You speak English well. Where are you from?"

"A dangerous place. I got away with words."

"'A dangerous place?'"

"Subject closed."

"But—"

"Respect my wishes, Erik."

"Sorry… No boyfriend?"

"Nope."

"Why not?"

"I'm saving myself for a man who doesn't need saving."

"Hah! Good luck with that in LA."

"What about you?"

"Me? Grew up back east. Came out here for college. Dropped out. Stayed in LA. Nothing exciting."

"I'll give you some advice, Erik."

"What's that?"

"This is the part where you're supposed to sell yourself. How is telling a girl you dropped out of college, drifted around, and there's nothing exciting about you supposed to get me excited about you?"

"I guess you're right… What are you going to do when this gig is over?"

"There's this company, Inglés Sin Barreras…they help Latino Americans speak better English. Maybe I'll work for them. And you?"

I think of the ad for the bukkake folded in my wallet next to my few remaining dollars.

"Honestly, the company closing down isn't a surprise…but I'm not really sure yet."

We sit in silence. She frowns and stares at my Nirvana T-shirt with a crooked smile printed on it while I stare at her upturned nose which crinkles when she frowns. I want to kiss her.

"*Bailamos!*"

"Huh"

"Let's dance. You're taking me dancing!"

"I don't dance well…at all."

"Do you always talk yourself out of getting laid?"

"Yes."

"Pick me up tonight."

"I don't have a car."

"We'll meet there. After, you can walk home. Safer than driving drunk anyway."

"It's never safe for me to walk drunk in public."

"What, are you in AA or something?"

"Yeah, African American."

"I don't get it."

"Never mind, it wasn't funny anyway. I have something planned."

"*Mentiroso!*"

"What?"

"Liar!"

A girl from another table walks up to ours.

"Hi, Erik."

"Hi, Patricia."

"This layoff thing really sucks, doesn't it? You're not gonna leave without giving me your—"

I follow Patty's eye line to Amanda who's shooting a soul-burning stare that I follow back to Patty who has turned and walked away.

When I look back at Amanda, her eyes are closed as she gyrates her hips, dancing in her seat to music in her head. "*Que fue?* You're scared. I know."

"What?"

As she moves to music only she can hear, I steal a glimpse of the curve of her butt as it wiggles on the bench, and that sight takes my breath away.

"What?"

She watches me, watching her. A smile. I look away, down into my glass where the cubes have melted and merged into a mini iceberg.

"Shhhh. It's okay, *Negrito.*" She nods at my shirt. "Where would Cobain be if he never found Love?"

I smile. "Alive."

ATTRITION

*ATTRITION \ə-TRI-shən\ [MIDDLE ENGLISH attricioun, from Medieval Latin attrition-, attritio, from Latin]
1: a gradual reduction in numbers as a result of resignation, retirement, or death.

2: the act of weakening or exhausting by constant harassment, abuse, or attack.

3: repentance for sin motivated by fear of punishment rather than by love of God.

Julio St. Lox and I put two MILFs through the paces on a pet-stained sofa when an effeminate pimp and an androgynous pixie enter the set. They stand off camera in silence, watching Julio and me work. Pixie girl hikes up her skirt, pulls her panties to the side, and fingers herself.

Flea, the director, acknowledges the pimp and his girl's entrance with a silent nod and continues filming. He pushes the camera in for a close-up with one hand, and mimes a motion that resembles shaking dice with the other: pop at will. Julio looks at me and we exchange nods. We're ready. We dismount from our women and stand shoulder to shoulder, stroking our dicks. The MILFs sink to their knees in front of us and angle their faces upward. Julio and I pop together.

Flea says, "Cut. Hold for stills."

Flea has swapped his video camera for a digital stills camera. The camera flashes as he snaps pics. When he's done with the stills, I pick some dog hairs, glued in place by lubricant, off my dick. The MILFs leave and the girl that came with the pimp replaces them, kneeling before us. She wraps her lips around my penis and works on me until I'm erect again.

Flash!

Flea checks the shot he just took on his camera's screen. "Who's the girl?"

Femme Pimp says, "Eris. She's street legal: her test is good through the end of the month."

Eris switches to Julio. She sucks him to get him going while she strokes me.

Flash!

Flea says, "Who's she shot for?"

"Alpha Man, Red Assholes Films…just a handful of scenes. It's slow for her, so I'm taking her around on sets for some go-sees to help her out."

I sit on the sofa and pull Eris on top of me, cowgirl. She's not the best piece of ass I've had but whatever, she's there. Julio sits next to me and pushes her head into his lap. Flea orbits us, pointing his camera.

Flash! Flash!

"I'm finishing up this *MILF Chocolate* movie," Flea says, "and then I've got *Brothas Love Phat White Ass*. She doesn't fit into the lines I'm shooting right now. What about Gideon Roads? Maybe he'll throw her into a bukkake."

Femme Pimp says, "Already tried. He's not interested. Don't you have a blow bang coming up?"

Flea sighs. "I guess. What's her rate per scene?"

The pimp quotes a sum that would be insulting for a mope. "Cut that in half, and maybe…"

The pimp points to Eris, bounding on my dick. "Come on, look at her fuck! Hey, you wanna try her out yourself?"

Flash!

"I'll pass."

Julio gets up from the sofa and leads Eris by the hand down a hall. I follow them to a bedroom door, and when Julio opens the door a team of dogs and cats escape and run past our feet. When the last beast has exited I pull the door by the handle and it creaks shut behind me. Eris climbs onto the bed and gets on her hands and knees. Julio mounts her. After a while we switch off and I mount her.

The bedroom door creaks open.

Flash.

⇨ ⇨ ⇨

As I'm parking my car, I notice the brakes feel soft and I make a mental note to get them checked. The driver's side door doesn't lock, but nobody's going to steal a rusted-through car with a carburetor. It's the end of a workday, consisting of two Viagras and, including Eris, five girls on three different sets. The reek of pussy, ass, and sweat clings to me the way cigarette stench lingers on a chain-smoker's clothes and fingertips. I'd have preferred to shower after last scene with Julio and the MILFs, but dog hairs and set grime infest my clothes. (When was the last time you saw porn stars stop to fold their clothes? Never, we rip them off and toss them on the floor.) It made no sense to clean up only to put them back on again for the drive home. I feel greasy. My pores feel clogged, like I'm suffocating through my skin.

Home for Amanda and me is a duplex on a hillside cul-de-sac of Melrose Hill. Named one of LA's ten best neighborhoods, you could live your entire life in the city and never know this tree-lined oasis exists. No traffic. Neighborhood children's laughter sparkles in the air as they chase after the ice cream truck. The fact that Amanda and I don't live in the Valley was a conscious decision to compartmentalize my work, and keep it away from our home life.

When I enter our home I leave the front door open behind me and take a moment to open some windows. A breeze sways the curtains, and light from the setting sun fills the space. Our sofa, dining room table, and bookcase all bask in the golden light.

My mail is laid out for me in a neat stack on the table. Bills. Checks from different studios. An envelope from my bank. Inside it is a check from a studio and letter stating the check has been returned for insufficient funds. I scroll through contacts in my cell phone.

"Good afternoon, The Wad Fathers Studios, Charon speaking. How may I direct your call?"

"This is Tyler Knight. Let me speak with Scowl Pacino, please."

"Regarding?"

"A bounced check."

"Please hold."

While on hold, I read more of the letter. The bank will charge a returned check fee to my account.

"Scowl isn't available, but he said to just go ahead and redeposit the check."

"My bank charged me a fee, and I want to be reimbursed."

"Go ahead and redeposit it and we'll mail you another check to cover the charge."

"Fine."

Amanda calls to me from the bedroom, and I go to her. A parti-colored bowling shirt, wrapped in dry-cleaning plastic, hangs from the bedroom doorknob. Date night. Amanda is buttoning up a matching bowling shirt in front of a mirror. She catches me in its reflection.

"*Te amo.*"

"Te amo."

I walk past her and into the master bathroom without stopping to hug or kiss her, and she makes no attempt to embrace me. Shower first; a protocol we never break.

Amanda enters the bathroom but keeps her distance. "You smell like cat piss."

"Yeah."

"How was work?"

"Not going to talk about it."

"You never want to talk about it."

I kick off my shoes. "Correct."

"Why?"

"'Why?' You know why."

"How are we supposed to have a normal relationship if you never want to talk about anything?"

My clothes weigh me down like spilt crude on a baby seal's white fur. I peel off my shirt, pants, socks, and underwear, and stuff them into the hamper. "We talk about everything, just not my work. You know that, so stop asking me."

Amanda glowers at me as I pour a cup of blue mouthwash and gargle. I swish the minty alcohol over my tongue and teeth. It has a pleasant burn inside my cheeks.

She says, "This is not healthy, Erik."

I spit out the mouthwash and foam fizzles in the sink.

I say, "I don't want to bring that shit home with me. What we have together is the only normal thing in my life, and I'm not going to poison it."

She scoffs and points to my clothes rotting away in the hamper.

I say, "Can we talk about this after I take a shower, please?"

"Whatever."

I pin the shower knob to "H" and steam thickens the air. I lather up, rinse, and lather up some more. With some pumice scrub, I excavate the muck that has seeped into my pores. Next, I soap up the fingernail brush and scrub the left hand, then the right. Then I work some dandruff shampoo into a lather, scratching it into my scalp with my fingernails. It has a cooling menthol tingle and scent, so I let the foam sit in my hair for a while. I place my hands on the wall, lower my head, take deep breaths as the hot water massages my neck and back.

Looking down, I see Amanda's scrunchie on the tub sill. I don't want to fight with Amanda, and she doesn't want to fight with me… She just wants to feel involved. Loved.

Clean clothes, including the bowling shirt, are laid out for me on the bed.

I say, "I'm sorry."

"I know."

"You hungry? Let's go eat first."

She smiles. "Okay, but it's got to be drive through. I can't be seen with you in that shirt, ha-ha."

We hug, then kiss. Her lip gloss tastes like green apples.

As we separate, something about my ear catches her attention. She picks it out. A dog hair.

⇨ ⇨ ⇨

I'm WALKING TOWARD THE Bon Voyage motel in the Valley. The motel has a reputation as a house of ill repute. Entire apartment buildings along this stretch of the street serve as drug dens. I used to live on this block, and not long ago I nearly died here, too.

An LAPD cruiser on the other side of the street flashes its lights, cut across four lanes of traffic, and drives up the sidewalk and screeches to a stop in front of me. The doors fling open and two screaming police officers rush out, aiming their guns at my chest.

It only takes about four pounds of pressure to pull a trigger, firing the gun and sending a bullet into its target. Anyone with firearms training knows that you never place your finger inside the trigger guard unless you intend to shoot. Both cops approach me with their fingers inside their trigger guards, wrapped around their triggers.

One cop screams, "Get on the ground! Now!"

The other cop contradicts his partner's command, "Don't move!"

The normal range of my voice is bass. In an attempt to sound less threatening, I raise its octave and make it resonate from my nasal cavity rather than my chest. "Could you make up your minds, please?"

"Put your hands on your head, turn around, and get down on your knees!"

I do.

People walking on the other side of the street look at me and point. Cars slow down to get a better look at me. Drivers crane their necks as they pass by, hoping for the worst outcome so they can tell the anecdote later.

A cuff bites into my wrist. My arms are twisted behind my back, another cuff snicks into place around my other wrist. Hands push me forward, and without free hands to break my fall, I fall onto my face. A knee digs into my back, pinning me in place like a butterfly specimen mounted on display.

The cop who cuffed me asks, "You have ID on you?"

I measure each word. "In my wallet, sir."

"Any needles or sharp objects in your pocket?"

"No."

Hands dig into my pocket and free my wallet. The information on my ID is read off into a walkie talkie.

The cement has scrapped my cheek and it stings. I'm probably bleeding but I don't dare move. I keep my cheek flush with the sidewalk. After a moment, there's chatter on the walkie talkie.

A cop says, "This ain't him."

The other cop says, "You sure?"

"Yeah, wrong guy. Cut him loose."

The knee in my back lets up, cuffs are removed, and I stand.

Red and the blue alternating lights from the police cruiser strobe across their faces. Their name tags say Borjas and Madero.

Borjas reads my More Than Waffles T-shirt and says, "I've been meaning to try that place out. Is the food any good?"

I don't respond. My hands are at my sides, my posture is slumped. I control my breathing, and remain still.

Borjas shrugs and returns my IDs.

Madero says, "Let's go."

They walk back to their squad car with its still flung-open doors.

The first time the cops drew their guns on me I was fresh off the plane, standing at a bus stop in front of the college I was attending.

To the LAPD, if you look like me, you're a criminal, ipso facto. Whenever you're stopped by the LAPD while walking, it's:

1) "Yes, sir. No, sir."

2) No direct eye contact.

3) Hands out of pockets and no sudden movements.

If you're stopped while driving, include:

4) Hands at ten-and-two on the steering wheel.

5) Look straight ahead.

6) Do not move.

You must be accommodating to the police while they reach inside your chest, rip out your humanity and dignity—sometimes at gunpoint—and discard them on the sidewalk, and at the slightest perceived provocation, close the book on your life.

It's the twenty-first century, but I don't feel free... Certainly not free to enjoy many mundane things others take for granted, like an evening stroll without concern of the predators in navy blue enforcing a de facto curfew... Always wondering, Is today the day I don't make it back home to Amanda? *It wears on me day after day, week after week, year after year. Trapped in—and by—my own skin. I want to scream.*

"Hey!" I say, "Are you two going to tell me what that was all about?"

The words have left my mouth before I realized I've shouted at them. I don't care.

Madero pauses behind the driver's side door. There's the LAPD decal with "to protect and serve" printed in cheerful font on the door.

Madero says, "Yeah. You almost got shot, homie."

He shuts the door. The flashing lights cut off and they speed away.

Eris answers the door after the first knock. Rashes cover her skin and her clavicles jut through the fabric of her dress. She smiles, revealing yellowed, film-covered teeth. *How the fuck could I have missed these details last week?* I didn't miss them. She's changed.

She steps aside, allowing me to enter her motel room. Mismatched furniture. Thrift store paintings hang askew on the walls. Threadbare blanket on a mattress. Nicotine-stained curtains, drawn shut. You could cross the room in two paces.

I say, "Are you okay?"

She scratches the back of her hand, then picks at a scab. "Not really. I finally got a scene last week, but Reginald—remember the guy who was taking me around to sets?—He has my money and his cell phone is disconnected. I'm so sorry for having to call you, but I'm all by myself here and I can't pay rent and I don't know what else to do." Her eyes lower to the floor.

Earlier today I did a scene and they paid me in cash. I give the money to her. "This should help for a while."

Eris looks up at me, smiles, and hugs me. "Thank you."

She falls back onto the mattress, peels her panties off and opens her legs. There are sores around her vagina. "I have an itchy pussy but you can still fuck me. Oh! Don't worry about the cream, it's just Vagisil… Do you have a condom?"

I say, "No, I don't, I just came here to help you. Besides, I know what it's like."

She picks at a scab on her inner thigh. "Ha-ha, how could you know what an itchy pussy is like?"

I force myself to look at her eyes, not her crotch. "No, I uh… I've been in your situation before."

"I was kidding, Tyler."

"Oh. Sorry."

Eris says, "I can suck your dick if you want."

"No, I'm cool."

She pulls her panties up and folds her hands in her lap. "Can you just…sit with me for a while?"

There's a sad desperation in her eyes. I capitulate and sit on the bed next to her.

"Okay," I say. "For a little while."

She stares at her hands. I fixate on a cigarette hole burnt into the curtain. Neither of us speaks. Eris places her hand in the space between us, palm up. A clear gesture for me to take her hand in mine. I don't. She retracts it.

I look to the door. Amanda and I agreed that I do what I must to keep the bills paid, as long as it's confined to set. Amanda's trust in me is absolute. God knows, I haven't been perfect—just being here is a violation of her trust. A police car passes by the window. Its lights paint the ceiling red and blue as it speeds by. I walk to the door and open it.

Eris calls after me, "You're the only person in the Valley who doesn't try to take advantage of me. You've got a kind heart, Tyler. You're a beautiful snowflake."

The door clicks shut behind me, and it's all I can do to keep from breaking into an all-out run. In the lobby I pause at a trash can, take a condom out of my pocket, and toss it in. At the heart of every snowflake is a grain of dust.

⇨⇨⇨

AMANDA WAKES ME WITH kisses, and we make love. I wait for her to climax, then I roll off of her without climaxing myself. I've got a full day and it's important to save it for the camera.

We've got time before either of us has to be anywhere, so we dress and take a walk together through Griffith Park. Our favorite place is Ferndell Trail, a lush arboretum with bridges that cross a rolling stream. Sunlight cascades through a canopy of giant sequoias. Dragonflies with stained-glass wings flitter in light. We sit on a bench, and listen to water falling over rocks.

⇨ ⇨ ⇨

USUALLY MY CALL TIME is set up so that by time I walk on set we're ready to roll camera, and I jump right into the scene. I dropped my first Viagra of the day on the drive over.

When I enter the house I notice the lights aren't set up, the video equipment is still in their boxes, and plastic bins are scattered across the floor.

Flea and Trisha Marie, my scene partner, are sitting on some bins. Flea stares at his cell phone. Trisha, still dressed in her street clothes, is smoking a bowl of kush.

I say, "We running late?"

Neither of them responds.

"Hello?"

Flea looks at me and says, "Daniel's test came back positive. He has HIV."

"What do you mean, positive? I thought he was still shooting Brazil with Alpha Man the Elusive Scoundrels crew…"

"They came back, and he took his HIV test a few weeks early."

"Shit…did he get infected over there?"

"Nobody's sure yet, but probably."

Trisha pulls out a prescription bottle filled with kush from her jeans pocket and starts repacking her bowl.

I say, "How's he taking it?"

Trisha says, "How the fuck do you think he's taking it, Tyler?"

Trisha makes room for me on her bin and I sit next to her.

I say, "Alpha asked me if I wanted to go on that trip, but Amanda said no way... That could have been me. Anyone else from the Elusive Scoundrels crew infected? Alpha? Mitch Adams or Malik?"

Flea says, "No, they're clean." He shakes his head. "I feel terrible, man. Daniel is such good guy."

"Yeah."

Trish passes the bowl to me. I take a hit and hold the smoke in my lungs. I offer it to Flea, but he waves it off. I take another hit and pass it back to Trisha. Flea goes back to staring at his phone, and Trish and I pass the bowl back and forth. A wave of euphoria washes over me and there's a tingling sensation in my teeth.

Trisha empties her bowl and scrapes the resin with a car key. She says, "I don't mean to sound insensitive, but..."

"Right," Flea says, "What do you guys want to do?"

Trish says, "I'm already here. Let's fuck."

I shrug. Flea stands, opens the plastic he was sitting on, and pulls out the rape kit.

⇨⇨⇨

The scene is over and I'm driving on the freeway, talking to Amanda on the cell phone.

She says, "Is anyone else infected besides Daniel?"

"Nobody knows, yet."

She says, "And people are still shooting?"

"I guess. My scenes for tomorrow are still on, and I'm still booked solid next week. Nobody canceled."

"You're going to cancel your scenes."

I say, "That's a lot of money, babe."

"Are you fucking kidding me? Don't be an idiot. You're not working until everything is figured out. Not until it's known whom he worked with since he came back from Brazil…this is exactly why I didn't want you to go on that trip. Those putas over there are nasty, and you can't tell me they test the same as you do here in the States."

"Yeah… I'll be home soon."

"Te amo."

"Te amo."

⇨ ⇨ ⇨

A FEW PHONE CALLS placed to others in the industry reveal a few details: Magnanimous Adult Industry Medical, the adult industry's HIV/STD testing center, has released Daniel's *real* name to the general public; M.A.I.M. also set up a quarantine list for the people who have worked with Daniel since his return from Brazil. This list is posted on the Internet for all to see; Porn industry message boards are filled with rumors, half-truths, fear mongering, and blame. Everyone from industry members to fans has their opinion, but nobody knows what's going on.

I've been spending the past few days hanging out at home with Amanda. Right now, she's out grocery shopping and I'm playing an online game of Counter-Strike.

My phone rings. It's Dana Divine. I log off and answer.

"What's up, Dana?"

She says, "Remember Eris, that girl you and Julio had fun with on Flea's set?"

"Yes."

"Daniel worked with her before you fucked her. She's HIV positive—"

I feel like I plunged through thin ice and into a freezing lake.

"—you need to retest right away, and—Tyler?"

I say, "Yeah...yeah, I'm here. Are you're sure?"

She says, "Alpha Man shot her with Daniel and Mitch Adams right when they returned from Brazil—I think it was a double anal cream pie scene. The quarantine list just got updated. It says she's positive.

"Anyway, Flea took some pictures of you and Julio having your way with her. Flea shared the pictures with Alfred, and I saw them, so that's how I know you've been exposed."

Flash!

"Thank you for telling me, Dana."

"Just so you know, Alfred posted pictures on the Internet of you fucking her. I told him not to, but he never listens to me..."

I say, "I gotta go, Dana."

This has to be a mistake...confusion about what's going on... I Alt/Tab away from Counter-Strike and log onto the quarantine website. The list is a chart of sorts. Daniel's name is at the very top as "Patient Zero." Below his name are the names titled "First Generation", people who have had direct sexual contact with Daniel. Now, there's a "Second Generation" list of people, those who have worked with the first generation, adding scores of people to the list. Eris's name, like Daniel's, has its own branch.

This can't be happening to me. This isn't real. Okay, relax, calm the fuck down and think... Wait, she did seem different when I saw her last...thinner...those sores! But, that can't be from HIV...could it? There's no way she'd be symptomatic that fast...right? What the fuck do I know? Nothing. Fucking HIV... Why me?

The girl who answers the phone at M.A.I.M asks for the names of everybody I've had sex with since my HIV exposure.

It's impossible to remember everyone because of the sheer volume of work I've been getting lately, and even if I could, I don't know all of their names. Often times, I don't bother to ask the names of everyone on the scene. I can't think straight, and after I give her a few names I draw a blank. We schedule an appointment for me come into M.A.I.M. tomorrow morning to retest tomorrow.

Amanda… We had unprotected sex many times since my exposure. Goddamn it! What do I know about female-to-male transmission? What are the odds of me getting HIV from Eris, then me giving it to Amanda? What's the incubation period? From what I understand, it's extremely difficult for a man to get infected through vaginal sex with an AIDS infected woman. I don't know a damn thing about how Daniel may have been infected. If it turns out that I'm HIV positive, I've put Amanda's life at risk the same as if I took a loaded gun, spun the barrel, and put it to her head. Christ, the only thing she's guilty of is loving me.

I call Amanda's cell, but I hang up before it rings.

⇨⇨⇨

M.A.I.M's OFFICE IS ON Ventura Boulevard near a coffee shop and a pet store. Inside, you could easily mistake the reception area for that of a dentist office. The waiting room is full.

When it's my turn, I tell the girl at the front desk who I am, and that I've been exposed to HIV. None of the other people in the reception area react to what I've just said. Conversations continue. I'm invisible. The receptionist gives me a clipboard with some forms, and I hand her my driver's license. The forms include spaces for personal information, the types of tests I am taking today (HIV, gonorrhea, chlamydia), and a waiver of privacy so that my test results may be disclosed. My hands shake as I write, so much so that I have to ask for a second set of forms. When I'm done I hand the clipboard back and she gives me a plastic cup, which I take into the bathroom.

I fumble with my zipper, and it takes concentration to steady my aim so that my stream makes it into the cup. I screw the lid back on the cup, wash my hands, and splash some water on my face. I compose myself, leave the bathroom, and head for the blood-drawing stations.

I sit in the chair and roll up my sleeves for the nurse. She gasps when she sees the scarred-over craters in the crooks of my elbows. The holes are right at the spot where a junkie would shoot heroin, and they are large enough to push a pencil through. She doesn't ask. She composes herself and ties a rubber tourniquet around my arm. The nurse swabs the area with alcohol and stabs at the scar tissue with a needle, but it does not penetrate. I make a fist and a vein bulges on my forearm. She stabs the vein and the needle glides in easy. Blood spurts into the collection tube, and it starts to fill.

The scars inside the crooks of my elbows are souvenirs from my homeless days when I needed money for food. Blood is life, and I've sold just enough life to stave off death. Whole blood is made up of red blood cells, white cells, and plasma. They only let you sell whole blood once every few weeks because your body needs time to regenerate its lost red blood cells. When you donate, your identification is shared in a database so you can't game the system by going from center to center before enough time has passed. It takes weeks for the human body to regenerate lost red blood cells, but plasma, however, is replenished quickly and may be sold twice a week, so I switched.

The reason the scars are so large is because the gauge of the needles they stick in your veins for plasma collection are wide enough to drink a milkshake through. They have to be to prevent clogging. When you donate plasma, you're hooked up to a machine that sucks your whole blood out of your vein, spins your blood inside a centrifuge machine to separate your red blood cells from your plasma. The machine keeps your plasma and returns your red blood cells back to you through the needle. This process repeats itself for several cycles until your plasma donating quota, based on your weight, is fulfilled. If you're a larger man, you must give more plasma per visit than a smaller man, but your pay doesn't scale accordingly. You get paid exactly the same. For a man my size, it takes many repeat cycles of sucking, separating, and returning, and I could be hooked up to the machine long enough for me to watch a movie. You learn not to eat fatty foods before you donate, because excess fat in your blood may clog the needle, slowing the process even further. Now do you understand why I hate needles?

When I've filled the collection tube with blood, the M.A.I.M. nurse removes the needle, swabs the area and puts a band-aid on. This is to be the first of many HIV tests I have scheduled over the coming weeks. I'll have the results for this one in a few days.

⇨ ⇨ ⇨

I'VE SEQUESTERED MYSELF TO my bedroom while waiting for my test results to come in. Waiting in a room to find out if I have a disease that may kill me in a slow and painful fashion, I can't handle the idea of going out in public and interacting with other people as though everything is okay.

Amanda checks in on me, asks if I'm hungry, and opens the drapes and windows. She gives me some space, but not much. She knows me better than anyone else does—that I tend to brood, and in a moment I may be a danger to myself. She's seen it happen before, and for far less. She leaves, but keeps the bedroom door open.

She returns with a game of Monopoly. She picks the thimble; I choose the shoe. While counting out the money, a lock of hair falls in front of her eyes and she smooths it back behind her ear. She looks up at me, hands me my starting money, and smiles. Just looking at her smiling at me shatters my negative mood, and leaves me with no choice but to smile, too. She picks up the dice and rolls.

⇨⇨⇨

FEW PEOPLE RETURN MY phone calls these days, so I log onto an online porn forum and sift through the gossip for any information. I read that some industry people say they can't understand why this is being blown out of proportion; apparently, I have AIDS; some male talent not on the list price gauge, charging two and three times their usual rate; Daniel has gone missing; a second girl is infected with HIV. I log off and switch to the site for the HIV quarantine chart.

The online quarantine chart has grown. It confirms a second girl has tested HIV positive under Daniel. This brings the total of HIV infected, including Eris, to three people. On the chart, my name is listed under Eris as "First Generation" exposed. A "Second Generation" list with other people's names grows under mine.

There's a girl I worked with whose name is not on the list. Trisha Marie. I should to call her before I call M.A.I.M.—better she hears it from the source than from a porn gossip board or from some M.A.I.M. employee. But I don't have her number.

I make some calls. Nobody who answers the phone and will actually talk to me has her number. After leaving a few more voice mails I give up.

There's a news special on TV about HIV in porn. I watch it while I wait for people to call me back. The anchor, while getting some things right and raising important questions, digresses into ad hominem attacks on Daniel and Eris, because it's easy. I turn the TV off.

⇨ ⇨ ⇨

I'M ON THE PHONE with Jack Hammer. He's telling me about the porn industry "town hall" meeting that just took place, and how there was an agreement on an industry-wide moratorium on all shooting until the quarantine list has cleared.

He says, "Some other ideas were brought up, too… No more anal cream pies, oh, and no double anal scenes, because of the risk of the anal lining tearing. That, and prolapse."

"Yeah, we'll see how long that lasts. What else?"

"Some studios, VELVET and Decadent, are going condom-only, and they're insisting that other studios do the same, but…"

"Yeah."

He says, "There was a lot of push-back from some of the gonzo studios on the condom thing. Their argument was, 'Yeah, condoms might be a bit safer for the talent pool, but it would hurt business because nobody wants to buy porn with condoms. And since we all need strong product sell-through to earn a living…'"

"Let me guess: '…why make things difficult for everybody by using condoms? M.A.I.M.'s testing and protocols are working anyway…' Jesus, Hume's *Guillotine*, anyone? There are some smart folks in our business. People went along with this?"

He laughs. "Yeah, pretty much. I was thinking, *Check out the emperor's new condom...*"

⇨ ⇨ ⇨

IT'S DATE NIGHT AND Amanda and I just finished watching a movie. She insists that it's important to keep our routine and hold onto normalcy in spite of—and especially because of—the events unfolding around us.

While she's in the lady's room I wander around the gift shop. I pick up an art book with works by Francis Bacon, a painter I've never heard of. I turn to the page of the painting, "Three Studies for Figures at the Base of a Crucifixion." The first impulse upon beholding it is to drop the book where I stand. Three contorted figures, more beast than man, shriek in a claustrophobic room painted a hue between orange and blood red. The painting is a triptych, so even though they appear to be in the same room, each figure is confined to agonize in the isolation of its own panel. The description says that Bacon got his inspiration from Aeschylus' *Oresteia* and the three Furies that hunt down Orestes for his sins. From the effect this reproduction in an art book has on me, I can only imagine the impact standing before the lush paint of the original would have.

We drive home through the gloaming. Amanda talks on her cell. The imagery of that painting is still with me. How Bacon captured raw human emotion and foisted it upon the viewer... I've got to learn how to paint.

I glance in my rearview mirror, and what I see triggers an adrenaline dump. My mouth dries and my pulse speeds, but I will myself to remain calm. I check my speedometer, and when I reach an intersection I step on the brake and come to a complete stop. Then I signal and turn. When we get to the next intersection, I signal, stop, and turn again. My brakes are still soft because I've been putting off getting them fixed, so I apply them early enough to compensate for the increased stopping distance.

Amanda ends her call and puts her phone in her purse. She says, "Why are we driving in circles?"

I point to the rearview mirror. "Those cops are following us."

Another intersection. I turn. The cops turn.

She says, "No they're not. Why would they be following you?"

I come up on another intersection, and this time I apply my brakes a touch late and the nose of the car edges past the white line. There's a clarion scream of a siren and a spotlight blasts through our rear window. The light is intensified by the rear view mirror, filling the cabin with the brightness of the sun. I pull over, turn the engine off, then return my hands to ten-and-two on the steering wheel. The cops cut the siren off but they leave the spotlight focused on us.

I say, "Don't say anything, Amanda."

"Okay."

A cop stands at my window, slightly behind my left shoulder. He says, "How are you doing tonight?"

I know he doesn't give a damn, this is a feel-out question designed for the police to gauge the attitude of whomever they pull over.

I say, "I'm doing well, sir."

"What are you up to?"

I stare straight ahead. Through my windscreen. Focusing on a billboard a block away. Hands at ten-and-two. Digging my fingernails into the steering wheel.

He says, "Do you know why I pulled you over?"

"No sir, I do not."

"You were driving too slowly."

"Okay."

It's a vacation billboard. People frolicking on a white sand beach... "License, registration, and proof of insurance, please."

I say, "My registration and insurance are in the glove box. My girlfriend is going to reach into the glove box and get them, sir."

Amanda scrambles the contents of the glove compartment, including traffic tickets from the previous times I've been pulled over this month, in her search. Finally, she finds the papers and hands then to me. I take my right hand off of the steering wheel to accept them. Then I reach across my body with my right hand, left hand still gripping the steering wheel, and pass the documents across my body to the cop. With slow and deliberate movements, I use my right hand to pull my wallet out of my pocket, extract my license, and hand that to him with my right hand, also. I return my right hand to its place on the steering wheel. He goes to his cruiser. In the passenger-side mirror I see another cop from the neck down, posted sentry at the back of the passenger side door. His thumbs are looped in his belt.

Amanda's phone rings. She fumbles in her purse to answer it.

I say, "Get your hands out of your purse."

"But, I'm just getting my—"

"Look in your side mirror. See that cop there? You want to get shot?"

The headless cop in the mirror no longer has his thumbs hooked into his belt loops. They are now at his side, elbows bent slightly as if he's dying to say "Draw pardner!"

She says, "No, I'm sorry."

She turns to toss her purse onto the backseat. The headless mirror cop flinches.

I say, "Stop moving!"

In my driver's side mirror, I see the first cop, back lit by the spotlight, walking toward us. His hand goes to the butt of his gun as he gets closer. The steering wheel is a circle of butter dissolving in my hands.

Here we go… Okay, without looking, what clothes am I wearing? Baseball cap, T-shirt, shorts with a draw-string… They'll take the drawstring out… My shoes have laces…no, they'll probably take my clothes and shoes and put in county blues and slippers… I say, "Amanda, if they take me into custody—"

"But you didn't do anything!"

"If they arrest me, call my mother so she can contact her attorney."

Her voice quivers. She tries to hold back tears, but fails. "Don't worry, Papito. I love you, we have each other."

The cop is at my window again, "Okay, you have no warrants, but—"

His hand still rests on the butt of the gun.

"—you still never told me what you're doing in this neighborhood."

I say, "If you read the address on my license, you'll see that I live nearby, officer."

"You did a rolling stop at the last intersection. Here's a ticket for that. I'm also giving you a 'fix it' ticket for the crucifix dangling from your rearview mirror. It's a hazard."

He hands me the tickets and returns my documents. I reach across my body with my right hand, take them, then return my hands to the steering wheel. The cops return to their car. They keep the spotlight on us and wait for me to drive away first. I stuff the insurance, registration, and new ticket into the glove box with the other tickets. Then I rip Jesus off of my rearview mirror, turn the key in the ignition, and drive the last few blocks home with great care.

⇨⇨⇨

WHEN I RETURN HOME from my final HIV retest, I close the door, shut the blinds, and head for the bedroom for a nap. My mind won't shut off, and after staring at the ceiling I get up and log onto Counter-Strike. The server list of available games populates. The server I want is full, so I watch a game in spectator mode while waiting in queue to join in.

I Alt/Tab to the Internet. The quarantine list shows a third girl has tested HIV positive. It seems as though the list of names grows by the hour. The message boards have posts by talent who check the list several times a day to see if their name has been added. I Alt/Tab back to Counter-Strike and join in a game, but I'm not able to focus and my character keeps dying.

Normally, this time of day I'd be sparing with my friends at the boxing gym, but of course that is now out of the question… So is Jiujitsu, and a long list of other things I may never be able to do again if I'm HIV positive. Like making love to Amanda ever again… Assuming I have not infected her already.

I check my phone for returned texts or voice mails. None. I head for the kitchen, turn on the water, and occupy my mind with scrubbing dishes.

There's the sound of the front door opening, then closing. Keys landing on the table. Footsteps.

She hugs me.

Then she leads me by the hand to the table, where she picks up her keys, and out the front door.

Amanda and I walk together along streets of our neighborhood in silence.

The sun is setting when we end up at our favorite bench in Ferndell. We sit. The stream flows. Squirrels go about their business. Amanda and I are alone. She takes my hand into hers and squeezes.

⇨⇨⇨

IT'S NIGHT. MY FEET splash in ankle-deep water as I run in a swale behind an industrial complex. My socks and shoes are sodden, and the air is thick with the stench of burning flesh. Officer Madero gains ground on me. In his outstretched hand, a torch that glows bluish white that is so bright it hurts my eyes to behold. My lungs ache. Lactic acid building inside my quadriceps screams a chorus of pain, its volume rising with each step. I'm just outside of Madero's grasp and I feel the heat of his torch as its light falls upon my back and shoulders, casting my shadow before me. The light sears my flesh and singes my hair away, and my shadow on the ground in front of me catches fire. Its ashes flake away, rising on convection currents and into the starless sky.

A phone rings.

I sit up in bed and reach over to my nightstand for my cell phone. The caller ID says, "Unavailable."

I say, "Hello?"

"This is Trisha Marie."

"Oh, uh…hi."

She says, "I hear you have something to tell me."

I say, "Yes. Thanks for calling me back. This isn't easy to say…not that it will be easy for you to hear, but—"

"Get to the point. What do you want?"

I say, "You…you may have been exposed to HIV. By me."

"You gave me AIDS! How could you do that to me? My life has just started and now I'm going to die!"

"Trisha—"

"And you're the one that killed me!"

"Trish, I—"

"MURDERER!"

She doesn't say anything else, and neither do I. I listen, phone pressed to my ear as she weeps. She lets out a wail which echoes inside my skull and a light shines through the phone's earpiece.

I'm being nudged… My eyes open to Amanda shaking my shoulders. She hands me my ringing cell phone. It's M.A.I.M.

"Erik Robinson?"

"Yeah, that's me."

"Your final test results came back. HIV 'Not Detected.'"

I hang up and tell Amanda. She nods. Then she gets up and goes into the bathroom and the shower hisses. The door shuts.

When she returns she's wrapped in a white towel and her hair is held up by her scrunchie. She sits on the bed and looks at me.

"So, now what, Erik? You planning on going back to work?"

"The quarantine list hasn't cleared, and moratorium on shooting has not been lifted."

"'Moratorium', my ass. I know people are still shooting, and some people who are quarantined are still trying to get work with forged HIV tests. I read it on the message boards. Regardless, that's not what I asked you, and you know it. After."

I say, "After the quarantine list clears and the moratorium is lifted? No…I think I'm done."

"Good."

She goes to the closet and lays out some clothes on the bed. She begins to dress.

I say, "Who knows, maybe the industry will be better for this experience."

She turns to me and shakes her head.

"What?"

She says, "People don't change. Adversity doesn't build character. It reveals it."

⇨ ⇨ ⇨

AMANDA AND I LAY on our sofa. A warm breeze blows through the windows and the first movement of Beethoven's Ninth plays in the background on auto repeat. She sleeps with her head resting on my chest and our fingers are interlaced. On her lips, the hint of a smile.

Everything I really know about Amanda is from the day we met and onward. Details of her life before she first entered the States are black. While going through her things one day, I discovered the name on her university degrees are slightly different from the name on her birth certificate, which is a bit off from the name she used to introduced herself to me. Some things are best left buried, so I left the issue alone. Without her, I'd be dead or wish I was. That's all the clarification I need.

Once, while she thought I was sleeping she climbed out of bed, knelt beside it and began to pray in Spanish. Prayers of hope? Penance for past sins?

Maybe I'm her albatross… Maybe she's mine.

My phone rings. The caller ID says it's a director. I thumb the volume down before it wakes Amanda, and let the call go to voice mail. I listen to his message: "I have some scenes coming up for you. Call me."

Delete.

I turn the phone off and let sleep come.

A knock on our open front door by the mailman wakes me but not Amanda. I extricate myself from Amanda's grasp, ease her head onto a pillow, and greet the mailman at the door.

Past-due bills I could swear I've already paid, asking for their money plus late fee charge…and returned check fee charges tacked onto the original sums.

Then there are a couple of letters from my bank. Enclosed with the first bank letter are two checks from The Wad Fathers: the original check I redeposited, and a second check The Wad Fathers sent to cover the bounced check fee for the first check. They both bounced. The letter says my bank charged me returned check fees for both.

I rip open the second bank envelope. The letter says some checks I wrote (to pay the now past-due bills) have been returned due to insufficient funds. They're charging me fees for those, too. The sum of all fees and charges I'm slapped with nearly equals the amount of the original Wad Fathers check.

I grab my car keys.

⇨⇨⇨

I'm waiting for the light to change at an intersection. School just let out for the day, and a group of kids cross in front of my car. The girls wear knee-high boots, caked-on makeup, and carry fake designer bags. They walk to a Carl's Jr. parking lot where a much larger group of girls, most dressed like their favorite Hollywood celebutants, are hanging out. If these girls knew what adulthood has in store for them would they still be in such a rush to look grown up? The light changes and I cross and pull into The Wad Fathers parking lot, across the street from the Carl's Jr.

A procession of official-looking men streams in and out of The Wad Fathers office. The ones leaving the office carry boxes of files which they load into the back of an SUV. One of them holds the door open for me.

In the reception area, a man in a vintage "STYX WORLD TOUR" T-shirt plays grab-ass with a woman wearing pigtails, knee socks, and a backpack.

I say to the man, "Are you Charon?"

He says, "Yeah, and who are you?"

"Tyler Knight. Scowl Pacino passed me some bad checks. I want my money."

"You need to learn how to read." He points to a sign on the wall: "Talent checks may be picked up only on Tuesdays between the hours of 2:15-2:20 p.m. Failure to follow the rules may result in permanent ban from The Wad Fathers Studios."

I glance at my watch: 2:28 p.m.

"Fuck that, get me Pacino. Now!"

He says, "I'm sorry, but you just missed him. He left for Europe this morn—"

I take the bad checks from my wallet and hold them up. "I'm not here to fuck around with you. These checks bounced enough times and for enough money to be a felony. Either you pay me right now, or not only will I see you in court, I'll make it impossible for you to book talent from several agencies. The grief will cost you more than the value of the checks."

Charon says, "Hold on." He leads the girl by the hand into the inner office.

More men walk in and leave with boxes.

He returns with a three-to-a-page checkbook.

I say, "I don't think so. Cash."

He leaves again. When he returns, he's got a brick of hundred-dollar bills in his hand. He tears off the paper band and counts out my money. "Don't spend it all in one place. Scowl says you're not worth your rate, and you're not worth having to book two weeks in advance."

"Yeah, yeah," I say, "'The food is terrible and the portions are too small...'"

I take a counterfeit money marker out of my pocket and draw on a bill. The line turns yellow and fades.

I say, "If you really want to impress me, deposit that money in your bank account and pay your goddamn bills."

On the way to the car, I roll calls to the directors who sometimes shoot me for this studio, including Dana Divine, and I tell them all to beware of bad checks.

While driving home from The Wad Fathers, I decide to swing by Eris's motel room. I couldn't tell you why, and I've no idea what I'm going to say to her. As soon as I knock on her door, I find myself hoping she doesn't answer. She doesn't. The clerk at the front desk says she's moved out and does not know where she went. There's a feeling of relief.

Before I sit in my car, I notice something on the floorboard glinting in the sunlight. A dog hair. I remove it from my car and shut the door.

I'm cruising along the freeway, windows down, radio off, listening to the 350 V8 rumble when, in typical LA fashion, the traffic ahead of me slows to a crawl for no reason. I step on the brakes.

Nothing!

Red tail lights come up on me fast; pumping the brakes doesn't slow me. I thread the needle through slower traffic while stomping the brake pedal onto the floorboard. I don't bother with the horn because it doesn't work. Heart pounding, I pull the emergency brake, glide to the right side of the freeway and down the exit ramp. Coordinating driving, sobbing to Christ, and slowing with the hand brake, I pull off into a side street and kill the engine before the car kills me.

I sit still. Cars drive past me. People walk along the sidewalk. I wipe my face on my sleeve and then reach for the crucifix where it should be hanging from my rearview mirror, but it's not there because I ripped Jesus down. He's neither under the front seats nor on the back seats. He's not in the glove box, but the pink slip is there. I write a note on the back of a traffic ticket explaining that the foot brakes do not work, and I toss the note and the pink slip on the front seat. Leaving the windows rolled down and key in the ignition, I get out of the rolling sarcophagus and walk.

⇨ ⇨ ⇨

AMANDA AND I ARE napping on the sofa when the mailman knocks on the door. Amanda gets up from the sofa to greet him. She hands me the mail: bills, junk mail, and more bills. No checks.

Even though the last of the exposed people haven't been cleared from the quarantine list, the moratorium has been lifted and my phone hasn't stopped ringing, I've yet to step foot on a set. Among the work I've turned down is a director who wanted to shoot me in a premeditated sex tape with a celebutant. I hung up without even asking who.

Amanda and I haven't put much thought into what I'm going to do for money going forward. We've got money saved to last for a little while, but then what? The mailman will keep bringing bills. At least we have each other…things will work out.

We put our shoes on and take a walk to the ice cream parlor down the street. We finish them on the way back home, and when we return home we sit on our steps and watch the kids play.

My phone rings. Work. I let the call go to voice mail.

Amanda says, "Go ahead and call back. When you're done, we need to talk about how it's going to be from this point forward."

MARQUIS VALUE

IN THE DINING ROOM, an all-white backdrop hangs from the ceiling. Techno-pop blares as a Euro girl straight out of a James Bond movie gyrates to the beat and poses for the pretty-girl stills for the video's box cover. She flings her black hair and undulates her hips to the bass. Crew members who have nothing to do with the still photography stand around to chat her up as she bumps and grinds. Since she's not the girl I'm working with, I don't know her name, nor do I care.

Gil, the director, tells me the movie's theme is barely legal teens, and the plan is for two crews to simultaneously shoot two scenes. A crew will shoot softcore (in which the genitalia is hidden) on one set, while another crew shoots hardcore on the other. Then they flip crews to finish up what the other crew did not get.

I see Joe, a veteran performer. He walks over to me.

Joe says, "This fucking business, man… I haven't worked in a month. I have to get a real job if things don't turn around fast."

Going into the summer, I was booked up two weeks in advance. Exiting the summer, it's two or three days a week. This is the effect of piracy on the porn business. People don't want to pay for porn so they download it for free off of some Internet bit torrent site. Studios aren't seeing the same return on investment for their movies, so they're cutting talents rates and shooting less. I live well below my means, so I'll be okay as long as things don't get too much worse. But I know they will. Not wanting to leave things to chance or accelerate the decrease in my workload because I start failing scenes, I've been doubling up on my Viagra. I say, "It's slowed down a bit for me, too."

"Yeah, but you do a lot of features and big-budget shit, you're lucky. The rest of us are scraping for what we can get."

This is fucking depressing. I say, "Hey, I'm going to meet the girl I'm working with. See you around."

I walk away and take Viagra out of my pocket.

⇨⇨⇨

SITTING ON A SOFA is Rita Blue, my bubble-butt blonde for the day. We take stills for the box cover of the movie, standing on the all-white backdrop. We strip down to various stages of undress, caressing and kissing for the camera. When the stills photographer leaves we plop down on a nearby sofa and wait for the softcore crew to set up in the room. Joe and the Euro girl are already underway shooting hardcore on the their set on the other side of the mansion. While we wait, Rita unleashes my cock and sucks away. It's good to be Tyler Knight. Sometimes.

⇨ ⇨ ⇨

A FEW MINUTES LATER, the sex-stills photographer is ready, and Rita stops slobbering on my dick off-camera so she can go back to slobbering on my dick on-camera. The hardcore sex-still photos fly by fast. When they're done, I step out of frame so the crew can film Rita buzzing a vibrator on her clit.

Afterward, the crew sets up for the next shot. Rita rolls over, face down, ass up, and wiggles her ass cheeks. I mount her. I'm fucking away when Gil busts into the room. His normally unflappable countenance is grim as he explains the situation.

He says, "Joe is struggling. He asked the girl to help him out, and she told him 'You are a man. Just looking at me should get you hard.' We may have to switch girls, but I'll give him five minutes more."

"Gil, if there is no chemistry, don't fuck around. Switch us now. You don't want Joe to go into a mental death spiral because some girl is fucking with his head. I've been there."

Am I losing my goddamn mind, you ask? Why leave a perfectly good piece of ass to deal with some unknown quantity? Because I know how this will play itself out, and I can use this for leverage later. Both with Gil and Joe.

Gil says, "Can you do two scenes?"

When you're not working often like Joe, and you've no idea when your next meal ticket will come, the pressure to do well each and every scene can be crippling to the point of making you choke. Porn is a zero-sum business if you are male talent. I like Joe, but I'd like his money in my pocket more. If I say no, Gil will simply call another guy to take Joe's place. Remember when I said earlier, "If you're male talent, I'm not your friend?" Still, I play it cool.

I say, "If I have to, but I say switch girls first."

Gil contemplates this. While he thinks, I close my eyes to zone him out and pound away on Rita faster.

He says, "Okay… Start the softcore with Rita, I'll give Joe another shot, and let's see what happens."

"Okay, Gil."

Gil leaves. I stop fucking and Rita and I get dressed, only so we can undress again to restart for the softcore. We get three minutes into the softcore when Gil runs back into the room.

He says, "Yeah, we're switching. She asked him if he is a faggot because he can't get hard for her!"

"Roger that."

"Tyler, this girl is a piece of work…"

I grab a baby wipe from the rape kit and wipe Rita's fluids from my cock.

I say, "Don't worry, Gil. I can handle it."

Rita looks crestfallen.

⇨⇨⇨

I WALK OVER TO the dining room table that's been repurposed into an ad-hoc office to inspect this other girl's test and IDs. (You never, never abdicate the responsibility of vetting whom you're having sex with for both age and disease to the PA nor the director.) Satisfied that she's clean and eighteen, I grab a bottled water from an ice chest (I have two pop shots today, gotta be hydrated), and walk toward the other set. I take my time as I stroll past the scurrying crew. Joe shuffles up to me.

Joe says, "Fucking bitch!"

"Bro, clear your head. You have to focus on the task at hand."

"Yeah…yeah, you're right. You always know what to do, Tyler."

I take a swig of water.

"You owe me. Rita is a great girl, you'll have fun."

We bump elbows. He smiles and goes his way, and I go mine. I could have given him one of the Viagras in my pocket. I have plenty. But I don't.

⇨⇨⇨

THIS SCENE IS IN the den. I steal a glance at the clapper which is resting on a table. It says, "Euro girl stage name is Aisha Mar." Below her name is "Tyler" written in on masking tape.

Normally, a crew would bullshit about their weekends or whatever while we wait for camera to roll, but these guys, all veterans of hundreds of porn sets, have their heads all up Aisha's ass. Even the makeup girl, who orbits Aisha while reapplying powder to her face, is googly-eyed over her. I know what to do. Ignore her.

I whip out my cell phone and return texts. The crew and makeup girl leave. Apparently, the silence becomes unbearable to her because after a moment she says in her Slavic accent:

"I hope dick works."

I take my time to respond. Without looking up from my cell phone, I say, "Let's see what happens."

She says, "I not understand."

"I know."

I text and text, chugging water every so often. She probably thinks I'm gay, also. Perfect. The sounds of my cell phone keys clicking and her restless shifts on the sofa seem exaggerated in the otherwise silent room. My cell phone takes up my field of vision and I have not once looked at her this entire time. There is some arguing and yelling from the far end other end of the house, and a moment later Gil jogs onto the set. He paces back and forth like he has to pee before he speaks. Gil says, "Not gonna happen with Joe! I really need you for the other scene!"

Fuck yeah, motherfucker! A male talent's failure. I get his scene and his cash. Plus, when I crush both scenes it makes my "Marquis" value rise. I get called first for gigs, and I justify my higher rate. Both critical in today's market. "Sure," I say, "just give me fifteen minutes after I pop from this scene to recover. Most likely the softcore and stills will take twenty minutes alone."

"Thank God you're here!"

The crew returns and the cameras roll. Euro girl masturbates and coos.

She says, "You put cock in pussy now!"

I stand off camera, right next to Gil, directly in Aisha's line of sight, continuing to text in a show of faux indifference. With a wave of the hand, Gil gives me my cue. I turn off my cell phone, take my time undressing, stroll into frame and proceed to fuck her to within an inch of her life. My sneak attack may as well have been a Taser shot to her spinal cord, because she's frozen in place.

The best defense is a great offense, so I give her a merciless pounding. After a while, her internal circuit breaker flicks. Her eyes go from "Holy shit, I'm going to come!" to "Okay, you wanna play motherfucker?"

She snatches my cock and sucks, siphoning my soul out of my body. Spit flies everywhere. My toes involuntarily curl, which of course she notices, and doubles her efforts. She pushes me onto the sofa and lowers herself onto me reverse cowgirl. I'm not gonna lie, it is all I can do not to shoot my load. The vision of her butt cheeks bouncing right in front of me is not helping so I gaze up at the ceiling and count the stucco stalactites.

Pinned down, I steel my resolve not to be turned into a two-pump chump by letting her pop me too soon as she pounds me into the sofa cushions.

Aisha leans back and taunts me by whispering into my ear, "Pussy feel good, no? Want to come? I know, you not need answer…you come now."

Enough of this shit! I toss her off of me then bury my face between her legs, pausing to admire her pussy… Skin rivaled only by buttery upholstery of a Porsche. Dimples where her ass ends and the legs begin… Not one hair or as much as a stubble to be seen anywhere. I could die here.

I snap out of it and attack her swollen clit, but she pushes my head off as she approaches her apex. Poor kid is squirming away. Not so fast, girl. I bend her over the sofa, sink my cock into her snatch. She can afford to come as often as she likes, but I can't, and she knows this.

This game of chicken goes on for three more positions. Each new position gives her new and creative ways to put me in check, leaving me scrambling to castle and then counter attack. I see three moves ahead to where this is going. Best I can hope for is a stalemate.

The girl shoves my body onto the sofa and mounts me cowgirl for her coup de grâce. I'm a defeated man, resigned to my fate. She grins… She begins her victory lap on my cock. The warmth of her pussy starts the process of milking me dry. Her lips part and she purrs, gloating. She says to "Shhhh…" giving me a final push off the cliff.

Oh no she didn't! If I'm gonna come, I'm taking her with me.

I lock my hands behind her ass in a wrestler's Gable Grip, and grind my pubic bone into her clit. Balls deep. Both of us panting, locked together.

"Cut," Gil says, "That was fucking hot!"

I push her off me. "I'm Tyler Knight, goddamn it."

The crew laughs.

⇨ ⇨ ⇨

MOST PEOPLE CHOOSE TO actually fuck during softcore filming because it's the most practical way to hide the penis from the camera. Not us. As soon as the hardcore was done, the Berlin Wall went right back up between us. Whatever. I won't make it through the softcore if I have to fuck her. I have a close call when I have to reinsert for the stills, but I get through them.

Softcore and stills done. Pop shot time. Aisha drops to her knees and licks the side of my cock while I stroke my knob.

A pair of porn starlets, ostensibly barely legal teens, walk on set behind the camera. Ass cheeks squeezed into booty shorts. Knee socks. Baby doll T-shirts, one pink, one yellow, tied in knots, reveal their bellies. Pigtails. They stare at my cock, drooling. Pink Shirt pulls her shorts down and shows me camel toe underwear. The other girl rubs her friend's clit.

I pop. The teens wave and bounce off.

Aisha says, "You fuck good."

"Yeah…you almost popped me."

She smirks. "I know."

We shake hands.

Gotta keep hydrated. I kill the rest of the bottled water and ask a production assistant to bring me another which I finish in two passes.

⇨ ⇨ ⇨

THE LIVING ROOM. THE white backdrop is gone, and a dining room table has been pushed back into its place. Gil is attacking a sandwich.

He says, "Joe is gone."

The teenie girls and some male talent wait on the sofa. Small talk. One teenie girl rubs her legs together up and down, grinding her clit in subtle masturbation upon learning that I handled Aisha, and am going throw down on Rita next.

I avoid the girls, but it's not for the benefit of the other male talent. Sure, me putting my cock inside girls they have to work with, right in front of them, may fuck with their heads and intimidate them, but I don't give a damn about that. I have another scene to do, and money always comes first.

I make my way down a hall to wash up for the next scene. When I leave the bathroom, the Caribbean teenie girl with the camel toe saunters by. She rubs her round little ass against my crotch. I avoid touching her but I don't exactly back up either.

I say, "Careful little girl or I'll fuck you right here on the floor."

Teenie rubs her ass on me and says, "*Ooh*, fuck this young thing, Daddy."

"Careful, I ain't playin."

I slide my hands up the back of her stretchy shorts, drop to my knees, and cup my lips over her pubic mound…if I could bottle the aroma of young pussy in heat, I'd be rich… I blow hot breath through her shorts.

On cue, Gil appears, mock chastises me, and together we escort the giggling girl into the bathroom. I lift her up on the sink as Gil pulls down her stretchy short shorts. Her pussy glistens. I finger her as Gil sucks on her nipple…everyone panting…my cock screams to life again and I hold the tip against her butterfly wings-shaped lips, but I remember my day is not finished so I kiss her on the forehead and leave them.

Money first.

As soon as I shut the door behind me, Gil opens it and emerges, smiling.

He says, "I just wanted to see if I could."

Heh, male ego. It's still a long day ahead for Gil, and a little diversion is always tempting, but professionalism is paramount. Many other directors would have fucked her. I gained new respect for his restraint.

Gil says, "Anyway, thanks for not cock blocking. I appreciate the gesture."

"It's all good."

"Ready for the next scene?"

Right then, I realize the entire episode in the bathroom was a ruse for him to keep tabs on me so I don't fuck up and blow my load off camera. Clever motherfucker.

Teenie girl leaves the bathroom walking between Gil and me. She makes a point to touch our crotches as she passes.

"Yeah," I say, "let's knock it out."

On the way to the set I snag another water from the ice chest and chug it.

⇨ ⇨ ⇨

Rita smiles when she sees me. We don't wait for the camera crew to get ready. We fuck. We get the scene in the can in one take.

Once again, pop shot time. Same drill, but with a twist.

Rita does the lemon squeezer. She double fists my cock and corkscrews her hands while sucking, and I come harder than I ever have in my entire fucking life. When I'm done nutting, my bladder releases all the water I've been drinking and I soak her in piss.

She is drenched.

Rita says, "Cough-cough!"

Gil says, "HOLY SHIT!"

I drank a lot of water so the pee is clear and it's hard to tell, so I decide to play it off. "Ha-ha, man, where did all that come from?"

⇨ ⇨ ⇨

THE LIVING ROOM. GIL and his partner are going over the call sheet to see where they are in the day's shooting schedule.

I say, "You guys should have just had me do both scenes to begin with."

The partner says, "Did you actually fuck Rita again during softcore?"

"Yep."

Gil says, "What the hell did they feed you today?"

Teenie girl moans in the distance. My dick twinges.

"I'm the greatest."

Gil laughs. "Right now, you probably are."

Thanks for the cash, bitches!

⇨ ⇨ ⇨

I SIT IN MY Roush-tuned Mustang, parked in my driveway. Motionless. It's quiet. I sniff my fingers, spit in my hand, and rub one out to Teenie Girl's short shorts. But nobody pays me for that.

MOST UNCLEAN

THE HOME'S INTERIOR IS decorated in a way that suggests the owners are scratch-off ticket instant millionaires and have only recently escaped the weight of poverty. Sofa, still wrapped in plastic. New pool table with side-by-side stand-up Space Invaders and Ms. Pac-Man arcade machines. A spool for a coffee table. On the far wall, a dining room table sized plasma TV that's wider than I am tall, accessorized with a Wii, a PS3, and an X-box 360. Watching over all this, a velvet Jesus painting.

Lumbering toward me, a man whose stature suggests he grew up next to a nuclear power plant. Skittles-colored bodybuilder pants billow with each step as if he's some kind of

African genie. He's got on a too-small T-shirt with the V-neck that exposes his pecs.

The man thunders closer. His face is chipped onyx, slick with sweat that gives it a look of high-gloss polish. When he stops in front of me and extends his hand, I don't know if he wants to shake mine or curl me. I have to look up at a forty-five-degree angle to meet his eyes.

"Hi, I'm Frank." He takes my hand in his and squeezes. In my mind's ear, the sound of wet celery snapping.

"Yep. Nice to meet you."

Frank's head is between me and a bank of recessed ceiling lights. From my angle looking up, it's like looking into an eclipse. He shoves some papers at me. "Here's the releases and whatnot. The script for both scenes is there, too. Look it over when you get a chance. It's not too challenging."

Frank stomps off and I find space on the floor to sit. The paperwork is the boilerplate release and proof-of-age bullshit. Then there is the script.

Is this a joke?

The script is one page, two paragraphs, divided by "Scene One" and "Scene Two." I read the first scene description… *What! The! Fuck!?*

⇨ ⇨ ⇨

MY FACE IS PRESSED against the sliding glass door, hands cupped around my eyes to cut the glare. I look inside. She is there.

A chestnut-haired girl stretches on the floor with her back turned to me. She's got bubblegum short shorts that fail to cover her ass. She parts her legs and leans over each one to get a full stretch. No underwear. She turns to profile and shows off tits like Jell-O shrink-wrapped in skin which strain against the fabric of her baby-doll T-shirt. Jiggly Girl, oblivious to me because of the iPod plugged into her head, bounces off some jumping jacks.

There is a mist of dew on the glass from my breath, I wipe it with my sleeve to clear my view. She bounces.

I slide the door open, not concerned with making noise, and let myself in.

She doesn't see me at first. Not until it's too late anyway. To her, I just materialized out of thin fucking air to the soundtrack of Blink-182. It takes her a moment to realize what this is. Recognition melts to horror across her face. She runs, I chase. She trips, I grab. She rolls from her belly to her back in an attempt to fend me off, kicking with her sock-clad feet and scratching up at my face but it's futile. I'm too big.

She continues to struggle so I give her a backhand slap to settle her down. With a fistful of hair, I drag Bubble-Butt Barbie to the sofa, scoop her up, and dump her. Those juicy tits strain her shirt and there is enough space between the warp and weft of each thread that I can see her skin beneath. I rip it open. She screams. I smile.

I lace my hands around her neck and squeeze. She claws at my hand for a while before she goes limp and her pupils focus on the Infinity.

There's the taste of salt on my tongue as I suckle her fist-sized areolae. I unzip my pants and take out my cock. It's ripping out of its skin, looking like a shellacked table leg. Sliding down her body, I shove my nose in her camel-toe and take deep inhalations of expired fear. Next, I rub myself on her cleft.

She stirs, moans, and her eyes come back from the Void. I wrap her iPod cord around her neck and finish the job.

"Cut!"

The girl springs up, as alive as she was when she stepped off the makeup chair before we started. She laughs. I stare at the floor.

Frank says, "Fuckin-A, that was inspiring! You are an amazing actor, Tyler! I didn't think you had it in you!"

Great, I'm a psychopath. Swell…file that under shit I learn about myself I wish I never knew.

Sweat drenches my T-shirt's armpits. "I'm full of surprises." I break my gaze with the floor and look at my costar. "You okay, Stephanie?"

She pouts, and under different circumstances it would be cute. "Yeah, I'm fine. Frank, why didn't you let him stick it in me? That was hot!"

What?

Frank says, "No can do, honey. That's why I cut when I did. Snuff, or even portraying snuff, is no bueno. My viewers will be disappointed though. They are the ones that submit these scenarios, and I film them custom just for them."

"Seriously?" I ask.

"Yeah, thousands of people from all over the world. It's a hell of a niche. Not my taste but hey, it paid for my BMW so what the fuck do I care? Ninety percent of the shit the fans suggest ain't even close to legal, though. There are some sick bastards out there."

My erection is still going strong.

Yeah.

"Okay," Frank says. "Next scene!"

⇨ ⇨ ⇨

THE SOFA. SCENE OF my last transgression. This time I'm dressed like a teenager fucking around with the PS3 controller. The girl walks in.

This one is made up to look like a female Golliwog doll: skin blacker than mine, schoolgirl outfit, hair going every which way and tied off with plastic beads in places. She looks at me as she drools all over a lollipop.

Golliwog says, "I'm so glad Mommy and Daddy left us alone! You're the best big brother a girl could ever hope for!"

"Yeah," I mumble. "Thanks."

Little sister stands between me and the TV. Her skirt fills my field of vision. My sibling straddles my lap. No panties underneath. The heat of her vagina soaks through my pants.

She says, "I always get soooo jealous when you take your dates in Mommy and Daddy's bed." She slurps on the candy. "I think about all the naughty things you're doing and it makes my special place soooo wet." She grinds.

I look across the room to Velvet Jesus. I'll get no help there. "You're not going to tell on me, are you?" I mumble.

Sis slides off the sofa and kneels in front of me. "Oh no, brother. I would never do that! If we make a deal, that is."

I can't do this! Okay…use my imagination and it will be over soon. She unzips my pants. Hot little palms and fingers wrap around my cold penis. Golliwog's hands knead.

All I have to do is just sit here and lie back and turn my mind off… That's it.

I remember my single scripted line of dialogue. "Gee, baby sis. I dunno—this is soooo naughty! What if Mommy and Daddy find out?"

She strokes me. "I won't tell if you don't."

She takes me into her mouth.

I purse my lips together. Shut my eyes. Exhale. Go to my fantasy wank bank? Please. The shit I've done, that motherfucker's long overdrawn. I peaced it out and replaced it with my growing Flip Book of Horrors that's now as thick as a dictionary.

Her lips vacuum-seal my shaft, and her tongue whorls around.

I pull the flip-book off the shelf and I flicker fucked-up movies on the screen behind my eyelids, and the room dissolves away and there is no sofa, and no "little sister" and no Velvet Jesus.

I don't last long.

"Cut! Excellent, we got it."

"Here's your mon—"

Running down the driveway. Into the car. Upshifting onto the freeway with a series of clicks, I put the accelerator through the floor.

Pink shorts…meaty ass…tits…hands on her neck…heart slamming against my sternum like a vice cop kicking down a meth-lab door. My pants grow tight and uncomfortable, I reach inside to adjust.

I am trying not to thinking about the wet mouth with the hot breath and the soft tongue on my crotch.

And failing at it.

What am I?

INSIDE THE BOX

MY EYES SNAP OPEN and my first breath of the day draws like a steel rake on a sidewalk. A swallow to wet my throat pushes my heart back down to its proper place from where it was sitting between my ears. The thrumming fades. I notice the cell ringing. I paw the phone off the night stand and onto the bed as the dream blows away on a neighbor's Reggaeton music. I missed two other calls. All from my agent, Cindy.

I start the day off with a lie ("Good morning,") and reclose my eyes again, sifting through what my subconscious was trying to tell me. Futile, don't have the tools. I catch and release a thought back into the stream and pick up her words buzzing those little bones in my ear.

"—next week, and she said she would really appreciate it."

"Who's the girl?" I shout over the music.

"Stevie Dicks. She's on the agency's website. If she wasn't one of our girls I wouldn't even bother to ask… Are you having a party?"

"No, it's my neighbor. Look, Cindy, you guys know I don't fuck with blowjob scenes, and I sure as hell don't wanna commit myself to a full day for half rate when you'll most likely get another call for me to do a regular scene at my full rate for the same day."

Where's that other slipper… I gotta take a piss.

"I know, honey. It's her boyfriend's directing gig and she especially wants to work with you in an interracial scene. She never does interracial scenes! Aren't you excited?"

The cell is pinched in the crook of my neck. "It's a blowjob scene—" I toe the toilet seat up and pee. "—and no, not really. Frankly I'm getting sick of this "I-don't-do-black-guys-but-you-don't-count, Tyler" policy these bimbos have. But what the hell, I'll do it for you."

The tooth-rattling bass from next door stops right as I pin the words, "for you," to the back wall as they say in theater-speak.

"Thank yoouuu!"

I shuffle to the kitchen. "Yeah."

"Okay, sweetie. I'll email you the info!"

"Uh-huh." Back in bed, laying down again with the cell clamped between my shoulder and cheek. I don't bother to hang up.

I drift.

⇨ ⇨ ⇨

"Thanks, for coming. This will be…interesting."

"Sure thing, what's the set-up?"

We are inside Charlemagne's (owner of porn empire, Rustler) studio deep in Porn Valley. Specifically, in an all-white room. The absence of delineation from floor to wall to ceiling robs the eye of sense of depth or focal point and is disorienting. In the center of the white room sits a toaster-sized black cube on a white stand. If I didn't know the stand was there I'd think the black box is floating. A safe-sized cube sits on the floor next to the stand.

She says, "Think Kubrick's *2001*. The idea is for us to establish a master shot with this small box here and—"

Her words are severed mid-thought, she looks over my shoulder and smiles. Feeling the vibration of the foot falls, I turn.

He moves with the grace of Big Bird lumbering down the catwalk in Comme des Garçons swimwear. Heels punch the concrete with each step. He stops in front of us and drops the rape kit he is carrying onto the concrete with a tympanum-rupturing slap!

"Hey, Sexy," Stevie says to the boyfriend, "why don't you explain the shot to him."

"Yeah," he says, "So the idea is to shoot the small, black cube in this white room as if it's floating—"

Stevie slinks up to the little box and traces a finger on its surface like a *Price is Right* model.

"—and the black box *senses* her beauty. And who wouldn't, right? And the box, it gets an erection!"

The boyfriend dives into the rape kit and rummages around, tossing out bottles of douche, lube, and a packet of baby wipes. I got my usual wisecrack ready but it falls dead to the floor from my lips because—"And this is the box's cock!" He yanks a flopping, rubber dong out of the crate and thrusts it into the air with the hyperventilating exhilaration of King Arthur freeing Excalibur from the stone. He's waving my dick in the air above his head, face overcome with ecstasy as though overcome with the Rapture. Yes, *my* dick. Well, my signature sex toy, anyway. This is the first time I've seen the finished product. Their angle, why Stevie Dicks is making this racial exception is clear. I say nothing. Can't. He may as well have taken my dildo and slapped the clever right out of my mouth.

He takes a deep gulp of air before continuing, "This beautiful black cock will just materialize from the box and Stevie will suck it off! We then fade out, and when we fade back in, it's *you* inside this big box—"

He tosses the dong into the crate, trots over to the larger of the black cubes and hoists it over his head. He looks like a caveman poised to smash a rabbit.

In his excitement, he practically sings his next words, "—with-your-real-dick-sticking-out-of-it! Forced perspective! See the hole here? Anyway," he drops the box. It *thwaps* on the floor. "Stevie Dicks sucks you off, and then the cock—your cock—retracts into the cube!"

I stand there. My eyes dart from the little box on the pedestal to the "Tyler Knight Vibrating Dildo" then to the big cube and back to the phallus. Stevie walks up to me and drapes her arms around my shoulders. Our pelvises touch.

She coos into my ear, "Just think about your pulsing dick between my lips. My tongue is so soft."

It's as though a flashbang grenade has gone off at my feet. My mind is a virus-riddled PC stuck in infinite loop struggling to reset. All kinds of shit swirls in my head. The supa-fly Tyler inside me wants to tell both of them to kiss my ass, but the warmth from her muff transfers through her pants into mine. She plants a kiss on my cheek, and Stevie and her boyfriend leave me alone with the props.

In the end, I'm no less doomed than any other man beguiled by a femme fatale. I get in that fucking box.

⇨ ⇨ ⇨

THE LAST PASS OF tongue sends flashes of crimson rippling across the synapses of my god-rod.

I'm wearing that cube around my torso like a barrel as if I'm a busted banker from 1929. Dick sticking out of the hole.

Stevie jaws my wood like a beaver on speed. The sound of slurping drifting up in cherry-flavored waves from below.

Her tongue is a pink chamois soaked in hot bathwater but it's my dick she wrings with her two-fisted squeeze-and-twist action, slippery with saliva.

My knees buckle and I moan.

The whited-out room tumbling on to infinity before my eyes does not help with the onset of vertigo.

Needing a focal point, I choose my signature dildo-toy peeking out of the crate behind the director. Like I said, this is the first good look I've ever had on the finished product. This one flawed because on its side where the dye didn't quite take looks to be a case of space herpes. I don't know what's worse. This mutant replicock or the time I saw my grandfather's member doing the swing-along—Coral!—when I walked into the bathroom without knocking.

Awesome, now I have both images fucking with my head, chopping down my wood. A master class of self cock-blockery, my penis goes insta-Nerf. I've got an impossible choice. Look away and give her the satisfaction of popping me like I'm an amateur before the scene is done, or focus on Pop Pop's jingle-balls and get an incomplete for the day... I split the difference. I look away and when I get close to coming I let visions of grandpa-beef whistle dance in my head... The gambit is working. I alternate from *pink* tongue, to Rudolph The Choad-Nosed Reindeer.

Then it happens.

The dildo hops out of the crate, falls on its side and does a lopsided roll toward me... It stops at my feet directly underneath Stevie, just within my line of sight if I strain my neck to look over the edge of the box I'm wearing. It stands itself erect.

The replicock says, "Greetings Erik Robinson!"

I look down at Stevie who is still sucking away, then to the director crouched to the side filming it at eye level, then back to Stevie. Both oblivious.

"Only you can see me, Erik," it says.

"Who are you?"

"I am number seventeen thousand three hundred and ninety-one off the line. I was manufactured in the year two thousand thirteen."

I say, "That's nine years in the future... You're telling me you...came back in time?"

"Correct."

"Bullshit."

"You are having a conversation with a model of your penis, and you find the fact that I came back in time implausible?"

I try to pinch myself but with the cube around me it's impossible. I settle for closing my eyes and digging my fingernails into my palms. When I open my eyes it's still there.

"Fine," I say, "what do you want?"

"In the year two thousand nine, you will be encouraged by many people to start a blog—"

"What the fuck is a 'blog'?"

It says, "Web-log. Blog. It's an online journal. You will write stories to help you deal with your pent-up angst as you try to make sense of your place in the world, then you will write a book—"

"HAH! Me, a writer? Some douche that spends all day at Starbucks with a laptop and a chai latte? Like hell, I'm not gonna be that guy!"

"Please do not interrupt me, Erik Robinson, I do not have much time."

"Okay," I say. "Continue."

"Remember this. You can get away with entertaining with superficial anecdotes and lowbrow humor that appeals to the lowest common denominator to get a cheap laugh. Or, you can choose to challenge how people view things by opening up and showing what's inside of you. To humanize a people seen as expendable, voiceless cast-offs." The latex penis falls on its side and rolls back toward the milk crate. "It will not be easy, but your biggest breakthroughs as a writer will be the direct result of how willing to be naked, stripped, and raw with who you really are. As Erik, not Tyler. Do not shy away from showing your flaws. You will grow from this."

It hops back into the crate. "Finally, in two thousand nine you will write a story called "Bukkake" where you will sit in bed with writer's block for two full days, working on a single sentence. You will want to smash your keyboard on your front steps. Don't. The answer is, 'Take a step.'"

"'Take a step.' Got it," I say.

"Farewell. Remember. Read widely, and keep fucking!"

It falls silent.

What the fuck kind of send-off was that?

"—because we have enough footage." The director says, "It's up to you to pop whenev—"

Floating.

A bio-luminescent jellyfish, my ghostly glow blasts fuchsia and cuts the thick darkness of Challenger Deep.

I drift.

"We got it, that's a wrap," the boyfriend says, "Let me help you out of this box."

The dildo's in its box…inert. I'm losing my Goddamn mind!

After he helps to free me he walks away leaving me alone with Stevie.

I say, "Man, that was only the second time in my entire life I was able to pop on camera from a BJ."

She snatches a baby wipe from a packet in the rape kit and wipes her face. She says, "You should feel honored that I chose you. I never work with black guys."

She leaves. I sit and stare at the cube I was just inside of.

STREET CRED

THE SHACKLES RESTRICT ME to baby steps. I'm being moved into a holding tank in Downtown LA's Twin Towers. County jail. The chain gang holds a dozen of us, linked waist-to-waist, handcuff-to-handcuff.

My charge is Failure to Appear. I forgot about the pile of unpaid tickets I left in the glove box of my old car. The act of not showing up for court, even for a civil infraction ticket, is itself a misdemeanor. Eventually I was stopped while walking down the street; the police ran my name and came up with a bench warrant for my arrest.

Everyone in the chain gang wears county blue jumpsuits with "LA COUNTY JAIL" stenciled on the back. On the feet of some of the men are county-issued slippers. I'm the only one in street clothes: white linen slacks and sweater, and some sandals.

You may as well have put a "my asshole is snug" sign on my fucking chest.

We shuffle to the holding tank. A group of Sheriff's Deputies bark commands on top of each other, including "Face the wall" and "Spread your legs." When we comply, they take off our waist chains. A female deputy frisks me, hands roving up my inner thighs. She commands me to open my mouth, lift my tongue, then move it side to side. She removes my handcuffs.

Another deputy asks the racially-ambiguous looking prisoners, "Who do you hang with?" LA county jail segregates the races into separate areas for safety. Race riots are not uncommon inside. There are only four non Blacks or Latinos among us. Three white guys and a Filipino kid. In the Twin Towers, you may be grouped in with guys on the way to prison for God knows what and for how long, so what the hell is another few months added for stomping on a new guy? The lone Asian kid hyperventilates.

The deputies leave and shut the steel door. The dread of being buried alive and forgotten washes over my brain and soaks my amygdala. A few of the black guys stare at me and talk amongst themselves. I do my best not to stare back, choosing to focus on a point on the wall across from me. The Asian kid stands in the center of the holding cell, alone and weeping.

After a while (with the absence of clocks or windows, it's impossible to track the passage of time) guards open the door and snatch both me and the Asian kid away. I'm moved into the black men's tank. The guards crammed enough people to fill a high school gymnasium into a room the size of a classroom. One steel door…steel benches bolted to the floor…open-faced toilet with a drunkard passed out on it. Again, no windows, no clock. There's unoccupied space on the steel bench but I do not sit. When my legs get tired of standing, I pace about to get the circulation going. More people look at me. They talk amongst themselves.

One kid, tired of standing, takes a seat on the bench without asking. The "owner" of the open space walks over to the kid, and with a crisp right hand to the abdomen, he folds the kid over his fist. Other men are fucked with and punched on by alphas for various, if not unknown transgressions.

A man shits himself and walks around mumbling to his personal god. Nobody bothers him.

People who are not high up enough in the pecking order to secure bench space resort to sleeping wherever they can on the floor. My eyes feel dry and scratchy. There's unclaimed floor space next to the open-faced toilet but I'm not so tired that I would risk getting pissed on, let alone shut my eyes for an instant.

A pack of men, who have been staring at me and whispering amongst themselves since I entered, stands up. As they cross the holding tank towards me, other prisoners part like a school of fish compelled by swarm theory. The pack advances closer. I fold my arms across my chest, resting my chin on my fist so I can raise my guard in an instant without looking like I'm preparing a defense. They stop just outside arm's reach of me. My eyes mist over. My perception of time slows. To control my emotions, I focus on inhaling to the count of four, and exhaling to the count of four.

The group's alpha speaks. He says, "Hey, me and the boys was wondering—"

My voice creaks out of my mouth, sounding like two bricks scrapped together. I say, "Yeah?"

I can feel the eyes from all over the holding tank. Feel them as opposed to seeing them, because tunnel vision has set in, making me myopic to only what is right in front of me.

Alpha male continues, "Are you Tyler-mothu-fuckin'-Knight?"

My nom de guerre never sounded more beautiful!

"Yes. Yes I am!"

One of the guys in the pack says, "See? I told you, motha-fucka!! I knew he was that porn nigga!"

Another one says, "Yeah, I seen your black ass on Showtime last week! You was trimmin' the pussy of this light-skinned curly-haired bitch! What's the name of that show?"

I say, "Uh… *Zane's Sex Chroni—*"

"Yeah that's it! *Zane's Sex Chronicles!*"

A crowd gathers. Even Shitty Pants Man takes an interest and shuffles over.

Alpha Male turns to face the gathering crowd of prisoners and says, "Hey Y'all, check out my nigga! We got's us a celebah-tee in tha house—"

This can't be happening.

"—he makes da POOOOOOR-NOS!!"

Shitty Pants Man says, "Hey nigga, whachoo doin' in here?"

Okay, just go with this. Do not fuck this up!

"It's those racist mothu-fuckin cops, man!" I say. "I was just driving, and they just pulled a nigga over!" (If you've ever heard me speak, you'd laugh at the thought of me sound trying to sound ghetto.)

The members of crowd retort like the chorus of a Greek play:

"That's some *booool*-shit right there man!"

"Shut up, nigga! Let a nigga speak! Damn!"

"You better act like you know, fool!"

Alpha Male takes control, "QUIET! Let the Tyler Knight speak!"

"Thanks, dog," I say, "so as I was sayin'—"

And I tell my story to the guys, holding court on a metal bench. The story of the LAPD then turns into the stories of my career in porn. They stand in silence as I tell the *Bukkake* story, laughing at the right places. Shitty Pants Man looks as though he's going to puke, but all things considered this could be his normal state of being. One inmate calls bullshit on the veracity of the *Bukkake* story, saying bukkakes can't really exist. I remind him it's on DVD.

I don't dare stop talking. As time passes, the other inmates tell me their stories. Shitty Pants Man joins in, and turns out to be the raconteur. Many tales of their exploits remind me why I'm glad these guys are in here. My fellow inmate's stories turn into confessionals, and I'm dispensing sex advice, making shit up on the fly. I swear to Jesus to get every single one of them into porn when we get out of lock up.

When the crowd thins, Alpha Male says, "Hey TK, don't worry. Me and my boys, we got your back. Lay down and get some sleep. Ain't nobody gonna fuck wit choo."

The inmates clear more space for me on the bench. I lie on the bench, doing my best to rest my brain with my eyes wide open. Apparently I doze off for a bit, because when I open my eyes there is a pile of plastic-wrapped cookies at my feet. A cookie shrine.

Alpha, watching me as I wake up, says, "We figured you was hungry, TK, so we got you some cookies."

Looking around the tank, there is evidence that guards delivered lunch as I slept. Some prisoners eat apples. Others drink cartons of OJ. Nobody else but me has cookies. This is not the time to tell him about my low-carb diet.

Alpha and his gang watch me work my way through a half-dozen cookies from the pile. The door opens. A couple of deputies enter and shout out a few names to see the judge. They shout my real name among them.

As I walk to the door, several of my new buddies shout their email addresses and Facebook pages at me. One of them says he will send me a friend request on Facebook. (He actually does.)

As I'm processed out, a deputy cuts my prisoner identification wristband off with safety scissors. Outside, I squint. The sun is up but the day on the calendar is different. I see Amanda waiting for me on the steps. She hugs me.

Across the street is the property return office. My personal effects, including my cell phone and wallet with my IDs, have been lost and the clerk tells me to wait while they look for them. When I ask how long this will take, the response is, "However long it takes."

I say to Amanda, "Let's get the fuck out of here."

We leave.

A few blocks away is Plaza Olivera, the oldest street in Los Angeles, made back when the city was just a mission. We find a cantina and sip mojitos, watching the foot traffic from an outdoor patio table. The setting sun colors the Los Angeles sky with colors not possible without smog. When the first round of drinks is finished, I order another. Then another.

She says, "How much longer are you going to keep doing porn?"

"I don't know. Job market sucks. Not a lot else out there."

"That's bullshit. There are opportunities out there if you look for them. But you have to start looking now and give it time. Dig your well *before* you're thirsty, Erik."

"I'm still doing well enough. For now. I'm up for a lot of awards this year again—"

"Who won the Academy Award for Best Supporting Actor this year?"

"I dunno. I can't remember."

"Neither can anybody else, and the Oscars were just three months ago. So, do you think anyone really gives a damn about porn awards? What have the awards you've already won gotten you? More money?"

We pause the conversation while the waitress brings us our appetizers. Neither Amanda nor I touch the food.

I say, "No."

"Those people don't give a damn about you."

"I know."

"Wait until you have a few off performances and then see how they like you. Those pills you take can't be good for you."

"No."

I occupy my hands by wrapping them around my mojito.

She says, "Porn is easy money—for now, anyway. You're just lazy."

I take a sip of my mojito.

I say, "It's not easy money."

She says, "What the hell are you hanging on for, then? What do you want out of life?"

Then I chew a mint leaf. "Fuck…I don't know."

"Well, what about my health?" she says. "How many porn-related HIV scares do you need to put me through before you think of someone other than yourself?"

"What can I say? You're right."

She stares at me. "I'm not going to wait for you forever, Erik."

HAPPY ENDING

Barney Blaze sends me a text message:
> Barney: r u avail 29th or 30th 4 a nuru massage scne?

Me: Either is fine. wtf is a "nuru?"

Barney: go 2 nuru-massage-dot-com. it's bad ass.

I go to my laptop.

Me: Oh. My. God!

Barney: U like?

Me: :D

I scroll down and unzip.

Me: Genius!

There is a video embedded, I play the video.

Me: I <3 u man!

Barney: Cool what day?

Me: BOTH!

Barney: lol just only need u for one.

Me: k. confirmed for 30th.

⇨ ⇨ ⇨

I HIRE A LINCOLN Town Car to pick me up and drive me to set: a postmodern architectural overlooking the bluffs of the Valley. The driver, Jacob, is a refugee from Soviet Georgia. He is missing several fingers: severed off in the same precise locations. I don't ask.

I'm early and no one else is there. After ten minutes, a rental car pulls up and a tanned Asian girl leaps out. Julie. Her pencil-eraser nipples press against her polo shirt. She's riled up and excited in a motivational speaker on PCP-laced Pixie Stix kinda way, which makes me excited. By the time the crew pulls up, I'm damn near chanting "I Can Do This! I Can Do This! I CAN DO THIS!" Between her Olympic gymnast body and her zeal, I'm fired up!

Inside, I do the usual paperwork while the crew sets up and the girl gets ready. That done, I scan the script. It's bullshit, I stop reading. This is a Tyler improv day.

I excuse myself to a bathroom and wash my balls, my pre-scene ritual. When I return to set, everyone's ready. We start with me outside.

⇨ ⇨ ⇨

KNOCK-KNOCK!!

Julie says, "Yes? What do you want?"

"Hi, I'm here to talk about your insurance policies for your—"

"Password. You got the password?"

I say, "Err…nuru massage?"

"Come in!"

She takes me by the hand and guides me inside to a sofa.

I say, "So as I was saying, I have a lot of policies that could benefit your business."

"This is a massage parlor, you bumbling idiot."

"I see, I see... Well, you have employees, right? Let's talk about annuities—"

She pushes me down on the sofa, and says, "No."

"No? You're not even going to let me finish telling—"

"Look asshole, if you want a massage it's a hundred and fifty bucks!"

She undoes her robe, revealing golden skin, and lets the robe slough off her shoulders and onto the floor. She places her hands on her hips, pouting. Her nipples stab the air.

I say, "You take Discover card?"

"Cash, motherfucker!"

She leads me into a bathroom, undresses me, shoves me into the shower. She soaps me up well, then passes me the soap so I can lather her up. Her skin is toast-brown with patches of cream where her bathing suit cover. If she were wearing one. Her skin is glistening and my cock is bursting out of its damned skin. She drops to her knees and licks and kisses my knob just a little bit.

Christ, I'm supposed to keep the gag going talking about insurance?

I clear my throat and say, "You know, you live in mud-slide country—"

"Shut the fuck up!"

Problem solved.

She rinses me off, cuts off the shower and guides me over to the hot tub filled with bubbles. Bubbles part and pop as my feet break the soapy water's surface tension. My body warms up as I lower myself into the tub. She sits on the ledge behind me and wrap her legs over my neck, pussy lips suction-cupping to the space between my scapula. Her feet stroke my cock, which periscopes up through the suds. I surrender my body to the white noise of relaxation and pleasure. First my arms...then my torso, releasing control as I work my way down. My legs float. I see Barney waving at me from behind the camera to keep the dialogue going.

Fuck off, I'm taking a Tyler moment!

Julie lowers herself into the tub and swim-crawls to my side. She stroke-sucks me. I'm looking at her tan-lined ass bob in and out of the tub; each time it rises above the water line sheets of water cascade off her cheeks. I'm about to lose my fucking mind. I talk about deductibles, anything to take my mind off of what this kid is doing to me. She gets out of the tub.

I watch her from my place in the tub as she pulls out an inflatable air mattress and a wooden bowl. She kneads a clear gel-like goo in the bowl, raising her hands and letting the slime slide between her fingers and drip down in foot-long globs. The slime, thick and viscous, is like nothing I have seen on this earth. Julie rubs the goo on her body, seemingly merging the liquid into her skin. She looks like she is melting as the translucent slime drips and runs through crevasses of her ass and tits and onto the mattress. Jesus. Fucking. Christ! How much of this can a man take!

Barney waves for me to get out of the tub and join her. I go to say something about insurance, but I'm running out of material. I lie face down on the air mattress. Julie loads her hands up with the primordial sludge and slathers it on my body. The slime—so cold at first it's jarring—warms to my skin temperature. After a few passes, she turns my back into a fucking Slip'N Slide, massaging my body with her body. I feel her tits trace a line up my spine, and I'm about to pass the fuck out from the blood rushing to my dick.

Julie yells, "Turn over!"

I pause at the apex of the roller coaster looking down, and the anticipation speeds my pulse. I obey. I look up to see this golden nymphet…foamy and slimy…stalactites of slime swaying to and fro on every possible plane of her body…my reflection in a shiny tit smiling back at me.

She lowers herself onto my body and mounts me. As she makes an upward pass, I feel her hot breath, her tits and then her steamy pussy lips slide on my cock.

"SO!" I say, "This stuff is very slippery and may present some workplace hazards. May I suggest a liability poli—"

"If I let you fuck me, will you shut the fuck up?"

I say nothing. This is the correct answer. We aren't scripted to fuck, but there is no way I'm turning this down. She lies on her side. I spoon behind her. She reaches for my dick and rubs the head on her labia for what seems like a full century, teasing me with her folds…and slips it inside her.

squish-squish-squiiiiish…

Our bodies slide frictionless on the air mattress as we drift weightless. It's a bit of a challenge to gain leverage to thrust when both of you slide in unison, but I'm motivated and figure it out. I feel her hot ass press against my lower abdomen with each pass. I'm not going to make it! Gotta give it at least two positions.

squish-SquISH…

I yank my cock out of her, guide her onto her back, then glide into position between her legs. I slide her up and down the mattress as we continue zero-gravity space fucking.

SQUISH-SQUISH-SQUUUIIISSSHHH!!

Losing all concern for the camera being able to see, I hunch over her turning myself into a man blanket, lying flush with her, chest to chest. One hand cups her ass underneath us, the other hand wraps a fist-full of wet hair. Her hips bucking, mouth cooing. Weightless. Primal.

Julie kneads me with her Kegels, and it's just about over, folks. I pull out of her hoping I can gather myself and go longer. Just seconds from withdrawing, my dick dripping with slime and pussy juice, I come delayed-reaction on her pubic bone and belly.

⇨ ⇨ ⇨

I STAND INSIDE THE hi-tech shower, hands on the tiled wall, watching the goo spiral down the drain. Conflicting emotions wash over me.

The feeling is ninety-proof cherry-flavored cough medicine because the day fast approaches when I no longer do this for a living, and some MBA who was teething when I was in college tells me when I can do life-sustaining things such as eating lunch or peeing. Excitement for what the Act II of my life and writing has waiting for me. Reality tempers those feelings… because at any given moment The Darkness will throw a burlap bag over my head and kidnap my life, holding me hostage and inert months at a time. Most days I still fight in mortal terror against The Darkness which seduces me to thank my sponsors and step in front of a bus on a day to day, moment-to-fucking-moment basis. Because one day I will lose that fight. A curtain of fog clouds my mind and imprisons me into a solipsistic hell of my own thoughts forming fractals into infinity. David Foster Wallace explained this feeling by relating the phenomenon of people leaping from burning buildings to their deaths. How a jumper knows he will die, but he jumps anyway. And how this forces the observer to consider what experience could be so horrific that anyone would opt to escape it by jumping to their death. I personally don't think about jumping because I believe things can't possibly get worse… To the contrary, I contemplate it because I believe things probably will.

I feel the pull of the whirlpool twisting and sucking between my feet. The micro torrent wants to suck me in and down the drain and speed me down its gullet. I step out of the smart-shower and it cuts off behind me. A long sigh escapes from my mouth…I gotta see somebody about this. How could I hold together if I lost Amanda? What if she got tired of waiting and I return from set to an empty home? I'll give her an exit date from this business…and stick to it. So few people who do porn for so many years make it when matriculating back into the real world. The recidivism rate for porn performers rivals that among career criminals for the same basic reason. It's all they know. Doesn't matter what I am going to do for a living. As long as there's Amanda to come home to…if I keep on this path, one day when I get home from set she won't be there. She's the last vestige of normalcy in my life.

I take my waiting check off the counter and fold it into my wallet. Then I hide from myself behind sunglasses, hop into the backseat of the waiting Town Ca, and gaze out the window as Jacob takes me to Amanda. What is this feeling? It's not new. Oh, yeah. Fear.

FROM KBC NEWS (REDACTED):

JUNE, 2009

SoCal Porn Actress Tests HIV Positive

A Southern California porn actress has tested positive for HIV, reigniting the concern that the adult entertainment industry is not protecting [its] talent from sexually transmitted diseases.

"There has been a person who has tested positive. There were exceptionally few partners, inside and outside the industry. All partners are currently testing negative and in adult employment quarantine. All required reporting has been complied with, as have the M.A.I.M. and industry protocols. The investigation is ongoing. This is not a major event," Nichols, an executive from

M.A.I.M., said, according to ATM Magazine, the adult industry trade periodical.

Max Barnes, senior editor of ATM, said the actress was an older woman who was only hired on rare occasions.

He called the case an "isolated event," saying she did not contract or spread HIV to or from anyone in the adult film world, a testament to the protocols the industry currently has in place.

TIGER BY THE TAIL

"**H**EY HONEY, SHYLOCK AT VELVET just called. They're rescheduling tomorrow's scene."

"Sure, what day did they have in mind?"

She says, "Today, three hours from now. Are you available?"

I'm unwashed, three days growth covers my face and I'm standing knee-deep in a pile of dirty laundry at the laundromat, which is full today, so I only have one machine. The first loads of white clothes are already soaking.

Fuck.

"Same movie?" I ask.

"Yeah, apparently there's some drama on set and he wants to see if they can get the scene shot out today."

"'Drama'? That's never good, Cindy. What kind of drama?"

She says, "I asked but he wouldn't say. I have to call him back to let him know if you're available right away."

Even if I only wash and dry the clothes that are already soaking I'll have little time to get ready and make it from where I am in Hollywood, the set on the far end of the Valley near the LA/Ventura county line. And it's going to be rush hour when I head out. My printer's out of ink so I have to run by an Internet cafe to print a copy of my HIV test but doing that won't leave time to run to the pharmacy to get my in-case-of-emergency Viagra in the event the girl I'm working can't lock her psychosis down long enough to shoot a sex scene. The test is mandatory; the drugs, only somewhat. Although I've done hundreds of scenes drug free, I never, never, do it without the insurance in my possession. Still, this is a chance to add to my fuck you stack…my savings that erodes month-by-month as I dipped into it because the DVD porn studios are losing their asses to the free-product fire sale via the torrent websites. Fuck it, it'll be okay.

"Whatever, that's cool," I say, "it's better than a cancellation."

"Okay, Hon."

She hangs up and I text the driver to tell him to pick me up at the agency today instead of tomorrow, then I go to the vending machine for a mini-box of powdered detergent. I put the quarters in and the box of Tide drops. In the interest of saving time, I decide to wash the remaining dark clothes with the whites. After stuffing them all in the same load together, I add the detergent and hope it will be okay. My lips move as I read the detergent box:

"No time to separate the whites from the coloreds? Use Tide! It keeps the whites white, and the colors from running!"

The machine rumbles and I'm leaning my back against it staring at the picture on the box when the cell phone vibrates in my pocket, breaking my trance.

"Yeah."

"So, okay. I just spoke to Shylock and he says the scene is going to stay on for tomorrow."

"Same girl?"

"Apparently."

The lady at the machine next to mine is pulling her items out so my hands dig into my laundry bag and pull out the shirt and the pants. I say, "Who is the girl, anyway?"

"Don't know, honey. All he would say is, 'She's new'… whatever that means."

We hang up and I text the driver telling him to ignore my last: the scene is still tomorrow, and as I send the text off the cell vibrates in my hands. My agent, again.

"Okay, scratch that," she says, "the scene is back on for today."

I sigh. "Cindy…"

"I know, dear. Same call time and location. Can you make it?"

I stuff the shirt and jeans back into the bag. "Yeah."

⇨ ⇨ ⇨

I TAKE THE SUBWAY to the Valley, where my driver awaits me at my agent's office. It usually takes a few moments for people to figure out where they've seen me before. It's like watching the process of thought on a game show contestant's face as they come up with the correct answer right as the buzzer goes off. The facial expressions are often my only warning to slip from "Erik" into "Tyler" mode. For this person, a weasel-faced man with a guitar slung over his shoulder, flash of recognition is instant.

He says, "OH SHIT!" the micro-second he steps onboard and sees me.

The other rush hour passengers on the subway car look over to see what the commotion is. The train doors snap shut behind him.

"I CAN'T BELIEVE IT! Y'ALL NIGGAS KNOW WHO THIS NIGGA IS UP IN THIS MOTHAFUCKA WIT US?"

I place my finger to my lips in an attempt to shush him down. He gets the hint but gives me a surprised look, like: *You're on TV, what do you expect, nigga?*

"Tyler Knight!" He stands right in front of my seat. He smells like he took a bath in Colt 45. He says, "Me and my shorty was just watchin you get down on them hos in your *Tyler's Wood* movie last night!" He smiles wide and his lips, framed by a goatee, look like flapping vulva with teeth. "Yo nigga, you got how that nigga, Tiger, be talkin' down cold!"

Many of the passengers have turned away, but a few of the nearby riders still burn holes into my face with their eyes. I think of ways to make myself small in my seat. Then I think of pressure point neck pinches like they do in the movies to knock him out.

"Thanks," I say.

He says, "That scene where you was all dressed up like a BITCH! What was that? A French maid, right? Yeah, nigga, you was DRESSED LIKE A BITCH!"

He makes a fist to give me a pound, and in hopes of placating him I make a fist and bump knuckles with him. The train speeds under the Hollywood Hills. I want the train doors to open. I'd take my chances and jump out. "Tyler, you was dressed up like a whore maid from like, France n shit, wearing all that make-up? AND THEN YOUR ASSHOLE WAS HANGING THE FUCK OUT! And then. And then. And then-then-then, them FAT-ASSED PORNO HOs? They had the whips n shit? Nigga, that was some cold shit right there, nigga—"

He laughs.

"THEY BEAT YOUR MOTHERFUCKIN' ASS! AND YOU WAS DRESSED LIKE A WOMAN!"

A pair of wild-eyed surfer dudes with questions on their lips are pushing their way toward me through the crowded subway car.

Pussy Mouth is still talking, "—WHADDAYA THINK THAT NIGGA, TIGER, AND THOSE STANK-ASS MISTRESSES THINK ABOUT YOU PLAYIN THEM IN THE POOOOOOOOOORNOOOOOOOOOOOS?"

Over the PA system the conductor's metallic voice says, "Next stop: Universal City."

My eyes dart up and down the train until they settle on a sign that says, "You never know, the person next to you on Metro could be an undercover cop!" and I mumble, "I'm the least of his problems."

Only a few people stand between me and the approaching surfer dudes, and this close, it's clear there's something off about them. The train slows down as one of them, pushing a passenger out of the way, opens his mouth to speak; the train door slaps open; I bolt off the train and up the stairs and go through the turnstile and up another flight of stairs and into the sizzling sun of the parking lot where I see my driver's waiting car; I rip open the car door to the eardrum rupturing sound of techno, dive in, and slam the door shut.

The driver accelerates, snapping my neck back, and my head thuds against the headrest and we're out of the parking lot barreling down the freeway on-ramp picking up speed; he threads the needle between slower cars and merges onto the freeway. He uses The Force to weave a through-line past the slower traffic while he fucks with the stereo with one hand, and uses his "free" hand to pull up GPS on his iPhone, steering with his knees. In a Texan drawl, he says, "What's with the on again, off again nonsense with VELVET?"

He slows down and looks up from his cell phone and up to the road, and steers with a part of his body that's actually above his waist. I relax my asshole by degrees.

"The fuck if I know," I say, still catching my breath from running up several flights of stairs, "New girl. Guessing they wanna shoot the movie before she has a vision of Jesus moment about making porn and disappears." I say to the passenger side window, as an afterthought, "It smells like pussy in here."

"Yeah," he says, almost irritated, as though I'm pointing out that water is wet, then, "Who's the girl?"

"Nobody's telling me shit, dude."

We drive past the VELVET building. Its garish neon sign blares right across the freeway from the Universal Studios family theme park.

"What if they call you while we're on the way and cancel again?"

I glance at my cell for any missed calls while I was underground and out of service range. None.

"Fuck 'em. They can tell me in person."

⇨ ⇨ ⇨

THERE ARE NO LUXURY cars or grip trucks lining the driveway and street, no equipment-carrying crew members wandering back and forth from truck to house or any of the usual signs that scream "porn shoot location", so the driver almost circles past the house. This home, situated at the back of the cul-de-sac on the top of one of the highest hills in one of the farthest points in The Valley, is unremarkable.

Since there's no way to be sure how long this will take, I tell the driver I'll text him when I'm done. I watch him fly down the hill to his next pick-up. The engine buzzes as the car twists along the road that snakes along the hill below me. Doppler shift stretches the sound of the exhaust out to nothing. Silence replaces the buzzing, and tiny red dots flare up as he on occasion taps the brakes.

My hand twists the front doorknob expecting it to yield as they always do so I can help myself inside. It doesn't. Walking around the property reveals the curtains over all the windows are drawn shut, and the garage, door pulled down, is also locked. As I make my way back to the front door I pass my eyes over the neighborhood… No activity. I give the front door a gentle knock. I wait.

⇨⇨⇨

ANOTHER HOUSE, YEARS AGO, I entered and noticed a faint scent of jasmine and cinnamon in the air. I wandered around calling out for the director so I could fill out the paperwork, not finding him (or anyone else), then decided to look for a bathroom so I can clean up before the scene. The home's interior was decorated with rococo furniture was incongruent with its mid-century-minimalist architecture. I followed the sound of a TV, which led me to the master bedroom…a Louis XV, four-poster bed with heavy velvet drapes dominated the room…a twentieth century television set with rabbit ears sat on a cart…paintings with serious-looking men in powdered wigs loomed from the walls, and an ottoman, with a copy of *Reader's Digest* and a National Audubon Society pamphlet resting on it, sat at the foot of the bed. There was a gilded writing desk with the roll-down top. Sitting on it was what looked to be the start of a handwritten letter (who still hand writes letters?) on personalized stationery…and three volumes of Collier's Encyclopedias.

The scent was stronger in the master bathroom. The bottle of Chanel No. 5 on the counter told me why. The lone towel, monogrammed, which hung on the rack, was still damp... As if it was just used. There were no fresh ones, so I couldn't take a shower, so instead I snatched a clean washcloth, also monogrammed, dropped my pants, soaped the cloth in the sink and proceeded to clean the space between my scrotum and legs. Next, I lathered up my dick making sure to clean under the foreskin well, wringing the washcloth into the sink, and splashed fresh water over the cock to rinse it off when I noticed I could no longer hear the TV set. What I did hear were tentative footfalls on carpet, then—"Please! Don't!"

I spun around to face a woman with damp, thinning hair, clutching her monogrammed bathrobe shut with trembling liver-spotted hands. Her milky eyes dropped to my hanging penis, and my heart squeezed and released, squeezed and released, wringing out all its blood before sopping up more like the washcloth dripping in my hands, and visions of spending the rest of my life in a six-by-nine cell flashed. I mumbled something like, "sorry, wrong house", as if that would explain everything when you discover some black guy washing his balls in your sink and leaving curly pubes and tan water in the basin. I pulled my pants up and brushed past her and out through the bedroom and into the foyer—the bedroom door slammed shut behind me—and I bolted out the front door and into the August humidity that stole my air like a punch to the gut between breaths, running across the lawn as my pulse screamed in my ears. Running. Monogrammed washcloth still in my hands.

⇨⇨⇨

THE SCRAPING SOUND OF metal on metal rings out as a chain is undone and locks turn and tumble. I confirm the address on my handheld PDA. The door opens. Through its crack comes rock music, and I expect Shylock or a familiar face from the crew to greet me. Instead, a fresh-scrubbed woman with her hair pulled away from her face in a ponytail, wearing onion-skin running shorts and a T-shirt stares at me. Expressionless.

"I, uh... Hi," I say, "I'm looking for one-oh-eight Lemongrove Court?"

She looks from me, to my laptop case slung over my shoulder, then back to me. She says, "This is it." An involuntary exhalation of relief blows past my lips.

She turns, leaving the door open, and swishes her hips into the home. She says, "Lock the door behind you." Firm ass cheeks covered by flimsy fabric churn as she walks. I follow.

Even though there's music playing somewhere, out of habit I lower my voice to a whisper whenever I enter any shoot house. "I never ring doorbells in case cameras are rolling. Don't want to ruin the shot."

She sighs. "Whatever. That's the least of this production's worries today."

We turn a corner. One song ends and fades into the next.

"I'll ask you to please observe the rules of my house while you are here. You'll find them posted in the kitchen."

She leads me into the kitchen where she hands me off to Shylock and then disappears around a corner. A door slams.

On the counter behind Shylock, the NBA finals play out on a muted TV. The announcer introduces the starting lineup. "Good to see you!" Shylock says. "Thanks a lot for being patient, dude."

Shylock reminds me of a young Donald Sutherland during his hippie phase. We shake hands.

"No worries," I say, "thanks for thinking of me."

He chuckles. "Oh, I didn't. You were requested by female talent."

He hands me the paperwork and I hand him my IDs and HIV test. I say, "That's cool. At least I know whomever I'm working with really wants to be here."

Shylock looks at me, and a smile flashes across his lips as if he remembers a funny punchline. When I finish with the forms I hand them back to him.

He tosses the paperwork into a folder without giving them as much as a glance, and says, "Okay, so I'm the set's designated 'safety officer,'" he makes quotes with his fingers, "because Cal OSHA is on everybody's asses from the HIV outbreak last year. Please note the hazardous waste bin—"

He points across the kitchen the way an airline steward points to the emergency exits. There's a red fifty-gallon garbage container with the word BIOHAZARD and the accompanying symbol stenciled on its side.

"—and," he continues his pitch in a mock gameshow host voice, "I'm supposed to show you a video on safety protocol—"

"I've seen it, bro."

"Thank God." He trots to the sliding glass door and gives a dramatic wave of the hand, and says, "And behind door number one…the girls."

The sliding door leads to the backyard. On the other side of the glass and off to the side are three bikini-clad women. They gyrate their hips in front of an infinity pool that seems to cascade off the grassy cliff and into the Valley below. Bass pumps, a camera flashes every now then, and women dance and change poses with looks of ecstasy on their faces. Except for the woman in the middle. Her lips are moving and she looks to be waving her pointer finger at something in front of her, as though she's having a bad conversation with a pixie only she can see.

They look familiar in the abstract. I say, "Who are they?"

The woman in the middle plops on the ground, legs open, and swats at the air around her head while the other two continue vogue-ing for the pictures.

"Those," Shylock says, "are Tiger's mistresses."

My gut sinks, like I've woken up just in time to feel myself rolling off the bed.

"But. They're…" Of all the questions swirling in my head I should have asked, I ask a stupid one. "I have to have sex with all of them?

"Of course not, dude." He points. "Just the one in the middle."

The woman in the middle pulls up clumps of grass.

He slides open the glass door and the music is intermixed with a wailing car alarm from somewhere down the hill. "Come on, dude," he says, "I'll introduce you to them."

⇨⇨⇨

I'M SITTING ON A stool clutching a wrinkled-to-hell call-sheet, still in the kitchen because I told Shylock I didn't want to interrupt the stills for the box cover. The real reason is that I need time to work through my "Surprise, motherfucker!" moment, and I'm hoping Ashton Kutcher pops out of the red toxic waste bin with a camera in his hand, laughing his ass off, telling me, "This is all a joke! You just got *Punk'd!*" He doesn't.

How much do these women know about me satirizing them in my *Tyler's Wood* movie/ Is that the reason I was requested? For revenge? Why didn't VELVET just tell me upfront what the movie is about? If they did, would I have shown up?

The photographer, Tom Tom, whom I've not seen in years, enters through the sliding door. We hug and talk, and this makes me feel better. We catch up, laughing about a time when Stan put a suction-cupped dildo on the trunk of his car, and Tom Tom drove along the freeway and all the way home with it flapping in the wind, only to discover it when he got home. I saw him on set the next week and said, "In five years it will be funny." We hug again and he goes off into another room to set up the lights. On the TV, Pau Gasol drives to the basket, makes the shot, and draws a foul. The first mistress bounces into the room and stops at my side, close enough to feel heat radiating off her body and onto my arm. Because I'm seated, her tits hang eye-level at my profile and I have to crane my neck upward to see her face.

She says, "Hiiiiii!" and tells me her name.

I'm doing my best to match the name against the women I've satirized in my porn parody *Tyler's Wood*. I look up into her smiling face. If she's one of the women I've lampooned, it doesn't seem to be bothering her.

"Tyler."

"Pleased to meet you!"

She offers her hand and we shake, then she just stands there. Smiling.

Silence.

She smiles. I smile. Seeing me smile, she smiles even harder.

Outmatched, I break her stare and let my gaze drift down until my eyes snag on some Asian characters inked onto her skin. Capitulating to the pressure of the silence, I say, "Wow, uh, nice ink. What does it mean?"

"Loyalty!!" she says down to the top of my head. "I'm loyal to a fault, which has always been my problem because I put other people before me like that asshole, you know who, but that *dickhead* stopped returning my texts after all the time we shared together—can you be*lieve* that? I mean, I'm super loyal. I'm not the kind of girl to go kiss and tell—"

"Uh huh…"

"—and yes I really used my real name with the media because I'm really a real person and I have nothing to be ashamed of because why should I be—"

I feel like I've run up ten flights of stairs breathing through a snorkel. I look up at the woman and her eyes are half-lidded and transfixed in rapture as she details her relationship with Tiger and I realize she's not looking at me. She's looking through me.

"Boy!" I slap my palms on my thighs. "I sure am thirsty! I'm gonna grab a Red Bull from the ice chest, can I get you a drink?"

She takes a breath, then says, "*Oooh*, that's so sweet. No thank you! But you know you could *never* buy me a drink in public because people will say we're *dating*—"

I escape across the kitchen and at the sliding glass door I'm intercepted by a woman whose mottled hair dye job resembles the coat of a German Shepherd. The Woman in the Middle. I can't get out. She can't get inside. Our eyes lock, and it occurs to me she's not trying to get inside—she timed it so we'd meet face to face at the doorway.

She says, "Our sex scene is going to suck."

"Wow," I say, "that's just swell."

"I am *not* looking forward to having sex with you. Not at all."

I attempt to maneuver around her. She mirrors me, blocking my path.

She says, "They told me you used to be a model." She looks me up and down. "That had to be a very long time ago because you're losing your hair and there are bags under your eyes and your face is kind of fucked up."

"Yeah, I get that sometimes."

"What happened to you?"

I squeeze past her. "Porn."

⇨ ⇨ ⇨

STANDING BY THE ICE chest and sipping a bottled water through a goose-necked straw to prevent smudging her lipstick is another mistress whom I recognize. TMZ plays a segment of her in heavy rotation. "Hi."

"Hi."

We both smile and introduce ourselves and the small talk is easy, and my eyes trace the angles of her well-cut cheekbones, and my fidgeting hands need something to do so I lean down and take in the view of her toned, flat belly, snagging a sugar-free Red Bull. Her pheromones sway me giddy and my penis presses against my pants. I adjust.

Lawn chairs flank the patio table. I sit. A 270-degree view. The sun-bleached buildings in the Valley's basin glint pink in the setting sun. The infinity pool's water crackle and splash while I sip my drink. The car alarm stops.

Shylock steps outside and sits next to me.

"You have to be anywhere tonight?"

"Not really."

"Cool, we're going to shoot a girl/girl/girl scene first, then a boy/girl, then a boy/girl with you and your mistress."

I'm silent for a moment, then, "Dude! What the fuck?"

"Yeah, I know, man. I'm just glad you're here. Your girl is a serious flight risk, so we moved the scene up to today before she skips town. Nothing but drama all day."

"Figured as much. Is she on something?"

"She's just shy." He stands up and pats me on the shoulder. "This is scoring you big points with VELVET, bro. Seriously, we appreciate it." He disappears into the house.

Everyone has gone inside the house. It's quiet.

The door slides open. The mistress I met in the kitchen stands there, naked except for a Negroid strap-on dildo that looks so much like my penis that I have to look twice.

She yells, "Tyler, look!" and hops up and down, swinging her hips the way you would with a Hula Hoop so that the phallus swings round and round like a propeller. Giggling, she takes a step toward me!

"Don't do it!" Shylock snags her by the arm, drags her inside, and slams the door shut. From inside the home the music cuts off and I hear somebody yell, "Rolling, quiet on set!"

⇨⇨⇨

THEY FINISHED THE FIRST scene. I'm in a back bedroom thumbing through a copy of *Fahrenheit 451*, distracted by the game I'm not really watching either. It's the halftime break and the camera pans to Kobe's wife, then pans to a fan holding a sign that says "THE MEDIUM IS THE MESSAGE" before it cuts to a commercial.

Shylock enters.

"The mistress in the scene before ours is cleaning out her pussy. As soon as she's done we'll rock out that scene. Then we get to yours."

"Sure."

⇨⇨⇨

THE LAKERS FILE OFF the court in victory. Tom Tom pops his head in the bedroom to say it's time to shoot the sex stills. I follow him to master bedroom.

It was my call to shoot sex stills *before* we shoot video because:

A) With this girl, it's best to feel out what I'm dealing with first, and it gives me an opportunity to warm her up (if this is even possible).

B) The girl is "new" and probably has no clue about how to fuck on camera, so I want to block out the positions to map out the scene before the videotape rolls. A game plan.

C) Frankly, I'm not feeling this girl at all and I don't have my "in case of emergency" Viagra. It's best to get warmed up during the stills in the event of me struggling when we get to deep waters.

I wash my balls in the master bathroom because I've been sitting around on set for hours and I'm not so fresh. Not for her benefit, for mine. I'm not giving this woman any excuses to stand between more money added to my fuck you stack.

⇨ ⇨ ⇨

THE GIRL HAS MELLOWED since earlier in the afternoon. A lot. She's quiet, but considering the alternative, it's preferable. We start the still photographs clothed, and Tom Tom directs us as we undress each other as though we're telling a story. Actually, I'm doing the undressing for both of us…it's as though someone cast a hypnotic spell on her. Tom directs me to kiss her. I spy some black, curly, pube-like hairs sprouting from her chin. I don't kiss her.

My pants lie crumpled on the floor next to the sofa, and she's naked, lying on her back with her legs closed. Tom Tom tells me to go down on her, and when I open her legs I see her cunt.

Maneuvering her through the sex stills is a bit tricky because it's as if she has no bones and I'm fucking a slug. Otherwise, we finish without incident, and we redress in silence for the video.

⇨ ⇨ ⇨

"ACTION!" SAYS SHYLOCK, AND the girl snaps out of her trance as if someone has flipped a switch. She tears her clothes off, then mine, then she drops to her knees in front of my hard penis, opens her mouth, sticks out her tongue, leans in close…and licks my *thigh*. Up one leg—avoiding my genitals—then down the other leg.

The camera man/director says, "Hold the roll! Honey, what are you doing?"

Diva says, "What do you mean?"

Shylock, holding the C-light says, "His dick. Put it in your mouth."

"No."

"No?"

"I'm afraid I can't do that. *Nuh*-uh. Nope. Oral sex is out of the question."

This is not funny, but I can't stop myself from laughing.

Shylock says to the director, "Cut camera."

The director says, "What do you mean, no blowjobs? This is porn." He turns the camera off. "Porn!"

She says, "I hate this! I told Mandy this morning in VELVET's office I never give blowjobs because they're super-duper scary, and she made me feel like I was stupid."

She cries.

"Well, I'm not stupid!"

This woman is fucking with my money! Time for some Jedi mind tricks.

I say, "Nobody thinks you're stupid, Sweetie. Right now you're the most important woman in the whole wide world and we just want you to look sexy and beautiful." I hug her. "Isn't that right, guys?"

They look at each other and nod.

The girl says, "Oh-*kaaaay*." Then she brightens up. "Hey, why don't you guys have me dressed up like how Tiger likes it? He likes it when I dress like a little school girl with a rollerblade on one foot and a Gestapo boot on the other, and then I punch him in the dick, and then—"

"Uh, no." Shylock says, "This is just your word, and we can't substantiate any of this. We try avoid lawsuits and cease and desist letters whenever possible."

"It's okay, he's really terrible in bed anyway. Did you know he likes to dress up like a woman and I spoon-feed him his own ejaculate?"

Goddamn it! With that visual in my head, my erection is a balloon with a slow leak. "Let's just get back to the scene, okay."

We resume the scene. Because VELVET needs footage for the softcore and since there's no BJ involved the mistress and I spend ten minutes hugging each other in silence. Hugging. No kissing. I'm flaccid, bereft of Viagra, and I've got nothing from my scene partner to fall back on to get erect again. I step off camera to get a bottle of lube from the rape kit, then grab the girl with one hand cupping her ass, and my other hand stroking my dick. I squeeze my eyes shut and imagine her as someone else. Doesn't matter who. My nana would be an improvement.

"What are you doing?"

"The pervert hug."

"What's the pervert hug?"

I squeeze her ass and continue stroking, eyes still squeezed shut. "This."

"I'm an escort, but I've only had sex with three men in my life. When you stick your thing in me, you'll be the fourth."

Shut the fuck up!

I recover my erection and we rock out a few positions, but I'm losing my ability to keep it up.

I say to the director, "Do you want a transition into the last position, or just be there?"

She says, "Transmission? Is that like, Ebonics or something?"

The director, Shylock and I exchange looks.

I say, "Sure. Ebonics."

Shylock says, "'Transition,' Honey. We've all been making porn for a long time. It's shorthand for…never mind. Just follow Tyler's lead, okay?"

"Why is everyone talking black all of the sudden? That's rude to speak a foreign language when not everyone can understand!"

Shylock says, "Soooo, Tyler, did the Lakers win?"

She says, "Who were the Lakers playing?"

The director says, "The Cavs."

"Nuh-uh!"

I say, "They mean Kobe tore his calf. It was a scary moment."

"You guys think I'm stupid but I know sports! Who was that quarterback that got drafted but he was traded because he sucks? You know, the big guy!"

The director says, "Hmmm. A big football player? Who could that be?"

During the banter I was able to stroke my erection back up, so I grab her and push her onto the sofa, doggy. "Place your outside knee where my hand is. Do *not* move it."

"Action."

I position myself behind her and angle myself as to offer the most open angle to view the forthcoming penetration. I'm about to insert when the smell hits me. Her ass smells like ass. Her asshole, winking at me as though something is pressing on its other side, is five shades darker than the rest of her. There is a purple, blood-filled bubble on her asshole.

Fuck you stack, Erik...the fuck you stack.

I insert in her pussy and fuck.

She says, "Wow, you're good."

"I'm a professional, now please be quiet!"

"You're suck a nice guy, Tyler."

"Hold still!"

"Say 'spray' to me. I love that word."

"Spray-spray-spray-spray-spray-spray-spray!"

"Oh my God, I'm coming!"

The director says, "Okay, cut...fuck it, we got enough footage."

Shylock says, "Fuck to pop, Tyler?"

I look at the juicy sphincter zit. "Christ, no! Setup."

They explain what a setup is to her. It's a cheat: I fuck, pretending I'm getting off, then I hop off of her and she drops to her knees in front of me. I make noises like I'm getting off. The camera cuts. She stays on her knees while I do whatever I have to do to ejaculate. In this case, because I'll get no help from her via blowjob, this means jerking off in a corner while I flip images through my head. When I'm ready, I'm to step back in place, the camera will roll, and I'll shoot my load. Editing makes it look like we never cut the camera.

She says, "Well, how will I know he's ready?"

"I'll say something clever like, 'I'm coming.' Don't move and it won't be a problem."

Stroking, and stroking, and stroking. My body does not want to give up the seed anywhere in the vicinity of this woman... How long have I been standing here? Jerking to pop isn't working so I push her onto the sofa, face-down-ass-up because it's the lesser of evils, and I try fucking her to pop.

Damn it, this isn't working either... I wish she never gossiped about Tiger's alleged perversions. Jesus, if they're true, what kind of shit goes on in that guy's head? Focus, Erik... Flush those images of out of your mind.

My eyes close, the sounds of her moaning beneath me fade to nothing, and memories of successful scenes begin to play in my mind.

A girl in pink shorts struggles under me as my hands wrap the headphone cord of her iPod taught against her throat... A tinny, far away drone of Blink-182 coming out of the ear buds. She wants to scream but the sound is choked off by a violent yank of the cord... I watch her tits jiggle as she kicks out and lashes side-to-side, and I feel myself growing in my pants. I look up and catch a glimpse of myself in the act in the reflection of the sliding-glass door that I snuck in through.

I roll off of her.

Shylock says, "Can't come?"

"Negative."

"No worries, dude. We'll fake it."

She squeezes her nipples. She says to no one in particular, "I'm pregnant."

Tom Tom takes a bottle of Cetaphil from the rape kit. His job is to squeeze the bottle, coordinating the spray of the white hand soap over the girl's ass while I pretend I'm ejaculating, all while the director and Shylock work the camera and the lights.

The camera rolls, I howl in fake orgasm, Tom Tom pumps the soap. We get it clean in one take. Somebody yells, "Cut!"

The mistress says, "I'm having Tiger's baby!"

⇨ ⇨ ⇨

THE CREW PACKS UP. The director already escaped the set and is long gone. Shylock's sits the kitchen packing the forms and documents. I stand there watching him.

"Shylock…"

He says, "No need to say anything, dude. We're surprised you got as far as you did. We got the scene and my boss will be happy. Seriously. Good job."

He leaves.

I text my driver to get me the fuck out of here and go out to the end of driveway to wait. This far away from the rest of the city, the sky is full of stars and the insects make their music. I know the porn critics will skewer me over this scene… It will look choppy because of all the stopping and starting, even with good editing… They won't buy the faked pop shot for a second, and the entire fucked up scene will be blamed on me because fucked-up scenes are *always* the male talent's fault.

Tom Tom pulls up next to me and leans out his window. He says, "In five years this will be funny." We laugh. He drives off.

ONEIRONAUT AT WREST

THE VAN LOOPS LAZY figure eights in the parking lot, tossing me side-to-side in its backseat while the Swap-and-Spit Girls spit and swap my cock. My mind relives this morning's fight with Amanda. The van flies into a curve too fast and teeth scrape my shaft, ripping me back into the present, and I remember to moan the way you're expected to when a redhead and a blonde are throwing a rainbow party in your lap. I'm not convincing.

The director says, "Cut."

Thank Christ. Me, shooting smut in the back of a speeding van with two white girls—bald cunts, panties around their ankles—is a game of "Pin the Felony on the Negro" waiting to happen.

While the girls wipe their mouths and reapply their lip gloss, Dana Divine, the director, explains the rest of the scene will conclude in her compound.

A typical pickup scene will have a pervert cruise the streets for a young lady whom he convinces to get into his van for sex. Today's scene is a reverse pickup. For the part we just filmed, I'm an Armani-clad executive out for a stroll when some girlies in a van skid to a stop next to me and fling open the door. Instead of baiting with a puppy, it's hiked-up skirts and glistening pussies. I drop my briefcase, dive in, and the car screeches off.

Tracy, the redhead, sops up the puddle of day-glo drool in my lap with a paper towel while the blonde, whose name I forgot, tucks me back into my suit pants, but I stop her before a zipper mishap occurs.

Perfume—Amanda's—coats the inside of my nose. Probably from this morning. When I'm together, I call her. It rings and rings. No answer. I regret this morning... What I'd give for another chance to do it all over again...

⇨⇨⇨

I SIT ON THE sofa. Dana sets up the lights and goes off somewhere. I hear Tracy and the blonde in the bathroom freshening their makeup, and then their pussies with douche. Right now is when I wash up and take a pre-scene piss, but I decide to wait until the girls finish. While I'm alone I call Amanda's cell again... Busy signal. I close my eyes...

...I open my eyes to a stiff dick and the extreme urge to pee, so I run to Dana's bathroom. Dreamlike smoke fades as I laser-pee a hole through the back of the toilet. I'm rock hard, so this takes some gymnastics.

I return to the set with the girls lay on a sofa rubbing their pussies.

Dana says, "Action."

⇨ ⇨ ⇨

I FEEL MY BONES sink into a sofa after the blonde gets up from riding me cowgirl and my eyes follow Blondie's ass as she walks away toward the edge of visibility.

Fading...fading, as Tracy lowers herself onto my rod and drapes her arms around my neck.

Tracy's mouth shapes the words "I'm next" then blossoms into a smile. Hands from behind me pull my shoulders down... it's Blondie. She straddles my face...

Blondie sits. Darkness.

⇨ ⇨ ⇨

IT's AFTER THE SCENE and Tracy and I sit on a bed. I rub her shoulders. She turns and kisses me.

Would things be any easier with a girl who's also in the business... I mean, seriously, could I handle it if Amanda went off to suck some mope's cock... Coming home with dick on her breath every day to pay the bills? And kissing me? That flake of dried come on her ass that she missed in the shower? Shit, how much better would my life look if I weren't in the business?

Tracy bends over. I insert in her pussy.

What would your life look like if you never met Amanda... There wouldn't be one... She saved you too many times to count... Jesus, what are you doing? You're such a piece of shit. Your entire life is a failure and you're not smart enough to break the cycle. Not man enough. Put your forty-five in your mouth and be done with it. Amanda's life would look better, that's for sure… But don't do it at home…can't let her find you. But if you just disappear she'll think you left her and that would only hurt her further… It's never too late to be a better man…

Tracy comes. I roll off her, get dressed, and drive home.

⇨⇨⇨

AMANDA SHOULD BE BACK from work already but the house is dark and the only sound is the ticking of the kitchen clock. I can still smell her perfume, though. I grab a bottled water from the fridge and sit on the bed and kick off my shoes. I strip down and listen to time, the betrayer of lives, tick away from the kitchen.

And *tick…*

I'm standing before a desk with a Newton's cradle, conservation of momentum manifested as steel balls in constant conflict with one another, crashing time…

Click-click-click…

Behind the desk hangs a mirror in a gilded frame. On the right side of the desk, a window with vertical blinds runs the length of the wall. The only light radiates through the blinds from the setting sun outside, which casts deep shadows, like long fingers reaching across the room.

A painting, also in a gilded frame, hangs on the wall to the left of the desk. It shows a man wearing medieval battle armor, mounted on a rearing horse with flaring nostrils. Tiny skulls piled at its feet. Plumes of smoke swirl around in a crimson sky. A plaque on the frame's bottom says: *Gilles de Rais.*

Click-click-click…

A laptop sits open on the desk. I walk around the desk's front to see its screen. There's a video camera embedded into the laptop screen's lip. The screen itself displays a document file…a contract. Scrolling down as I read, I learn the contract is an exclusive performing deal, and along with the performance contract is an agreement to have my body parts, specifically my genitals, cast and molded and mass produced into sex toys. My pulse quickens as I scroll down to the compensation section.

Click-click-click…

I read… My mouth dries and I have to reread it to be sure the numbers are right. The cardboard I stuffed into my shoes as inserts to cover the holes in the soles have long since worn through, so I can fondle the soft carpet with my toes. I read my compensation again. I'm on the edge of losing it, maybe even dancing, until I remember the camera in my face. I wipe my face and type my name on the space designated signature and click the send button, executing the contract. The contract on the screen dissolves into a real-time image of me from the video camera's point of view. The shadows cascading across my face from the window's blinds give the appearance of bars. The combined effect of seeing myself simultaneously in the screen in front of me, as well as reflected in the mirror behind me, renders the effect of two opposing mirrors angled in such a way that both the front and back of my head are cast into infinite regress. I swallow.

Click-click-click…

Amanda's perfume bottle sits on the desk. It wasn't there before, but now it is. There's a sensation that whoever was watching me from the other side of the video feed is no longer watching me… It's as though their presence is in the room with me.

Amanda's voice calls me from somewhere…I stand. My feet trod in hushed footfalls across the carpet and the world shakes…

"Papi, *wake up!*"

My bed…an empty water bottle in my hand. The kitchen clock ticks… Was I asleep? Amanda stops shaking me by the shoulders. She stands over me, dressed for work. She waves something in front of my face.

She says, "Whose red hair is this?"

I take it from her. Tracy's.

"I dunno…"

"How can you not know?"

I take my time sitting up and I rub my eyes to buy time.

"Jesus," I say, "It's from work. One of the girls from—"

I look out the window. Sunlight.

"—yesterday?"

"Why are you yelling, Erik? Don't yell at me. Never yell at me. People only yell when their guilty of something."

"I'm not yelling, damn it. I'm just sick of these questions the first thing when I wake up, fucking up my mood for the day. You know damn well I go to work and—"

"How many times do I have to tell you to shower those putas off of you before you get into our bed? You smell like pussy, and you bring those…those bitches into my bed—"

"I'm sorry, okay. Christ, I sat down and I must have fallen asleep or…"

Amanda moves the water bottle and sits on the bed beside me. She says, "Remember, the exit date from porn is coming up."

"I know."

"When are you going to marry me? Are you ever going to marry me?"

"I uh…I can't…not while I'm still working…"

The silence. It's a third person in our bedroom.

She says, "I already told you we can't go on like this forever, Erik."

She's right. This isn't fair to her…she deserves a lot better than me.

I say, "I know."

"I trust you."

…*my hands knead another woman's flesh*… "Yeah."

"Well?"

"…Amanda…"

"Asshole!"

She cries. Heels click down the hall. Keys jingle. The front door slams. A car starts.

But I'm not really alone…her perfume lingers.

And that clock ticks.

I sit in bed wishing for a do-over, but I don't know if that would do any good. I always repeat the same mistakes, three girlfriends running. I'm not any more clever today than I was yesterday.

I get dressed in my wardrobe for this morning's scene—a suit—and I drive to the Valley.

⇨ ⇨ ⇨

I CHECK MY CELL phone. It's time, so I walk along the sidewalk. I can still hear Amanda crying in my ears, which makes me tear up, and when I wipe my nose I smell her perfume on my hand… I'm losing my girl and I'm working twice as hard for half the money I made the year before… Diminishing returns all around… Screw this, Erik, you can turn around right now! Your car is right behind you. Get in it. Go!

A van skids to a stop next to me. The door swings open and a blonde and a redhead, skirts hiked-up, show me their pussies.

I drop my briefcase and I get in.

The door slams shut behind me.

QUIETUS

I CONTINUE MY FOUR-MONTH-LONG search on Craigslist for a job. Amanda and I agreed upon an exit date for when I'm to leave porn. That date is still a ways off, but I'm getting an early start because we're realistic about this current job market. Economists say this is the worst job market since the Great Depression. Even janitor gigs want five years of work experience. Verifiable, with references.

Porn has been waning for years. Porn people who were making $10,00 or $20,000 a month are getting evicted and their cars repossessed. Porn Valley is quiet. With the advent of bit torrent piracy, many studios have closed and the business has changed and will never be the same again. Unlike the music industry, the government won't intervene to save porn. Why should they? The Chinese saying goes, "When your enemy is destroying himself, get out of the way."

After nine interviews with no job offers, I see a posting for a financial services firm.

⇨ ⇨ ⇨

THE WOMAN LINGERS IN the door's threshold. Bifocals hang from a chain around her neck. She's engaged in conversation with someone inside the office.

"—and I know all the tax codes." she says, "And—"

"Thank you, Mildred."

"Oh, I see. Okay...so, I shall expect your call then, sir?"

"Probably not."

Her lips move, stop, and move again to a series of stillborn thoughts.

"That will be all," the voice inside the office says. "Close the door behind you."

The woman shuffles in a daze across the reception room, where she passes my chair. A run streaks down one leg of her hosiery and her shoe leather is scuffed. The woman stops, walks back to the office, and knocks on the closed door.

"May I come in?" she asks.

She waits. Video cameras loom from the ceiling, peering down on her.

She says to the closed door, "I don't know if you can hear me, but if you hire me I will work extra hours...off the clock... every day."

No answer.

"You see," she continues, "Jim...that's my husband, we have custody of our grandchildren, but he...well, Jim passed away...

And the bank sends these letters, so I'm afraid to open the mailbox anymore..."

She stands by the door, straining to hear a response. Silence.

Her shoulders slump, and she crosses the reception area once again to the front door and to the waiting elevator. It opens and she steps inside. The doors shut, swallowing her whole, and speeds her down into the bowels of the building.

At that moment, the office door opens a crack. A voice says, "Next."

⇨⇨⇨

I ENTER AND CLOSE the door behind me, sealing out the buzz of the sales floor. A man with an expensive looking haircut sits behind the desk, finishing a conversation with a businesswoman. There are two chairs in front of the desk, but I don't sit. I stop my hands from fidgeting so I don't crush the document I'm holding.

I scan the office for any clues I can use to establish common ground. Framed antique currency and gold certificates line the walls. Behind the desk, a photo of men screaming at each other in the Chicago Board of Trade trading pit...no diplomas or degrees or indication of his alma matter...no pics of a wife or kids. A keyboard and a bank of monitors. A tray labeled "RÉSUMÉS" on it, a stack as thick as a Sunday newspaper. A coffee mug rests on top of the stack of resumes, staining through the documents on the top with a brown ring.

The conversation between the man and the woman ends with a command from the man, then she nods to before disappearing through a side door. The man turns to me. With his slicked-back hair, he reminds me of a snake. He rears up in his chair like a cobra poised to leap across the desk and sink his venomous fangs into my face, and offers me his hand. We shake hands and I sit.

He says, "Do you have something for me?"

"Sure."

I hand him the single greatest work of fiction known to man: my résumé.

Snakehead skims the résumé, then says, "So you were a stockbroker, but that was a long time ago. I want relevant work experience that's more recent, and for the last eight years you worked for…" He glances at the document,"…Continuum, Inc. Films?"

"Correct," I say.

He waits for me to continue. When I don't, he says, "Care to elaborate on your duties?"

I stand in the eye of the orgy. An Asian girl vortex of flesh swirls around me, and I'm buffeted with the scent of assholes and cunt, and sloppy fuck sounds as skin slaps on skin. Through the tempest, I spot Alicia. I tackle her.

"Sure," I say. "Human resources."

He says, "If I were to call them right now, what would they tell me about your performance?"

"I'm a consistent worker."

He regards me for a moment, tosses my resume on his desk, and folds his arms across his chest. I mirror him, folding my arms across my chest.

"Give me a reason to hire you over the people that came in before you, and the people I'll interview the rest of the week."

He leans back in his chair. I lean back in my chair.

"When I was a broker," I say, "I raised millions of dollars in assets under my control. I'm a closer, and that's a skill set that never goes away and is always in demand."

That's actually all true. Next, I do what salesmen call the take away. It takes balls, because there's always a chance your bluff will be called: "Three other firms put offers on the table for me. I'm making my decision today."

"You're full of shit," he chuckles. "Jesus…the take away? Really?" He hands my resume back to me and stands. "You start training Monday."

⇨ ⇨ ⇨

IT DOESN'T TAKE LONG to settle into a routine. Aside from the other black guy in the office who cornered me at the coffee machine one day with a *You look familiar…do you go to my church?* Everything is swell. Although it feels good to earn a check from an honest day's work, I stare at the clock until it's time to leave every day, and Friday never comes fast enough.

I'm leaving the office when I get a few text messages from my non-porn civilian friends asking me if I'm okay because of the new HIV scare in porn. What HIV scare? I use my phone's web browser and search for answers…

Another male talent, Chet Cheeks, who crosses over and goes back and forth from gay porn to straight, has exposed the straight porn talent pool to HIV. M.A.I.M, following the 2004 incident, will not release the names of the exposed (not even to the at-risk talent pool or any other members of the industry). This furthers the confusion. This is the second HIV-related event in porn since HIV was brought back from Brazil in 2004.

Out of all the porn studios, only a few decide that it may be a good idea to stop shooting until there is a sense of who may have infected or exposed whom. For the rest of the studios, it's business as usual. They keep shooting.

⇨ ⇨ ⇨

THE END OF ANOTHER workday. After ten hours of collecting "fuck you, take me off your list," and "Bob is dead" while cold calling, it's time for the sales manager's propaganda meeting.

Everyone on the floor prairie dogs it from their cubicles to give him their attention. He paces back and forth in front of the flat screen TV as he speaks. The TV, on mute, is tuned to CNBC, where Jim Cramer is wrapped in foil like the Tin Man, arms waving in silence as he goes about his shtick touting Alcoa Aluminum.

The sales manager drones on about the importance of enthusiasm when the program on the CNBC changes to an investigative program about the state of the porn industry, trying to ride the ratings wave due to the newest HIV event. Of course, nobody is paying attention to the manager.

Several edited clips play out in silence. A girl dressed as Little Red Riding Hood prances across the screen. Fuck! That's one of my scenes...the one I won an award for ass fucking Little Red when I was dressed as the Big Bad Wolf... This can't be fucking happening to me... My asshole clenches as the girl skips through the foggy woods with her basket swinging, and I recognize my character's cue is right now, and my face feels hot. Red bangs and bangs on the cottage door...but the program cuts to the news anchor a nanosecond before my pornographic wolf man was to appear on screen. I laugh aloud. People turn and stare.

⇨ ⇨ ⇨

I'M ABOUT TO OPEN my email when I notice my cell phone flashing with messages that I missed from the night before. It's my mother. My uncle—her brother—has passed away. He was born with physical disabilities that prevented him from caring for himself, so my grandmother sacrificed her dreams to take care of him day and night for sixty years. Mom tells me Nana is in a lot of pain, too, and she doesn't have a lot of time left, either. I call.

"Hey Grandma, it's Erik."

"Who?"

"Erik."

Silence.

I say, "Um…hello?"

"Hello?"

"Yeah, Nana, this is—"

"Will you stop calling?" she says, "I paid the bill last week!"

"—Erik…"

"Erik!"

"Yes," I say, "Erik."

She laughs. I smile.

Nana says, "Oh silly, Erik doesn't live here. He moved out to Hollywood twenty years ago!"

"No, this is Erik—"

"Who?"

I whisper the rest of the sentence into the phone "—your first grandson…"

Silence. Then, I hear soft weeping. My grandmother says, "I'm sorry, but my son has passed away… My baby is dead…"

Click.

The connection dies, but I keep the cell phone pressed to my ear. After a while, I don't know how long, I set the cell on my desk. I walk to my bed and sit. I try to cry. But the tears don't come. I lie back and try to sketch memories of good days growing up in Philly with a younger grandmother. Then, the last conversation I had with either my grandmother or my uncle. But they don't come, either.

⇨ ⇨ ⇨

I MOVE THROUGH THE next few days on autopilot when Amanda gets me out of the house for a Halloween street festival a block from our place.

It's a Saturday night. The Ferris wheel spins. Laughter, screams, burnt popcorn, and lights fill the warm night air. Every little girl is a princess. I watch Amanda play with some neighborhood kids. There's hope and dreams in her eyes, just like the children's, because she never let life grind her spark down. How does she do it? Without her, I'd have thanked my sponsors and swallowed Drano a long time ago. The only thing that has kept me from doing just that most times was the pain it would cause her.

Amanda meets a few of her girlfriends from the barrio, and they chat in Spanish. Amanda holds my hand. The girls gossip, and I look at the other idiots tethered to their women's hands. These men just smile and say nothing as the girls complain about what losers their men are, and I feel as welcome as a roach at the bottom of your milk glass, so I kiss Amanda on the cheek, cut the line, and head for home. As I jostle my way through the crowd, a few college kids dressed as a hotdog, ketchup, and mustard bottles run up to me.

Mustard says, "Hey, aren't you Tyler Knight?"

"Not anymore."

Mustard and Hotdog laugh at this, and Ketchup shoves a camera in a passerby's hand and the pedestrian takes my picture with the comfort food and the condiments. I scribble some lines on a piece of paper that I pass for my autograph and the kids leave.

When I get home I open my email again. It's full. Fan mail. Hate mail.

⇨⇨⇨

It's Wednesday morning. I'm standing in front of the elevator with my Starbucks in hand. I'm three minutes late, one elevator isn't working, one is going up, and the one that's going down is paused at the tenth floor. I know when I get to the office there will be a confrontation with Snakehead. In his opinion, "You should be bursting at the fucking seams to get here an hour early!" The elevator dings and the door slides open and people don't wait for the passengers to exit before they pile in. I think about my laptop and the story about a Japanese porn set I need to rewrite. Then I remember my grandmother. The elevator door shuts. I turn around and leave the building. Then, I eat the sandwich out of the brown bag that Amanda made for me as I walk down the street.

⇨⇨⇨

ALTHOUGH I'LL TURN FORTY soon, I don't need a calendar to tell me I've got more road behind me than what's left to travel and that my body is winding down its operations. The white hairs growing out of my ear do that just fine. This is the point when most people think of their legacy. Certainly not those Lucite awards people give me for fucking. My friend, the late David Aaron Clark, tossed all of his ATM awards in the garbage. The ATM awards show was last weekend. Even though I'm always nominated for shit, I never go. Bragging about winning porn awards is like showing mommy what you did in the toilet. Hell, David wasn't much older than me when he died.

LA PULSE (REDACTED):

MAY, 2011
"Porn Clinic M.A.I.M. Closes For Good: Valley-Based Industry Scrambles to Find New STD Testing System"

M.A.I.M, the clinic that tests adult performers for STDs, has shut down and filed for bankruptcy, industry sources confirmed to the PULSE...

The AIDS Watchdog Foundation is calling on county health officials to enforce condoms at porn shoots in the absence of an STD testing regime...

We're told a privacy lawsuit challenging M.A.I.M.'s handling of patient's records was the last straw... The AIDS Watchdog Foundation, part of that suit, has been targeting AIM as part of its crusade against the industry's lack of condom use...

Mike Howoritz, an AWF director said, "Now that M.A.I.M. has closed—and the industry 'fig leaf' is gone—the responsible thing for the industry to do is to put performers' health first and require condom-use on all adult film sets. Testing adult film performers for HIV and other sexually-transmitted diseases is important, but has never been an effective substitute for safer sex and condom use. Performers were poorly served by M.A.I.M. and are poorly served by an industry that places profits above worker safety. If the porn industry won't protect its own workers, it is time for the Los Angeles County Department of Public Health— the government body charged with safeguarding the health and welfare of its citizens—to enforce condom use on all adult film sets in the County..."

AFFLICTION

I'M SITTING AT A kitchen table listening to a pimp explain to me that the Interracial Rate practice in porn—in which he can charge more money on behalf of his client if she works with a black man—is not racist. Because it's just porn. I nod and smile.

I could say, I won't do the scene with your client because she's a Jew. And as of now, I don't work with Jews, Muslims, Buddhists, or Xenu-worshipping Scientologists. But if I did, I'd charge extra money…let's call it my Inter-Faith Rate. And this won't be discrimination because after all, it's just porn. But I don't say this. I don't say anything.

Porn pimps charge a service fee from the studio. Then they charge a service fee from their client. Sometimes, they charge the client other fees: a housing fee if the girl stays at a "model house" with other porn starlets in his stable, and a driver's fee to shuttle the girls back and forth to set. As the economy shrinks, government agencies ratchet down, and piracy runs amok, studios and directors go bust all the time in Porn Valley. Even the talent pool struggles to earn a living. But the one segment of the porn industry that continues to thrive among the carnage is the porn pimp. The pimp never has to shoot a single frame of film, and he makes money whether the video sells one unit or thousands. It's the same strategy Levi Strauss used during the gold rush of 1849: mine the miners. By selling supplies to the miners, Strauss made money whether they struck gold or not.

The stills photographer and the director enter the kitchen. The director says the pretty-girl stills are done. He tells me I should get ready because she's now doing her "girlie things" (douche, enemas, birth control). I drop a Viagra and chase it with a Red Bull right there in front of everyone, making no pretenses of hiding it. Then I walk to the set.

⇨ ⇨ ⇨

KINO-FLO DIVA LIGHTS FOCUS on a sofa. This is the set for my scene, the scene that took place before mine, and the scene before that. There's a musk of sex in the air. It has the woolen sweetness of a fresh-turned field of topsoil and manure. I give the sofa a few passes of Lysol until the surface is nice and wet. You learn to carry Lysol with you when you're sick of mystery lesions appearing on your skin the next day, or antibiotic-resistant staph chewing holes in your flesh. I wait for it to dry. I wait for the Viagra to make my dick feel heavy.

The director and my scene partner, a MILF, enter. The director says action, then aims the camera at her. She closes her eyes and does a dance.

I squint my eyes, softening her wrinkles for a glimpse of what she was like at her apex: she was new to the business, signing autographs for fans at her booth in Vegas during her first porn convention, giving fans who've lusted after her all year their first glimpse of her. That night, a team of hair and makeup artists fussed over her. She stepped out of the elevator and crossed the casino floor. Hips swung, men stared. Her body, a weapon, severed thoughts and sentences before their first full stop. Out of the casino and into the waiting limousine that zipped her down the strip to the red carpet of the award show. Fans and photographers fought for attention. Flash bulbs popped. Later, awards in hand, she bounced from limo to club to limo, never once having to bother with money.

As the night continued, the number of people in her orbit increased. With each appearance, she generated angular momentum the way a figure skater draws her arms in close to increase her spin velocity. Or like a collapsing star.

The director, holding the camera with one hand, tosses a dildo at her with the other. It lands on the pleather cushion with a slap, snapping both her and me from our conjured-up private fantasies.

She flops onto the sofa, smears lube on the dildo, and plunges the phallus in and out of the rent between her legs with the enthusiasm of unclogging a toilet. I let a few moments pass before I step into frame. The scene begins. No clever dialogue filled with double entendre or sexual innuendo. I open my fly and let the cock loose. Nobody tells her to sink to her knees and put it in her mouth. Nobody has to. Both of us have played these roles many times before.

After she does me, I go down on her. She tries to kiss me. I stop her. I turn my head and her lips slide across my jaw. Some girls I kiss, others, no. Kissing is personal. Never mind the fact that I just rimmed her asshole. Whore logic.

We both press "play" on our pre-recorded outbound messages: I pant, she moans. I sit on the sofa and she mounts me cowgirl. Our bodies meet but neither of us are in them. I go to my fantasy land. God knows where she goes. Every three-point-five minutes we switch into a new sex position without being told. Our whore clocks are well-tuned. My fantasy plays out: Today, it's Libyan thugs gang raping a journalist who resembles my mom. What the fuck is that about? The rest of the scene plays out in silence.

⇨⇨⇨

THE SCENE IS OVER and she's talking to me... Something about the end of the world prophesied to come in a few weeks, but I'm not really listening. Instead, I'm staring at what looks like a cigarette hole burnt into her hoodie. What must it be like for a woman to live with power over men rivaled only by God for the first third of her life, build her identity over her looks, only to feel it slip away as time tumbles by? Feel the shift in how people treat her, as though getting old is a contagious affliction? Maybe it is. Shit, at mid-life, what do some of these girls—girls that weren't even born when I was their age—see when they look at me? Do they squint their eyes to imagine me at my prime? Less fat? A bit more hair? Doubt they even see me... Fuck, the scene ended ten minutes ago, and I'm still winded. I know why.

The woman says something about how nice I am, and how nice I treated her, and how very nice it was working with me. She mumbles something about picking up her kid. She hugs me and leaves with her pimp. I wait for a few minutes. Then I step out the door and disappear under a sky the color of wet flannel.

⇨ ⇨ ⇨

I'm on the floor of my parents' garage squirming and wailing and screaming as the man who gave me life is doing his damnedest to take it back. The concrete floor feels hard and chafes my skin, and the walls are filled with sharp tools. Both the floor and the walls serve to keep me in play as I'm driven end to end by the tart sting of my father's belt. The garage door is open. I could escape, but I don't. Where the hell would I go? It's open, and the neighborhood kids, who normally would be loud as they play, are silent. I'm sure they are listening. If they are, they'll hear my father screaming, asking me why I still wet the bed and how my parents wasted good money on a child psychiatrist, and how that money could have gone to more important things, and how it doesn't make sense that I can be so smart and flunk a grade, and just what the hell is wrong with me? School tomorrow will not be fun.

The belt snaps across my chest, catching me between breaths, and I fight for air that does not come. Instead, I'm rewarded with dust coating my tongue. I shake. Across the garage, I see a pair of gardening sheers. All I can think about is how I long to know their weight in my hands. And how hard I'd have to push to make this moment stop.

⇨ ⇨ ⇨

WHEN I WAKE UP, I go to the bathroom. It feels like I'm pissing shards of broken pottery. Chlamydia. Again. Which means Amanda has it. I can't count how many times I've got the clap over the past decade. That, and strep, staph, warts (those have to be frozen off), ringworm, pink eye.

She tells me how this is getting old, and how my work choice is endangering her health and even her life, and, from now on, I either wear a condom on set or I can forget about sex with her.

I tell her that wearing a condom on set, with the exception of maybe two studios, is not an option. It would be career death. She reminds me of the time I had unprotected sex with an HIV positive girl, then came home to have sex with her. How we both took batteries of HIV tests for months on end. How I risked her life and she stood by me anyway. There's nothing I can say. She's right. Always is.

I got a supply of Zithromax on hand from a stocking-up trip to Mexico—you learn to do that, too—and I self-medicate. Amanda tells me she'll see her doctor for an exam tomorrow. Can't say I blame her. About anything. Every time we make love there's the chance of a secondhand disease invading her body. Anything I say about continuing to risk her health—her life—is nothing but a rationalization.

She's not speaking to me, so I grab a book and head to the Starbucks on Vermont and Prospect. It's the only place where I can read or write without interruption since Amanda moved her mother and her mother's boyfriend into our one-bedroom home.

So, Tim, the coffee shop's Cliff Clavin who loves everybody and everybody loves, is there having a discussion with the other regulars. When Tim sees me enter, he walks up to my seat.

He says, "We got him."

"Who?"

"Osama Bin Laden is dead."

"No shit?"

Tim sits in the chair next to me. "Yeah, our special forces team raided his compound and took him out. Looks like all is right with the world again."

I say, "Too bad some Internet prophet is predicting the world is going to end soon."

Tim laughs. "You believe that nonsense?"

I shake my head. "Of course not...tell me about Osama."

⇨⇨⇨

I'M ON MY BACK, lying in a pool of sweat that oozed from the pores of three different people and some girl is riding me cowgirl, fucking me while some dude rims her asshole at the same time. On each up stroke, his tongue caresses her taint a Planck length from the back of my shaft. I can feel his breath on my balls when he exhales. The girl bucks and brays. Every time the man's tongue misses the girl's asshole, the wind from his tongue as it fans the air close to my dick. I grit my teeth and fuck.

"LICK MY ASSHOLE!" the girl says to the man.

And to me, she says, "Pound-me-with-that-black-cock! Don't stop! Don't stop! Don't stop! Don't—"

Before every scene I drop a Viagra. Every scene. It didn't always used to be this way. Before, it was only brought to set with me as insurance but the pill seldom left my pocket.

"—stop! Don't stop!"

But this was before 2008. Since 2008, if you're male talent, you're only as good as your last scene. Profit margins are thin, and studios don't have the chips to reshoot a failed scene if the male talent can't get it up.

"Don't stop! Don't stop!"

All the awards you've won in the past, and all the relationships you've fostered throughout your career mean fuck-all, because chances are, the people you've won the awards with and bonded on set with are gone. So for the last couple of hundred scenes, I dropped a V.

"I-love-black-cock-I-love-black-cock!"

There are no real directors entering porn anymore. No skilled lens men to replace the ones who get sifted out through attrition. What you've got now is a kid who was flipping a skateboard just last week when some studio gets him on the cheap and puts a video camera in his hand.

The ass licker says something. The fuck if I know what he just said. Have you ever felt the baritone vibrations of a man's voice resonating near your crotch?

Porn is a video game. You are not a human. You're a character. But once you clear the level by getting the scene in the can, you never progress to a new level. It's the same Goddamn level, the same Goddamn scene. Over and over and over again. And with new male talent who shoot their cocks up with Caverject in lieu of a learning curve, you cannot fail. Ever. So you gobble that magic pill, power up, and keep the ghosts away.

"Don't-you-mo-ther-fu-cking-stop!"

Today, if you haven't already guessed, is a cuckold scene. Husband and wife have marital issues. The usual: he's white and only Negro cock can satisfy her. But when I read today's script, I dropped a second V.

The script originally called for the hubby and the wife to "make out on the black man's cock" and "reconcile their marital woes by feeding each other dark meat." I don't play that shit. The script was changed. Now, the scene calls for hubby to get as close as he can without actual contact with me. If I had a third V, I'd have dropped that one, too.

The director makes a looping motion in the air with his pointer finger. Time to switch positions. Hubby lies on his back, then the wife lies on top of him, also on her back. His head pops out over her shoulder. This new thing…this two-headed, four-armed beast with tits parts its legs and watches me with anticipation. I squirt lube in my hand and give the cock a few backhand strokes to keep it up then I position myself between two pairs of legs. Hubby gives the wife a reach-around and rubs her clit. Then, he pries open her vagina for me to penetrate. Her innards are pink. His knuckles are hairy. Four eyes gaze into my face. I fight instinct and fuck it. In my mind, I'm plunging a stake into the heart of a monstrosity that shouldn't be alive. As I thrust, hubby grinds upward, in effect fucking me vicariously through the wife. His lips part as he stares into my face. I've had this look directed at me many times before...overt and unbridled animal lust...but almost always from women. He rubs the clit as I fuck.

Sweat from my forehead trickles into my eyes and burns, and drops of sweat fall, splattering onto the wife's chest. She's oblivious. She shudders as wave after wave of orgasms surge through her. Her foundation melts and her mascara runs in rivers down her cheek. She's melting under the set lights, and I'm cooking away in a reduction of my own perspiration.

I've had about enough of this. Time to go to usual mental triggers to block out this eight-limbed Hindu demon and get myself to the where I need to. After a thousand scenes, ejaculating, for me, is mechanical. It's as erotic and as personal as a sneeze.

I pull out and the wife drops to her knees and hubby drops to his knees next to her. Both of them, side by side with their faces angled up, mouths agape like ravenous baby birds. He's in the line of fire, but there's no stopping the tide. I soak them both.

I flick my cock, flinging a drop of come in wifey's face. Once. Twice. On the third fling, hubby nudges her aside and catches it in his open mouth. His eyes roll back to slits of white and a torrent of ecstasy washes over his face. My stomach flips and folds inside my chest. The camera is pointed at them, so I jog the bathroom and hover over the toilet. I dry heave into the basin. The sweat from the sofa soaks me to the bone.

When I return to set, the girl is clean and dressed. Hubby has my dried come on his chin.

The director and the stills guy tells me how great a performer I am, and someone congratulates me for my nominations for Performer of the Year for both the TLA Awards and the Urban X Awards. I'm tying my shoes and pulling on my T-shirt as someone comments how they wish I was the male talent for the earlier scene, because the guy for that scene was high and couldn't fuck, wasting half of the day. I'm not up for conversation, but when John, the lighting guy, wants to chat about a mutual friend, David Aaron Clark, who died of a heart attack last year, I snap out of my funk and sit. And we talk. Turns out, neither of us have resolved losing him.

⇨⇨⇨

EVERYONE IN THE HOUSE sleeps. Nobody is snoring. This is a rare moment of quiet, so I'm taking advantage of the opportunity to read without ear plugs. Then it happens. A hot and dull stabbing sensation pierces my chest. This is followed by a great squeezing, like a white-hot vice grip. The book slips from my fingers. My pulse thrums through me as though my entire body is a sub-woofer.

Bang ba-BANG bang BANG BANG bang bang bang!

I tell myself to relax and that this will pass.

BANG!!! ba-BANG BANG!

It's not passing. Two people in my living room…Amanda's sleeping right next to me. I may as well be on Pluto.

BANG!! BANG!! ba-BANG!!

My heartbeat pound in my toes…my fingertips…my eyes…
my teeth…my ears.

How do you bargain with a god with whom you've got no
rapport…a god that you're certain you've got nothing he wants?
Instead of pleading, my thoughts go to the absurdity of the
moment: one instant, I'm a rational thinking man, a member of
the human race reading the thoughts of another sentient being.
The next, all thought fades… I just am. A panicked insect, alone
and stripped of humanity… An animal that cannot run. The
veneer of humanity painted over our instinct is thinner than
you'd think.

ba-BANG!! ba-BANG!! ba-BANG!!

Salt drops well up in my eyes and pile onto each other, blurring
my vision like looking through a frosted window at dawn.

Just as soon as it all started, it stops. The rumbling in my
chest fades like a train that has just passed and is now a mile
away. My mouth is dry, and my entire body is numb and tingles
like a hand that's been slept on.

It came and went. The entire thing was so…sudden.
Human thought returns. Amanda still sleeps. I just lie there and
contemplate it all. You're a gazelle in a herd drinking from a
still pool when jaws spring from the water and grip your chest.
It takes you deep and twists you so that up is down is up. Then,
the crocodile lets go.

I brought this upon myself. When you abuse any prescription
drug you take your health in your hands. My prescribed dosage
of Viagra was fifty milligrams a day; at the peak of my career, I
took three hundred.

The first time this happened to me, I lived in denial. Who the
hell thinks they can have heart problems in their thirties? Since
then, I live with doom. When you look at it from the perspective

of my state of mind as of late, maybe it's the Universe giving me what I asked for so many times over the past few years…a way out. Until now, I wasn't sure if I even wanted to survive this. I mean, really, what's the fucking point? The only joy I get from life is during those rare bursts of energy when I write and paint for days on end, sequestering myself from society while I create, often forgetting to eat. These burst are always followed by much longer stretches when I can't get out of bed, let alone sit up to reach the keyboard or a paintbrush… My mind is my enemy hell-bent on my annihilation. I'd give all of the highs back for a taste of normalcy.

And no, I never sought medical attention—for either affliction. Before you judge me, I'm one of millions—*millions*—of the working-poor class of Americans with no health insurance. As such, we tend to avoid seeking medical care until it's too late.

It was well after the first time my heartbeat was on the verge of critical mass when I told some friends: Justin, a physician; Jeff, whose father was a cardiologist; Derek who escaped from porn purgatory; and my brother. It's not easy being my friend. Just ask any of the above people. I avoid social situations, often lying my way out of birthdays, drinks, bowling, or hanging out with the guys to watch pay-per-view fights. It's not unusual to go months, even up to a year without as much as a text message from me, and when you do see me I'm not really there. Who knows why I even bothered to tell the people I told, but I did. Maybe I really don't want to die and T. S. Eliot is calling my bluff by showing me a handful of dust.

I told all those people, but I never told Amanda. You think it's tough being my friend, try loving me. How would she feel that I told others before I told her? How would she feel if she learned of my affliction by reading this sentence? I wake her and tell her.

They say the average man thinks about sex every seven seconds. Death perverts my thoughts.

⇨ ⇨ ⇨

THE NEXT DAY I write out my will. Then I print a copy of important contacts and put it in my wallet, and take a walk. I don't have a destination planned, I just need to get out of the house and think. I have to lose weight. I can never take Viagra again. Ever. No matter fucking what.

My first stop is Skylight Books. Then I walk down the street to Starbucks and look to my usual chair. It's empty. I sit.

Soon I notice how quiet it is in the store. Bud, one of the regulars, walks up to me and stops in front of my chair.

"Tim died yesterday."

"Are you sure? I mean…I mean…how? I just spoke to Tim two days ago."

"He was in his office last night. He had a massive heart attack."

⇨ ⇨ ⇨

THE CAMERA MAN FILMS Jasmine Embers masturbating on a sofa. It's a live feed, as opposed to DVD, meaning, you log onto the web cam site, pay the fee, and you get to see everything in real time right there on your computer. You can even type in comments to the performers, which they can answer back. You can help the girl pick out her outfit, tell her how to masturbate, and if there is male talent present, you can direct the scene, telling them how to screw.

Jasmine goes through the commands of the viewing audience, as barked out to her by an off-camera woman who reads them from a laptop. I wait off camera, next to the barker, stroking myself to keep the motor running while I wait my turn to step in. Jasmine is one of perhaps four black girls I've even seen on a set, let alone worked with, in the past few years. Jasmine would be my female counterpart in porndom. I first met Jasmine way back when I was a contract star. We were both on set paired up to work with other people, but when I saw her, time ceased to exist. Never has a woman triggered such a primal and visceral response from me. Never. She was the Golden Ratio expressed in flesh and breath. I had to have her. Whenever a major studio has a need for an acceptable black couple, we are always paired together. Black talent are by no means a plurality in the adult industry, but there are certainly more than just a handful of us. (Plenty of other talent should get a chance to work for the upper echelon studios, not just the same six of us.)

Over the past decade, whenever Jasmine and I see each other, we fall right into step. Like we've got our secret club: her and me against the porn world. She was the girl who played my little sister in the "Most Unclean" story. No matter what happens, we've got each other's backs. She requested me to work with her in today's scene.

The girl's pre-game warm-up is over and the barker taps me on the shoulder and I step in front of the camera and go to the girl. Today is to be the first scene attempted without Viagra in… God, I couldn't tell you how long. This is a failed scene before I walked in the door…even before I woke up this morning. Not because of the girl. We've worked together dozens of times before and Jasmine is one of my favorites. Not because of the lack of drugs—well, not entirely. I am on set physically, but I'm just not there. I'm not really anywhere lately. I'm a Polaroid developing in reverse.

The blowjob goes well. I manage to keep focus on the girl and the sensations from what she is doing to me. My dick stays up. The barker conveys a command from a viewer for us to switch to doggy style. The girl gets on her hands and knees— my God, what an ass this girl has—and I position myself behind her and insert. It doesn't take long for my erection to wilt. After fumbling around in her vagina, I roll off her and walk off the camera. Jasmine picks up the slack by resuming her masturbation, and the camera stays on her.

Franco, the camera man, whom I've known a very long time, looks at me and frowns. He taps his finger to his temple, meaning, *It's in your head, dude.*

I nod to the affirmative. I take a Tyler moment, then step back into frame. Jasmine takes me into her mouth but it's no use. There will be no more sex from me today. I can only imagine that the fans viewing my live and real-time implosion are saying. The barker spares me the reading of their heckling.

The barker goes up to Franco and whispers in his ear. She then holds up a dry erase board with the message:

FAKE A POP SHOT IN HER MOUTH, AND STEP OUT OF THE FRAME!

Jasmine, still thinking of saving the scene (and me) says, "You can do it. If it helps, just pretend that I'm a white girl or a Latina girl or something."

It breaks my heart that right now she believes my problem of not being able to perform is because of her. That she believes I don't find her, the ne plus ultra of my feminine ideal, attractive enough because of the color of her skin. Our skin.

That my struggling through this scene is my passive-aggressive way of stating a preference of lighter skin and my boycott of black women. I want to tell Jasmine if we met under different circumstances, and if I wasn't with Amanda, I'd move heaven and earth to make her mine. But we didn't meet under different circumstances. And I cannot say any of this. The things left unsaid to people we care about, and the void those unspoken words leave, often have more impact that what is said. I take what the Universe has dealt. A true professional, Jasmine looks chipper for the always-watching camera, but I know better. The weight of her sadness grows in the space between us. I wish I were dead.

She drops to her knees and I howl as I deliver a fake pop shot into her mouth. She then lets saliva dribble down her chin. It isn't ejaculate of course, but the camera doesn't linger on it long enough to tell the difference.

When the camera cuts, it severs the connection between Jasmine and me. Franco packs up his camera equipment. Jasmine gathers her clothes and dresses in silence.

The director, now sitting behind his desk, asks if I can finish out one position and pop for the DVD version of this scene. I tell him there is no way. He lets out a sigh, then slides my check across the desk toward me and says that he will keep me in the rotation and give me another chance later, if only by my reputation alone, but the next time I have to deliver a pop shot.

This is not true. I will never see this man again. That's the way it is. My success ratio for scenes has to be 200:1. This is my first failed scene since the summer of '09.

He's asking me what the problem was. This is the part where many other male talent, caring only for self-preservation, place the blame on the girl, the heat under the lights, choice of lube, the sofa, Fibonacci numbers, anything rather than to take responsibility. They beg and plead to the director to keep them in the talent rotation—and to keep their failure silent from the industry lest they be banished to mope purgatory. But when you no longer give a fuck, you have freedom.

I say, "Jasmine is awesome, and this scene, in terms of difficulty, was a lay-up. I had an off day." I slide the check back to him and say, "I didn't earn this." I don't offer an apology, either. I just leave the house.

The sky is black. The air is warm. I'm walking down the driveway, thinking I should go back inside and find Jasmine and hug her and tell her how sorry I am, and that my failure had absolutely nothing to do with her. But I fear it may come off as a "Hey baby, it's not you, it's me" cliché, so I keep going. I'm walking when something pushes against my thigh and a thousand sharp pains spear my crotch. This time it's not Chlamydia. I walked into a cactus. I laugh and laugh and pluck the quills from my groin and thigh. A car passes, and the woman inside glares at the cackling black man in her neighborhood who is fussing with his crotch.

⇨ ⇨ ⇨

I GET A TEXT for a booking. It's a reshoot of a scene with jennifer dragon (spelled with lower-case letters), the contract star and director for Decadent Pictures. She directed me in something last month. Decadent is the only condom-mandatory studio in the porn industry. Its stance on condoms—proving porn's long-standing "nobody buys porn with condoms" paradigm wrong—is commendable. They put talents' safety first, and it takes balls to make a stand.

Not every male talent can work with condoms, however. Under the stress of a porn scene, when time and money are on the line, condoms make the job infinitely more challenging because at minimum, it reduces the sensation that may keep you aroused and in the moment. This, and the couples and female-friendly, woman-empowered content they shoot demands male talent who are fit and attractive, and believable as choices for the females in their films. As a result, the list of Decadent's approved male talent is shallow. These things present two problems for me. One: I just failed a scene since swearing off Viagra, and with a condom-only scene, what are my chances of success? Two: I put on a few pounds over the past few months.

I read the details: call time, location, wardrobe, then text back, confirming my availability.

⇨ ⇨ ⇨

I'M SITTING ON JENNIFER dragon's sofa. My girl for the day is off doing her girlie stuff and the other cast and crew are sitting around me talking. It's an equal mix of men and women, and most of us have been friends for years. It's relaxing—even comforting to see some familiar faces. While the conversation goes on, I'm actually contributing now and then. Sure, I'm aware that I don't have a Viagra on me, how can I forget, but it's not a great concern at the moment.

The conversation drifts from gossip to the prevalence of performance enhancing drugs in the business. How many of the top-level guys won't/can't perform without them and the new generation with their Caverject injections. I'm silent while this conversation is going on, but after while I speak up.

"Back when I was working at a clip of twenty or thirty scenes a month, I'd take a Viagra every once in a while...

Mostly days when I'd do two or three scenes scheduled for the day so I wouldn't fail any of them. Aside from last week, I can't remember when I didn't pop a V before a scene… That's a lot of fucking pills. Anyway, I'm fairly certain I've had at least two heart attacks over the last year. At minimum, there's significant damage done. If I take a Viagra today, you'll have a snuff film on your hands."

Someone laughs and makes an innocuous joke to break the tension, and the subject changes. I like these people.

When the girl returns, she goes through pretty girls on a white sofa next to a crackling fireplace. She's all legs and smiles, and while she poses, the men on set are transfixed.

Someone asks me, "What are you gonna do with all that?"

"Braid her hair and ask her about her day."

Laughter.

When the stills are done I take my place next to her on the sofa. My mind starts fucking with me. It screams, *WAIT! You can't perform without Viagra! Remember last week? You're gonna FAIL!*

The crew takes their place and someone yells, "Quiet on set." The cameras are pointed at the girl and me. The boom mike hovers above our heads.

I point to the fireplace and say, "You guys ever hear of Richard Pryor and Michael Jackson? Never put a black man's hair next to open flames!"

Laughter.

Jennifer calls, "Action!" The girl leans over and kisses me and the inner voice shuts up and the scene begins. We complete the scene, with condoms and no Viagra. The scene goes without incident.

⇨⇨⇨

I'M AT A BURRITO stand with Ken, a screenwriter who was a philosophy professor in a past life. Some girls take too long gathering napkins at a dispenser near our table. They try to be subtle as they stare at Ken. The way women react to Ken has to be seen to be believed. It's as though he's a Disney character and girls are woodland birds that eat out of his hand. He acts oblivious, but I'm sure he misses nothing.

Today, we meet to trade books. I give him a copy of *Permanent Midnight*, a rare book for me in that I've read it more than once.

Ken takes a few bites of an enormous burrito. I don't eat. My diet as of late consists of fresh fruit and grains. We catch up to what we've been up to. He tells me about a philosophy book he's working on. Then I listen to another idea he has for a children's book.

I say, "Shit man, that's a great fucking idea. This would go right over kids'—and for that matter, most adults' heads, but you could go Nabokov on the colors thing—"

"Nabokov was a synesthete—"

"Yeah!" I say. "Your idea is fucking brilliant."

"Thanks, man."

Ken, in between chewing, says, "Every story you've given me to read for my opinion, I notice the same Nihilistic theme."

"It's not so much an intent…I'm just trying to figure shit out."

Ken says, "There are modern-day Buddhist monks that spend a lifetime discovering newness of the bell."

"What's that?"

"They empty their minds… When you hear a stimulus… like a ringing bell, it's great, but each successive time you hear it, the effect of the bell's beauty is less. These monks, they meditate so that each time they hear the bell, even after a thousand times, the bell has the same newness of the first time they heard it. The effect is bliss. Bliss every time."

I consider this for a few moments. I say, "So, it's a discipline…"

"Yeah."

"A lifetime discipline."

"Pretty much."

A woman, walking a Pomeranian, slows down as she passes our table. This is her second lap around the burrito stand. Ken winks at her.

I say, "Fuck that. You're trading one sacrifice for another. And the stimuli are still the same. It's still the same bell."

"But it's not the same. By definition, everything in life, no matter how mundane or meaningless, is a new experience, Erik. Each moment that passes has never been and never will be again."

"Tell that to Prometheus…or Sisyphus."

Ken says, "The rock Sisyphus pushes up the hill is a bit different each time. His thoughts while toiling with the rock are different. He is not the same man pushing the rock."

"You're right. Each day, there's a bit less of him doing the pushing!"

Ken doesn't say anything to this. He smiles at me, then gets up from the table to talk to the lady with the dog. When I figure it out, I smile, too.

LOS ANGELES POST (REDACTED):

S EPTEMBER, 2011
"HIV Scare That Led Porn Industry to Shut Down a False Alarm"
The weeklong moratorium on the porn industry has been lifted after an adult film performer whose HIV positive test prompted the shutdown was released with negative results, according to a porn industry trade group.

COLLAPSAR

Col·lap·sar /kə'lap-sär/ noun [Astronomy Late 20th Century: from collapse, on the pattern of words such as pulsar] 1. An elder star that has collapsed under its own gravity.

2. A black hole from which there is no escape.

The waves of heat rising from the asphalt make the building on the other side of the boulevard flicker like a mirage. I toss glances left and right to time the traffic, then walk through exhaust fumes to the other side and through the building's front doors. Somewhere, bass drones from a chic-this-week hip-hop anthem. A line of people snakes across the lobby and up some stairs. Without slowing down I jog alongside of the line where it leads to double doors. The bass, now a full-on assault, reverbs in my teeth. Head down, feet moving, I cut to the front and flash my neon-colored wristband to the guard, who, in turn, lifts a velvet rope. I push my way through and onto the convention center floor. Bodies and booths everywhere.

Porn company logos and pictures of porn starlets decorate the booths. Bikini-clad girls staff most of the booths. They perch on stools while signing autographs for lines of men. Nurses, schoolgirls, and women in hot shorts weave through the crowd selling panties and pictures and DVDs. Hordes of men wander adrift in circles like reanimated corpses, mouths agape at the circus of flesh gyrating on stripper poles or patrolling the floor.

I turn my shoulders sideways, then back the other way as I squeeze through the crowd. A group of elderly men gather around an inflatable SpongeBob kiddie pool filled with oil and girls. The girls wrestle and slither and undulate in the pool like a snake mating ball for spectators whose cheers and shouts are drowned out by the *thwump-thwump-THWUMP* of the music.

I'm staring at a poster of me with airbrushed six-pack abs, and a girl, probably retouched, too, pulling me into bed. A pack of business-casual cubicle serfs encircles me. Their alpha thrusts a Sharpie and some cocktail napkins into my face. The pack leans in close and shouts questions over the music. Their breaths smell like happy hour at Friday's. The usual banal questions like, "What's it like banging so-and-so?" and, "How do I get into the business?" and, "I got this problem getting hard/staying hard/coming too fast—what should I do?" Alpha Serf shouts, "My dick is bigger than yours. If I did porn, I'd totally crush it! How much money do you make?"

I could tell these guys truths, but I don't. Nobody who asks about their fantasy ever wants to hear the truth. So I smile, sign, and tell them what they want to hear then push on. Flashes of light strobe like lightning above the crowd toward the far end of the floor. That's where I head.

⇨ ⇨ ⇨

THE RED CARPET RUNS between a wall plastered with event sponsor logos, and a bank of photographers, journalists, and videographers. The girls stop to pose as they strut along the shooting gallery. Reporters shout. Flashbulbs pop and sequins sparkle. Dan, the director for the *Tyler's Wood* movie for Poison Apple Pictures, claps my shoulder. With Dan is a couple of contract starlets, one from VELVET, the other from Poison Apple. As we step onto the red carpet, Dan yells how glad he is that I agreed to present for tonight's award show. I follow Dan and the girls onto the red carpet. We advance, pose, then walk some more. Flashes burst and pop. I want to squint. With no character or fourth wall to hide behind, I force myself to smile. A sweat drop tickles my forehead, but I resist the urge to use the hem of my T-shirt to wipe it. "What's it like living every man's fantasy life?" I smile, tell him to visit my blog and start with *Bukkake*.

An hour ago, I ate my dinner out of a laundromat vending machine. Later, I'll feed some coins into another slot to pay for my bus ride home with swing-shift workers, the housekeepers, and the transients. When I emerge at the end of the perp walk, my cheek muscles burn from smiling and my lips quiver and the lights and flashes seared white spots into my retinas.

⇨ ⇨ ⇨

THE AWARDS SHOW IS under way, and I'm backstage talking with the president of Poison Apple pictures. He holds the trophy that I'm about to present for the Studio of the Year award. He thanks me for all the work I've done over the years for the studio. This includes *The A-Team XXX*, where I played Mr. T; *Tyler's Wood;* and *The 8th Day*, which was the post-apocalyptic epic I had the male lead in. That won the ATM award for Best Picture and is considered one of the finest adult films ever made. And among the most expensive. The director, Ren Savant, had the stones to cast me and Poison Apple gave him zero pushback over it. If you've been paying attention to what I've laid out about the race paradigm in porn, you can appreciate how special this was. Casting me as the male lead of their "A" film for the year (with a production budget larger than gonzo studios' entire yearly budgets), in which it was not necessary for the character's race to be black, is no small thing. I'm already a spokesmodel for *Playgirl*. I travel to conventions all over the country and sign autographs at Playgirl's booth at the ATM show. Appeared in *Playgirl* magazine twice. I have sex toy deals and speaking engagements at universities. VELVET used me and Johnny Castle in their cable channel commercials alongside their contract girls. I've long escaped mopedom, but I've had a lot of help.

Before anyone can speak, the announcer on the other side of the curtain announces our names and the category we're presenting for, and the girls each take me by an arm and we walk onto the stage and to the podium. My breathing comes quick and shallow, and there's a buzzing in my teeth, and an escalating sense of panic fizzes over, screaming at me to RUN! People in the audience applaud and cheer. My hands shake as I read a scripted joke. It falls flat because of my delivery, but people laugh anyway. I announce the winner for Studio of the Year, VELVET, and there's more applause. Some VELVET studio execs lumber down the aisle and climb onto the stage. Someone snatches the trophy from my hand, and the girls take my arms and lead me off stage.

⇨⇨⇨

IT'S NIGHT AND MY sweat-soaked T-shirt clings to my skin like a greasy film, and the cars slog along the boulevard at a lethargic pace. I wick sweat from my face with the back of my hand, and when I lick my lips a taste of salt dissolves on my tongue. I'm walking to the bus stop when my cell vibrates in my pocket. I pray it's not the mistress... It's not. It's Dan, the director. He wants to know if I want to head to the after-party with a bunch of people for drinks... Fuck it. I could use a drink.

⇨ ⇨ ⇨

When Dan and I arrive at the restaurant, the after-party is underway and the red carpet has already ended. A pair of cookie-cutter blondes whom I could have fucked last week and wouldn't remember says hello to me and grabs Dan and pulls him inside. They melt into the crowd. I jostle my way into the restaurant, but I've lost Dan. A Latina who dyes her hair blonde saunters by. I do remember fucking her so I say hello. She sneers. I need some Dutch courage...I head for the bar and order a Stoli, kill it, and chase it down with another. And another. Some industry crew members come up to me and talk. Someone says he forwarded the *Bukkake* story to his civilian friends. More guys join the group and soon I'm surrounded by pornographers trying to guess who is who in some of the stories I've posted on my blog. Many of them can identify other pornographers by the behavior, idiosyncrasies, and character traits, but not one of these guys can recognize himself. Someone puts another Stoli in my hand. The conversation runs its length so I excuse myself and drift amongst the crowd.

Another male talent walks up to me. We've seen each other maybe three times in the past decade. Many of the studios that shoot him never shoot me because they never film black talent. He pulls out his iPhone and shows me a picture of my blow up doll. It's in bed and looking satisfied while a famous and very naked girl counts a stack of money. The doll was also on a late-night TV talk show. My effigy is more successful than I'll ever be. I ask him to forward the picture to my email. As he wanders off, a Czech-Russian model/actress/whatever in a white Lycra tube dress struts up to me, pulls herself in close, and drapes her arms over my shoulder…she smells like soap. She straddles my leg with hers, pressing her crotch against my thigh. The heat from her pussy seeps through my pant leg. Her breath blows in my ear as she speaks to me, and her accent is crisp and neat like my vodka. Most of her words are swept away into the background noise but the sentiment is clear. My eyes trace a line along the angles of her face…the planes of her cheek bones…the slope of her nose…those frosted glossy lips and her teeth as white as her dress. She grinds her pelvis into mine. I run a mental catalogue of every private nook in this place I can take this girl when someone yells, "Fight!" The restaurant empties into the parking lot. I take my time finishing the last of my drink. By the time I make it outside the fight is over and I'm left to sift through secondhand accounts. I ask a guy with a Justin Bieber haircut what happened. He says something about a fight between the only Asian male pornstar and another male talent. Then, he grumbles about that bottle-blonde Latina girl who is walking around sneering at everyone and "Acting like a cunt." I'm trying to figure out if these events are related when I spot Dan waving at me from across the parking lot. There are some contract girls in his SUV. I hop in and we speed off. One of the girls blasts Heart's "Crazy On You" and the girls all sing along as we enter the 101 freeway on-ramp.

⇨⇨⇨

EIGHTIES ROCK BLARES AND the bathroom overflows with water. Some porn starlets dump bottles of Mr. Bubble onto the floor and splash around, trying to make bubbles. Spilled vodka and champagne bottles, and room service trays with untouched food, litter every surface so I have to stand. Porn stars on the bed. Porn stars on the floor. *Flesh For Fantasy* begins to play and the irony is lost on everyone. A group of civilians whom somebody let in the suite huddles by the hotel room door, whispering amongst themselves and pointing. A couple of girls lead a male talent who keeps drifting in and out of consciousness to a chaise and dump him on it. One of them mentions some pills he took earlier. People gossip about other people who aren't in the room. In another conversation, a man I don't recognize says the words 'my lamborghini' louder than the rest of his sentence for the benefit of everyone else to hear. The civilians, having seen enough of their favorite contract starlets and male talent in situ, walk out as Billy Idol claims to sing for culture. I step over people and bottles until I find Dan sitting by the window with a VELVET girl, smoking cigarettes and looking out at the city lights. I tell him I'm going home. He gives me a somber nod, bumps elbows with me and says, "Thanks for hanging out." Then he looks out the window again. As I'm turning to leave the girl says, "You better not write about tonight."

I push my way through the crowd and out of the door and shut it behind me. Quiet. I walk along the stark white hallway trying to chew through my neon wristband but I give up. At the elevator, a couple my parent's age glares at me with derision.

Outside the hotel, the streets are silent and the air is thick and wet. A bus approaches. I board it and feed some coins into the slot. Brown faces stare at me. There's a sheen of perspiration on everybody's skin. No empty seats, so I stand and hold onto a pole. The bus is full but nobody talks to anyone else. I shut my eyes and feel the bus sway.

⇨⇨⇨

I USE THE ID badge on the lanyard around my neck and tap it to the panel next to the double doors. There's a beep and a click and when the doors open, a whoosh of cold air hits my face. I pass through the doors and enter the trading floor: a hermetically-sealed open space sprawling the length of a football field filled with rows of un-partitioned work benches laid end to end. All of this enveloped by floor-to-ceiling windows that distort the light entering in from the outside world, suggestive of bullet-resistant glass. Blond people chatter from scores of flat screens hanging from the ceiling every twenty feet tuned to Fox News. A commercial for our competitor begins to play, and in unison all of the TVs switch to CNBC. I pass row after row of workstations, each identical.

This is my second attempt at a real job since the economy tumbled into the Great Recession. I haven't quit porn entirely, but HR has made it clear that I cannot continue to come and go as I please and still keep my job.

Most of my coworkers, in a rush to log in on time, ignore me as I walk along the aisles. Every morning I show up to work at my day job selling commodities, focusing on precious metals, there's a risk that somebody will recognize me. There was already a close call with the FedEx guy last month. Thank God he caught himself. Hundreds of account executives and ancillary staff work on this floor. It's just a matter of time.

The firm hires twice a year. The ad ran for months, and thousands of people applied for my position.

I had to take a battery of personality, aptitude, and ethics of tests, as well as pass comprehensive background and criminal checks to get hired on. During the interview, I caught an upside down glimpse of the aptitude test results.

High ninetieth percentile on ambition, adaptability, leadership, sales knowledge, self-confidence. There was a red ink circle around my "Team player" score: bottom sixtieth percent. They took their time evaluating me, and waited until the day before training to hire me on.

Fifty-six other trainees started the three-month training program with me. I'm the only trainee who was selected to attend training who did not get in through a referral from somebody employed by the firm.

It's the first day of training, and the spot gold price hovers around $1,400 an ounce. When I arrive at the firm, I'm sequestered with fifty-six other trainees from the main trading area on a separate floor of the building. We walk through a gauntlet of corporate security and stand in a line. A man who introduces himself as Chuck chats with me. He tells me that he tried to get into the training program for three hiring cycles. Almost two years.

As the line progresses, I notice a quarter which looks fresh from the mint shining from the carpet. I step over it. Chuck bends down and picks it up.

"Look, Erik. My hiring bonus!"

I laugh. He pockets the coin.

After the last trainee is processed through the line, a procession of executives of various ranks of the firm's org chart introduce themselves to us. The last executive is man a resembling Fred Flintstone. He gives a well-rehearsed motivational speech ripped from an Ayn Rand novel about his humble beginnings in business without a college degree, how he grew the firm to ten figures in sales, and how the firm is a microcosm of America: the ultimate meritocracy.

Chuck is not sitting at his station when everyone returns from break. His name tag is missing from the top of his monitor. I remember Flintstones words, and the quarter Chuck pocketed from the floor this morning as we passed through the gauntlet of security personnel. It may be unrelated, but if that's the reason he was pulled from training, then the message was clear: We are watching you.

⇨ ⇨ ⇨

DURING THE THIRD WEEK, I return from lunch to discover the trainees gathering around an empty terminal. Name tag atop the monitor gone. The seat's former owner returned early from lunch complaining of chest pains. Then he clutched his chest and dropped to the deck. EMTs came and wheeled him out on a stretcher. All this before I returned from getting my venti Americano down the block. Not one person, trainee, security, nor HR personnel, deployed the defibrillators.

⇨ ⇨ ⇨

WHENEVER A SELECTION OF senior AEs and team leaders visit to speak about how they became successful, trainees lean forward in their chairs.

Today we are visited by Gideon Sachs. He relates how two years ago he was telemarketing newspaper subscriptions during the day and counting change for new guitar strings to play gigs at night. How he almost didn't make it out of training. Now he's deciding if he should spend part of his 1.2 million in earnings from the trailing twelve months on a Maserati to park in the driveway of his compound. Gideon walks us through a recent trade which netted him six figures, and how he uses the Socratic method to close deals. He recommends *The Secrets of Question-Based Selling*, and how his favorite technique is using third-party credibility from experts by referring to current events articles he culls from newspapers every morning. A compliance lady interrupts him and stresses that we must first vet any article through the proper channels for approval before using them as a sales tool. Failure to do so would be in violation of compliance.

Gideon says, "Don't be mistaken, the strong eat and the weak get culled from the pack." He leaves the training floor to training an eruption of applause.

⇨ ⇨ ⇨

THE TRAINEE RANKS ARE cut down to eighteen. Half of us who are left are at this point are expected to survive to the main trading floor. The tests now pit trainee against trainee in heads up competitions, like who can raise the most assets under control (money) from cold calls, and which one of us will be the first to get a hat trick—three trades in one day. Now, even if you pass the weekly test and hit your performance numbers, if your scores fall at the bottom of the bell curve relative to your peers, you get disappeared.

⇨ ⇨ ⇨

"SO, I TAKE MY wife to a disco. There's a guy on the dance floor, really getting down. Break dancing, moonwalking, back flips… the man is grooving.

My wife turns to me and says, "See that guy? Twenty-five years ago, before I met you, he proposed to me and I turned him down."

So I say, 'Looks like he's still celebrating!'"

Laughter.

"Welcome to the firm, and congratulations for making it this far into training. My name is Tiberius Trân. I'm a team leader on the trading floor. I used to be a vice president of Merrill Lynch, Pierce, Fenner & Smith. Before that, I flew planes stuffed with nukes. Now I'm here. Questions?"

"How much was our last paycheck?"

"Who are you, my wife?"

Laughter.

"Look, guys, since you guys started last, gold climbed from fourteen hundred dollars an ounce and now it's testing a new resistance level at seventeen hundred dollars. Any idiot can make money in this market. That's not important. What matters is how well you develop your skills in this room, your cash management, and the alliances you form starting right now with the people left in your class that will determine who survives the lean times and develops a career. Next question… You. Go."

"What kind of car do you drive?"

"What am I, invisible? I drive a Prius. It's comfortable. I like it… You. Yes, you in the Lane Bryant dress."

"I…I beg your pardon, sir. I did not raise my hand."

"Yes, I'm aware of that. I always get my most fascinating questions this way. Go."

⇨ ⇨ ⇨

IT's THE LAST WEEK of training and I'm tied for first place in new accounts opened with a kid from Stanford whom everybody pegged as the kind of guy who'd come back and spray the floor with a Heckler & Koch if he didn't make it past training. A mop of hair swept forward and over his eyes, he could be twenty-four or fourteen. He never says hello to any of the other trainees except me. Already, management pulled him aside for his antisocial behaviour, which is amusing since the personality tests they gave us had a heavy selection bias toward type-A, borderline sociopaths. A typical conversation with us goes like this:

"Good morning, Hansel. How was your weekend?"

"If it's possible to earn a million dollars my first year here, I'm going to do it!"

I sigh…fucking commission breath.

"Swell, have a good day."

"You're not going to beat my numbers today."

⇨ ⇨ ⇨

I LOG ONTO MY terminal. Gold tested another resistance at $1,800 before closing in the high $1,700s. Then I listened to a voice mail from my missed phone call. Before the message is over, I dial Tiberius's extension.

"TTB. Go."

"Hey, it's Erik from upstairs."

"What's up?"

"I got a possible new account who called me back—"

"How much is he considering?"

"Maybe start with twenty thousand dollars…I'm tied with Hansel and I can't fuck this up."

"Copy that. Give me the client's number."

Tiberius hangs up.

Moments later, Tiberius's extension flashes on my caller ID as my phone rings on silent.

"Okay, Done. Your new client did a hundred thousand dollars. A mix of semi-numismatic and bullion. He ordered three tubes of Swiss Francs, some Kennedy silver dollars, and some junk silver for his bug out bag. Three thousand eight hundred and forty-seven dollars in commissions for you. Zero for the home team. Good job."

I say, "Wait, we're not going to split the commission?"

"Negative. But I'm claiming you for my team when you get down to the floor. You showed solid judgement by not letting ego get in your way and turning over the trade. Good job. Gideon drafted Hansel. They deserve each other. Whoever else makes it through the training program will get divvied up among the other teams."

"Tiberius."

"Yes?"

"Thank you."

"You're welcome. Team leaders are not supposed to draft trainees, but I told the brass that I'm taking you under my wing. Just don't embarrass me."

⇨⇨⇨

I SIT IN MY pod and log on to the intranet trading system. Intranet, because we're disconnected from the Internet on the main trading floor. There is a bathroom located on the trading floor. Its door opens to a clear shot down the row of stalls for anyone passing by on the trading floor, male or female, to see. Aside from the suit on your back, nothing you weren't born with enters or leaves the trading floor. Not a pen nor a scrap of paper. Paperclips, tape, scissors and staples—all banned. You may only ever use the specific pen and pad of paper issued to you by the firm. Neither of which can ever leave your pod. No electronic devices of any kind. Cell phones are locked away. Violation of these rules subjects you to instant termination.

⇨ ⇨ ⇨

EIGHT FIFTY-NINE IN THE morning. The flat screen TV monitors switch from CNBC to an internal feed. It's time for the daily corporate propaganda meeting.

One of our corporate officers holding a microphone paces back and forth and shrieks, "Good morning and happy Monday, everybody! Hope you had a good weekend! Time to get back to work! Let's read the top ten producers for Friday. You had to earn at least three thousand and eight hundred dollars to make it to the top ten for the day... Coming in at number ten, from the new graduating class, Erik Robinson earned three thousand eight hundred and forty-seven dollars on Friday! Way to go, Erik!"

I get a round of Monday morning golf claps from my coworkers.

A nearby AE says, "You don't seem very pleased."

"They'll put me on a throne today, and tomorrow I'm a son of a bitch begging to keep my seat."

He gawks at me as though I've committed blasphemy.

The executive gives shout outs to the remaining top earners for Friday and divvies out their awards accordingly. Then, he shifts to the real reason people show up every Monday. The lottery. A series of cash drawings which occur every Monday. You get one ticket for each $200 increment of commissions you generate during the previous week. For each of your corresponding tickets drawn from a hat, you win $1,000 cash. Today they're drawing twenty tickets and giving away $20,000 cash. You can win as many times as you have tickets in the hat. Even if none of your tickets are pulled, you can still redeem them for ten dollars cash each. During the lottery, one of my tickets was pulled. During the worst recession in US history, I made $1,200 just for showing up to work.

⇨ ⇨ ⇨

I'M EATING LUNCH IN the outdoor courtyard with some other trainees from my graduating class, listening to them brag about their weekends.

McNally is saying, "...Tompkins and I took those two skanks—remember the girls that—"

"Yeah, we remember. They were in the parking lot," Cortez says, "Go on!"

"So, sixty seconds after we get those whores back to our room, I'm in the semi-hot one's asshole—no kissing, no pussy fucking. Straight to the asshole—while Tompkins is trying to convince the short, fat bitch that the piss spot on the front of his pants is just spilled beer—"

Laughter erupts around the table.

McNally continues, "So, I'm pulling an ATM when—"

Cortez says, "What's an 'ATM'?"

"Ass-to-mouth. Jesus, you gotta get out more, dude—"

One of the senior account executives, a Megan Fox look-alike, walks by our table. All the men stare at her ass.

Levinson says, "Oh my God, did you see her ass?"

"That's the greatest ass I've ever seen in my life!" Tompkins says.

The Fox look-alike turns around and catches the table staring. She scoffs and continues on.

"Eh, that's nothing," McNally says. "I'm getting a girlfriend experience from this porn chick whose ass is—"

"Wait, what?"

"What? What 'what'?" McNally says.

"A 'girlfriend experience.'"

"Are you fucking kidding me, Cortez?" McNally says. "How can you not know these things? These porn chicks, they hook on the side, but they make you wear a condom. But most of them, if you toss a couple bills their way, they'll fuck you bareback. That's the girlfriend experience. Business is slow so they'll do whatever they can to make ends meet—"

Levinson asks, "Why would you do that?"

"Do what?"

"Fuck a porn chick bareback?" Levinson says. "Those girls have diseases."

McNally sighs. He says, "Nah, dude, they test for everything like once a month. Besides, condoms fucking suck. It's cool."

Levinson says, "Erik, you're always so quiet? What did you do this weekend?"

"Went out for a few drinks. Nothing special."

"You get laid?"

"Nah."

McNally says, "Hang out with us next weekend. We'll get you laid, dude."

⇨⇨⇨

THE CONTRACT STARLET SITS in a chair playing with her pussy. She says, "You wanna put that big black cock inside this tight white pussy, don't you?"

I'm sitting in another chair, stroking my dick. I say, "Sure."

"I wanna feel your mahogany inside me soooo baaad!"

This girl requested me for the scene. But we're on opposite sides of the room masturbating. This is the only way she will do an interracial scene. Under no circumstances will there be any physical contact between us. I sit two paces away from a flesh-

and-blood porn star, but I'm rubbing it out to the memory of a civilian: the Megan Fox girl at my day job.

The director gives the signal for dual climax, so the contract starlet intensifies her masturbation and fakes her orgasm. The camera turns on me, so she gets on her hands and knees to show me her ass for visual stimulation. Her ass looks a bit…off. Then I see them under her cheeks. The scars from ass implants. I close my eyes and focus an image of the day job girl's real ass. I pop.

⇨⇨⇨

KEN, THE PHOTOGRAPHER FOR the scene, and I sit at the kitchen table. The contract girl is at the table, too.

Ken says, "I heard you're off of the Viagra. That couldn't have been an easy scene. Good job, Tyler. "

"Thanks, man. These past few scenes without drugs…it's like learning how to perform all over again."

He nods. I stab my fork into my salad and put it in my mouth.

Ken says, "I've never seen this business so segregated. It's ridiculous."

"You think it's getting worse?"

"Yeah. I mean, who's left from your generation of black male talent? You, Darkus, and Rex?"

"I had my day in the sun," I say.

"Yeah, but then there are scenes like this one. Across the room with no touching? Seriously?"

The contract starlet's fingernails click across her iPhone, texting. If she's listening, she doesn't seem to care.

"The business is racist," I say. "Knowing that, you can either chose to accept it for what it is or you can do something else with your time, because it will never change."

The girl gets up from the table and leaves the kitchen.

Ken says, "The people in porn sure do change. I shot Tina Allen the other day. What a fucking nightmare."

"I heard the stories."

"She was such a sweet girl before…"

"Before she won all those awards?"

"No," Ken says, "No, she was still cool after the awards. It was when Travis screwed her over. You hear about that?"

"Uh huh. It was on that mainstream film he directed, right? I know them both…It's hard to know what to believe, really."

"Well, yeah. It was a slasher film, but yeah. Travis actually went to film school. He had these ideas on how he can change the business." Ken laughs. "Want to know what Travis is doing now?"

"What?"

"I heard he's filming girls getting pies thrown in their faces, then fucked."

I laugh. "Well, there you have it."

We sit in silence.

I say, "Have I changed? I mean, for the worse? You've known me for years."

He takes a bite of his salad and pushes it aside. He says, "I wouldn't say I know you, Tyler. You never open up to anyone. But yeah, I'm sure you have. Hell, I know I've changed, too. Man, Tina was such a nice girl…"

"Yeah."

Ken says, "I always tell my friends back east…you know the ring, Precious, from *Lord of the Rings*?"

I nod.

"I tell my civilian friends that this business is like Precious. It slowly corrupts everyone."

⇨ ⇨ ⇨

I SAY MY LINES, "It's time to go," and walk down a hallway and out the door.

The director says, "Cut! That's a picture wrap for Tyler Knight and Ryan Lancer."

As Ryan Lancer and I are heading to change, a blond, Calvin Klein model–looking kid orbits us. The kid, porn's next generation of male talent, asks us questions about performing and asks for any advice we may have. Ryan is patient and answers every question.

I say my good-byes. Part of me is glad these people are here because I'll never step foot on another porn set.

Vlad, the director, says, "If going straight doesn't work out, you always have porn to fall back on."

Jake, the cameraman, says, "You spend eighteen-hour days on set with the same cast and crew years on end, you become a dysfunctional family."

The way this business corrupts people, the Decadent crew is one of the few cliques that has managed to not fuck each other over.

Ryan asks me if I'm ready. We leave the studio and drive off into the night.

⇨⇨⇨

"BUT YOU'RE A LEGEND," I say. "You've got to be a hero for every man who would interview you."

Ryan takes a deep drag and blows smoke out the car window. "Therein lies the problem." he says. "Those kids who saw my work, they're sitting across the desk from me and they're thinking, 'There's no fucking way I can hire this guy. If something happens, like an HR problem, it's *my* ass.'"

The Mercedes glides onto the freeway on-ramp. This time of night, the nearest car going our direction is a red dot of light ahead of us.

I say, "So, you're out? For good?"

"That last divorce fucking crushed me. Wiped me out. That was the last straw. When my directing and performing contract with Decadent expired, there was nothing keeping me here. Getting as far away from the Valley is the best thing for me. Away from the drugs... I'm healthy, now."

"That's fucking great."

The lane lines glow white under our approaching headlights and disappear one after the other as we pass them.

Ryan says, "You got a woman?"

"Amanda...been together ten years."

"That's a long time. She in the business?

"No. Civilian."

"And you've made it work for the entire time you've been in the business."

"Yeah... She took me in when I was homeless and despite everything... AIDS scares—remember that HIV outbreak in o-four?"

"Uh huh."

"I was first generation exposed, and she... I put her life at risk so many times and I fucked up so many different ways and she never gave up on me. She..."

My eyes sting. I look out the window and watch the exit-ramp signs pass by my window.

Ryan whispers, "We're damaged goods, bro."

We exit the freeway and merge onto traffic on Ventura Boulevard, the main artery of Porn Valley. We pull up to the hotel. We park and get out and a valet gets behind the wheel and drives off. Ryan and I stand a car's width apart, looking at each other.

I say, "What are you gonna do?"

He's silent for a while. Then, he says, "I'm staying in Arizona. Maybe start some kind of business. Then after that…shit, I don't know. You?"

"I'm going for it. I'm working a full-time gig while I finish my book."

He smiles. "Good for you, bro. Good for you. Remember, whatever happens…whatever happens, you get out of this business while you've still got something left, and don't look back. If you can't do it for yourself, do it for Amanda. She's waited long enough."

I nod.

"By the way, my real name is Erik."

"I know. I'm Gary." He laughs.

He crosses the distance between us and offers me his hand. In all these years of bumping elbows, I can't remember anyone who has ever offered me his hand to shake. I take it.

I say, "Nice to meet you, Gary."

He laughs. "What the hell, I've known you a decade, right? Good luck with the second half of your life."

Gary, still holding my hand, pulls me into a hug. He lets go and lights another cigarette. "We were the best in the world at what we did, Erik. The experiences we've had…nobody can ever take that away from us."

I watch him walk through the hotel's double doors.

The bus is coming and I have to run across the street, dodging traffic to catch it. I feed some coins into the slot and find a seat. Then I text Amanda.

Me: It's over. I'm out.

Amanda: Really? You promise?

Me: Yeah.

Amanda: I'm so proud of you! Te amo!

Me: Te amo, mujercita.

⇨ ⇨ ⇨

IT'S FRIDAY. THIS WEEK saw America's credit rating downgraded for the first time in history. The equity markets are in turmoil and the precious metals markets, the markets I trade, broke new record highs. It's draining, but doing an honest day's work feels good. When I exit the building I check my cell phone for any missed calls that came in during the day. Two texts. One text is from Frank, the director of the scenes when I strangled a girl with an iPod cord, and the scene when I got blown by my baby sister.

Frank: How's my favorite psychopath? Are you avail—

Delete.

The next text I missed is from a director who wants me to reprise my role as Tyler Wood. He's always been kind to me so I text him back.

Me: No.

Delete.

If you want to take the shortcut out of the office building complex you have to walk by a restaurant's outdoor patio. It's happy hour, and a group of senior account executives sit at a table with some well-dressed women. Dane, one of the senior brokers who took me under his wing, waves me over. He introduces me to everyone, and everybody says hello except one man who leans back in his chair with his arms crossed. He's got an expression that says, "What's that smell?" on his hang-dog features and his clothes appear three sizes too big. He reminds me of a pissed-off Humphrey Bogart.

I say, "Hello."

When Pissed Bogart speaks, his voice surprises me so much I think it has to be a joke. It's the voice of a whining six-year-old.

He says, "What exactly do you do here?"

I say, "What do you mean?"

Dane says, "Erik's a new account executive. He's got skills. He made the daily top ten a couple times."

People at the table congratulate me. Pissed Bogart stares.

Pissed Bogart says, "What's with the twelve-hour work days and the suits? You trying to impress somebody?"

"I'm compensating for my small penis."

Laughter around the table.

Dane says, "That was funny. You come up with that just now?"

"It's old material. This is just the first time you're hearing it."

Pissed Bogart says, "I used to wear suits every day and come in early. But now that I'm a senior account executive I don't have to. I come and go as I please and I still made over $200,000 last year. What did you do last year?"

"Porn."

More laughter.

Pissed Bogart says, "You think you're clever?"

"No. Excuse me, gentlemen."

I walk away.

I'm waiting at the bus stop when a van drives by. On the side it says, "Better to be a somebody for a day than a nobody for a lifetime."

The bus arrives. I board it, feed some coins in the slot, and take a seat.

REDLINE

"**L**OOK AROUND YOU… THOSE of you who are here are men and women of character. You will be rewarded when things turn around. Gideon and everyone else who abandoned you are not your friends! Once you leave us for another firm, you can never come back," says the executive with soap-opera patriarch looks clutching the microphone as he prowls the near-empty trading floor during the morning meeting.

This speech is well-designed to simultaneously manipulate both fear and greed emotions of its audience. It's an effort to stem the mass exodus of ranks as a diaspora of AEs fans out into the wilderness of smaller competing firms, and control those who stay.

"...when the guy or gal who used to sit next to you left for another firm, they abandoned you. If he calls you, it's not because he cares about how you're doing. He is not your friend. If he cared, he would have stayed by your side as we fight through this. He's only fishing for information. About what specials we're running. What exclusive products we're offering. Our marketing... You all signed NDAs. Make no mistake, anyone who consorts with an AE who left for another firm is considered fifth column. Don't do it! We monitor your social media. We have friends everywhere. We will know!"

During my first few months at the firm I witnessed gold rocket to an all-time high of $1,923 an ounce, where clients loaded up on it at the top. Now, with gold prices in free fall, some of my clients call a half-dozen times a day, crying, threatening suicide and, more than once, outright murder. After the firm settled a lawsuit for unfair sales practices, fines, and a Federal injunction against the firm took effect. A squad of court-appointed monitors marched into the firm one morning and took over the firm's internal compliance department. Then the city sued the firm in an attempt to force it to move its headquarters outside of the city limits. We were issued pre-approved responses by management to read to clients whenever they called to ask about the firm's legal issues and its solvency, which was often. All employees are outright banned from speaking with the media. I've heard rumors of reporters ambushing employees in the building's lobby.

"...and just remember that the grass is not greener at another firm. Gold is down for everyone, not just us. And yes, we lost our celebrity spokespeople, but that's okay. Only true believers are welcome here! Stay true to the message, people... Gold cannot be printed. Gold cannot be debased. It cannot lie to you. It's not subject to counter-party risk, and it is the single greatest store of wealth known to man!" The executive stops in an aisle and rotates 360 degrees, scanning the faces. He double-fists the microphone and bellows, "God! Guns! Gold!"

"God! Guns! Gold!" shrieks an AE from the trading floor, and with that, the trading floor stands and burst into cat calls, cheers and applause.

The members of Tiberius's pod, which consist of me, Tiberius, his son-in-law, a middle-aged beach babe, and the contrarian USC MBA who sits next to me are the only people not joining in the cheers. We exchange nervous glances as the extant members of the trading floor—highly educated people— sip champagne flutes of Kool Aid, pinky up, while marveling at the emperor's finest livery.

It feels like I'm trapped in a fucking cult.

⇨ ⇨ ⇨

I'm WORKING THROUGH LUNCH today like I have every day for the past month or so. I forgo food and sleep, working every second of every day allowable, getting off the phone only to pee. Most AEs make about a hundred calls a day. Yesterday, during a twelve-hour shift, I made 315 calls. I'm confident that's an all-time record.

On occasion I take a walk around the open-air man-made lake in the center of the building to ctrl + alt + delete my mind. I've timed it do that a lap tales me about eight minutes from the moment I leave the pod to return. My phone shows a stack of messages, one from Vlad.

Vlad says, "Hey, man, so I'm making this *Men in Black* parody. I want you for the Will Smith part."

My own words make me nauseous leaving my mouth. "I can't. I've got an office gig working seventy hour weeks, and HR won't give me time off."

"Are you sure? It's the lead in Decadent's big movie of the year."

"Who's playing the Tommy Lee Jones part?"

"Ryan Lancer, of course."

Well, damn. So much for his dream of entrepreneurship out of state.

"Of course…"

Vlad told me that I could always return to porn if going straight doesn't work out… Is this working out? I think of the defibrillators…the armed guards…the waiting telephone and the prospect of leaving another two hundred thirty-second voice mails with the occasional, "FUCK YOU, TAKE ME OFF YOUR LIST!" Barked into my ear to snap me out of my ennui.

Doesn't matter, I promised Amanda.

"Yeah, I'm sure. Thank you."

This is one of many parts I've turned down since going straight, but if you keep saying no to people, eventually they'll stop asking.

I've got a callback scheduled. A true believer from the deep south who, in yesterday's conversation, spewed red-hot vitriol over the current administration and swore that in a year's time the world would go "Mad Max". He's one of the few people not to hang up on me as soon as I identified which firm I worked for, so I waited his tirade out.

I dial his number. He answers and I reintroduce myself. After some small talk, I pivot to the trade. You never present the product until the client agrees that status quo—keeping assets 100 percent exposed to the dollar—is not an option. Until they agree on that, you've got nothing. The trick is to phrase it as a series of open-ended questions so that the client comes to the conclusion on his own accord. The Socratic Method.

I say, "Mr. Briggs, yesterday we touched on the fate of the PIIG nations and how that could impact the dollar. Please share your thoughts about that with me."

"Why don't you share your thoughts with me about your firm's complaints?"

"Even Disneyland has complaints, and they're the happiest place on earth."

"Cute. Look, kid, I'm already sold. Let's get down to it, shall we?"

"How much were you considering?"

"One million dollars."

Holy shit! Even if he buys all bullion the commission will be nice... But if I can get him to go Swiss Francs, the bid-ask spread is greater and the commission is $50,000. I take out my Gideon Sachs–inspired article book. "May I share an article with you from *The New York Times*? It's about how people just like you discussing their futures at their kitchen tables consider certain types of gold to purchase as portfolio insurance."

"Do you sell nigger insurance?"

"Uh...excuse me?"

"Nigger insurance. That monkey swinging from the Whitehouse chandeliers and all his kike cronies are ruining our economy!"

Fuck this! My finger swoops down over the End Call button, but it hovers to a stop before it clicks the connection. Relax... One-million-dollar trade. That's up to $50,000 to you, Erik.

I say, "Would you like to discover which types of assets people who share your concerns are considering when converting their dollars into metals?"

"Cut the bullshit sales talk! Where do I wire my fucking money?"

I read the wiring instructions to him over the phone. I can always close him on which types of metals to buy after the funds hit the account.

"Okay. Call me tomorrow at the same time, and we can talk about which 'assets' your nigger-loving Jews are hoarding."

Click!

People begin to trickle back in from lunch. I feel like I just felt up my grandma… Fifty grand will save my ass, but still… The firm passes out metric sheets so you know where you stand in relation to everyone other AE in the firm. I'm in the top decile for new accounts opened. Bottom decile in earnings. Missing $4,000 this month would make it three in a row for me, which would mean I'm terminated. This is the last week of this month, and I'm goose egging. I've got nothing else. Screw just not getting fired, I need to eat… But "niggers" and "kikes"? Who the hell talks like that? Fuck that cocksucker! Okay, if he wires the funds and I don't do the trade, the firm will yank the account from me and assign it to somebody else. You're doing the right thing, Erik. I'll tell Tiberius when he gets back from—

"Do you have a problem following directions?"

The accent tells me who is behind me without having to look. I spin my chair around and look up. The president of the firm. He's a near-exact facsimile of Arnold Horshack, the class clown from the sitcom *Welcome Back Kotter*, right down to his Brooklyn-accented voice. Except this Horshack is as hilarious as the Battle of Somme. He loves to sneak up on people to embarrass them in front of everybody. No transgression of corporate protocol is too trivial for him. In fact, the more trivial the better. The message being, Just imagine what I'd do if you really fucked up! His is the third century BC Roman strategy of decimation, where centurions would gather up a populace, line them up, and walk down the line, executing every tenth person on the spot. "Come with me."

He walks up the aisle of pods. As I follow him, the trading floor, conspicuous in its silence, begins to hum with activity the way people do when pretending to ignore a spectacle.

We enter his office. Our scene plays out behind the floor-to-ceiling glass wall. He sits behind his desk. I wait.

"Sit down."

I do.

Horshack says, "Not only did you ignore the protocol when asked about our legal issues, you misquoted an article used for a third-party source."

"I did?" My voice cracks as I speak and I hate myself or it.

Horshack says, "Yes. It was a *USA Today* article, not *The New York Times*. You can read, can't you?"

"Yes."

"Go ahead and get your third-party sources."

"My articles?"

"Correct. Bring them to me. Now."

He knows every article ever approved for third-party credibility because he is the one who approves them, and they are all a mouse click away on his PC. What he's really doing is tasking me. You know when Chris Hanson on the TV show, *To Catch a Predator*, tells the suspect to "Take a seat," or when a telemarketer tells you to "Go ahead and grab a pen"? The action they demand is irrelevant. It's all about establishing psychological control. By tasking me in front of everyone to "Come with me," and then let everyone witness me leave his office a moment later to return with something he made me fetch goes beyond control. It's Horshack's personal brand of public flogging. He knows that I'm aware of what he's doing. Doesn't matter.

I feel my fists clench in my lap, but if I don't obey, I'm as good as fired and forfeit the commission on the trade.

Everyone has returned from lunch by now. I feel all the eyes on me, I leave his office, walk down the aisle, fetch my article from the folded flip book, and walk back up the aisle to Horshack's office.

"Close the door."

I do.

"Sit down. Do you have something for me?"

I hand him my article. He glances at it, then makes a show of turning the sheet over to inspect its backside, which he knows is always blank.

"What's this?"

"My article."

"This is one article. Maybe it's my fault for not being clear. I want the booklet of every article you've ever accumulated since you stepped foot on this property. Go get them."

⇨ ⇨ ⇨

I DIDN'T SLEEP AT all last night. If that million hits the account, I can say fuck this firm and take a few months to decompress. I can buy Amanda a decent engagement ring! I can't think about any of that until I see that Mr. Briggs wired the funds... Don't get your hopes up, Erik... Can't jinx this.

Before I reach my desk I can see my phone blinking red. A message. When I reach my desk, I see a printout waiting for me. A wire confirmation! I decide to skim the wire confirmation first.

Client: Jackson Briggs... Funds available to trade: $977,000.

Hell. Motherfucking! Yeah!

Confirmation in hand, I put my headset on and listen to my message… Ravinder Singh, my backup AE, asking me to call him back when I get in. I call.

Ravinder says, "Your client did the trade."

Look at my watch…6:25 a.m. My appointment with Mr. Briggs isn't until noon. What the fuck! I just gave away $25,000 by splitting a million-dollar trade with my backup AE! Whatever, Ravinder is a lot better than me on the phone… That's still $25,000.

"Mr. Briggs is really something else. He asked me about my ethnicity saying, 'What kind of name is Ravinder?' and I almost hung up on him until I pulled up the funds to trade in his account. Anyway, he went all bullion for storage. All of it. Look, man, I'm sorry. He was adamant."

"Whatever, man. We split…twelve grand? It's my only trade for the month. Could be worse."

"You're not listening, Erik. Bullion for storage."

"So?"

"It's non-deliverable gold, so you only get paid part of the storage fees. The commission isn't one-point-twenty-five percent. It's twelve and a half basis points… That's one thousand two hundred and twenty one dollars and twenty-five cents."

"I see…"

"Which, of course, we split since I did the trade in your absence. So that's six hundred ten dollars and sixty-two cents net to you."

"Six hundred and ten?"

"And sixty-two cents, yes."

"You're telling me that after paying taxes, my check for the month will be…four hundred dollars? Net-net? On a million-fucking-dollar trade?"

"Hey, I don't make the rules, man. You know the firm only really pays on deliverable numis and semi-numismatic. Shit, even if he went physical bullion, that would have been better."

I hang up, then run the numbers on my calculator… Do you remember when I almost walked away from a $400 scene because I wouldn't let April call me a nigger on camera? Everybody has their price. Turns out mine is $406.25. I feel sick. I bury my face in my palms, close my eyes, and try to control my breathing.

"Is that a hoodie you're wearing?"

Horshack.

Hoodies are a violation of dress code. I forgot to take it off when I entered the trading floor. I begin to shake like a fever has come over me. I can't trust myself to answer his question, so I pull it off. By the time I pull it clear over my head, Horshack is entering his office with a retinue of sycophants.

I get up from my station, exit the trading floor, walk across the atrium, and find an unoccupied Grand Comfort to sit in. A pair of AEs walk past me on their way to the trading floor doors. One of them complaining to the other about how long it's taking to get his Vacheron Constantin Patrimony back from servicing. As dawn breaks, my unfocused gaze drifts outside the window… A family of ducks waddles into the man-made lake that probably cost more to build than the GDP of Paraguay. I'm balanced on the tipping point of losing my shit, but I'm in public so I hold it together.

Tiberius enters the atrium. He chooses the chair next to me even though the one directly across from me is closer.

He pretends to check his Tommy Bahama watch that his kids probably bought from Costco and gave to him for Father's Day while I dry my eyes. All gestures to allow me to save face.

He says, "Do you play chess?"

"Uh… I mean, I know how to play, but I haven't played in years."

"Same here. I'm much better at poker, but I still play once in a while. Anyway, it's accepted that there's only been two American's ever who have become World Chess Champions. The first was Paul Morphy. The other, Mr. Robert James Fischer."

"Fischer was paranoid and walked away from the game."

"Correct. I find Morphy more fascinating, though. Unlike Fischer, Morphy had no formal lessons. When he was a kid he learned at the kitchen table by watching his father play his uncle. By the time he played his first game he already possessed a masterful understanding of chess. He beat everybody in town, and then in the region. When local masters, including a Civil War general, challenged Morphy to a game, his father had to place a box on top of a chair so he could see the board and reach the pieces. Morphy would crush all of them. Sometimes in as few as six moves. He would go on to become the greatest living chess master of the era.

"So, one night at this dinner party Morphy saw a painting hanging on the host's wall. It was a picture of a kid playing the Devil in a game of chess. Ostensibly for possession of his soul. The kid in the painting is playing white and the Devil playing black, of course. The host of the party sidled up to Morphy. He recounted to Morphy the legend of the picture: That not only is it possible for white to escape certain checkmate, but there is a way for white's position to actually win the game in a handful of moves.

"He told Morphy that many chess masters came through his house over the years and studied the position of the pieces on the board in the painting. Not a single one of them found a solution, and for years it was accepted that it's impossible for white to win.

"Morphy, possessed by hubris, took that as a challenge. He just couldn't let it go. While everybody else at the party was having a good time, he camped out in front of the painting working out solutions in his head. Late into the evening, he called everybody in the room and announced to all the guests that he had found a solution. He, then, walked them through his solution, move by move. He did it! He beat the Devil at his own game!

"Before Morphy could publicize his solution he went home, drew himself a bath, and he got in the tub. The temperature difference between the bathwater and his body was so great that when he lowered himself into the tub, it shut down the world's greatest brain before yours can process this sentence. Death by stroke. Just like that."

Tiberius punctuated the point by snapping his fingers. He smiled, pat me on the head, and walked toward the trading floor doors.

⇨ ⇨ ⇨

INSTEAD OF GOING HOME I decided to walk along Hollywood Boulevard to clear my head. Above the retail stores on Hollywood and Highland, a text crawls across a horizontal LCD screen for the Hollywood Stock Exchange that tracks the buying and selling of shares in celebrities whose values are reduced to box office and Q scores while the hoi polloi beneath in sweat-sodden T-shirts clinging to greasy skin jostle against me from all directions, chortling as they recede into the night. I slip into the current of the crowd, streaming all directions and going nowhere. A grandmother standing on stack of pamphlets advertising LIVE NUDE GIRLS! acts as a breakwater for the flow of humanity flowing around either side of her. She asks passers-by, "What happened to time?" A young gee with neon lights glinting off his grill and shrouded in a hoodie hiding his eyes twists through the crowd and slaps a pamphlet into my chest that says, "WHEN YOU DIE…" and on its reverse, "YOU WILL MEET GOD!" What's happening with my life? I'm not a young man anymore. Every decision I make affects the lives of other people. Shit, I'm fucking trying… Not good enough. Am I'm worthless? Taking up space? Why do I keep fighting? Maybe the best thing to do is just… It would have to look like an accident, and let Amanda get the insurance money… I'm so tired. I'm so tired…

So very tired…

In front of the Chinese Theater, Billy Jean blasts from a street dancer's boom box with LEDs flashing all colors of the rainbow fire in synch with the beat. The one-gloved street dancer pops and locks and children play and husbands spin and twirl their wives. Another street performer wearing a tuxedo covered in mirrored shards of glass dances in a circle of spectators and I see my face in a thousand fractured fractals, distorted and warped as he grooves to the beat. Passing cars' headlamps throw the light into my eyes. Sounds comes to me, muffled and distorted. There is a pressing and throbbing around my skull as though it's submerged under water at a depth of ten atmospheres and pressures of water assault and press against my skull from all sides. The light around me magnifies until all edges, all of sight blurs…and everything. Goes. White.

Ringing!

When my vision restores itself I'm stumbling around a few blocks away on Hollywood Boulevard and La Brea, where I turn south toward Sunset. I make it to a 7-Eleven and pull the door shut behind me.

Silence. I hide my shaking hands in my pockets and head for the refrigerator where I stand with my back to the store, facing the glass doors but avoiding my reflection while pretending to examine my choices for bottled water—

"Tyler!"

A fan, probably. Not now! Can't ignore him. That never works and I'll come off like an asshole… Smile. Be kind…

I turn around. Nobody is there. The store is empty.

Can't be. Where is he… He was close enough for me to feel breath blowing hot in my ear as he spoke!

I stumble from the store and dash across traffic and into the backseat of a taxi parked outside of the Comfort Inn.

He pulls away from the curb and asks where I'm going… Where am I going? When I don't answer he pulls over to the curb and turns in his seat to face me. I fold my hands together to hide the shakes, and whisper my address. I look out the window as neon lights and distorted pictures pass over it.

The driver steals glances at me in the rear view mirror. As the taxi glides along the street and passing under the street lights, my head goes from being shrouded in shadows to lights of Sunset strip splashed across my profile and I shut my eyes but colors paint the insides of my eyelids.

Light, dark…light, dark behind my eyelids…as we creep. There's a screaming in my skull and bile forces its way up and sears my throat but stops there. Horns blast and the cab jolts to a stop and lurches me forward, tipping bile upward that's bitter and stings on my tongue like mouthwash.

I open my eyes. Sunset and Vermont. Close enough. I glance at the meter and jam bills in a slot of the Plexiglas partition bisecting the cab and open the cab door to a cacophony of traffic and slouch my way toward Sunset Junction and home in Silver Lake.

⇨ ⇨ ⇨

I close my bedroom door with care and leave the lights off. I kick off my shoes and lay in bed on my belly with a pillow over my head, waiting for the screaming in my head to stop. As the pain in my head fades, memories of today's humiliations push their way into the foreground and slash at me like razors whipping around in a maelstrom. I try to bring to focus hazy memories of good times with Amanda instead... The imagery flickers behind my eyes like a zoetrope projecting stop-motion images on muslin before they fade because there's nothing for them to latch onto. Even though we live together, I've left Amanda out of my life and kept her at arm's distance for the better part of a decade...

I hear the door click open and click shut. Amanda pats me on the foot. I sit up.

"Que fue, Papito?"

My life in isolation ends right now. I say, "I'm starting to hear things that aren't there...I'm not sure I can tell what's real and what's not anymore."

She sits on the bed and takes my foot in her hand. "You're having another nervous breakdown."

"Yeah...probably."

"You've got to quit this job. I want you to quit."

"Okay."

"I mean it. You're not going back to that place."

"Okay, but what else am I supposed to do, huh? Go back to fucking?"

"I don't know… We'll figure it out later, but now you're getting in my car."

"Where are we going?"

"There's a free health clinic across from the school down the street. It's on Sunset. They offer mental health services."

"But, what if they decide to hold me? Can't they, like, keep me there for seventy-two hours?"

"Then you stay a few days. If you don't get in my car, I'm going to leave you."

"I'm scared."

"So am I. But I'm here."

"Heh…"

"What's funny?"

"So much for, 'I'm saving myself for a man I don't have to save.'"

"Come on, Erik. Let's go."

⇨ ⇨ ⇨

"I'm sorry, Miss, but he needs a referral from his primary care physician."

"This is a free clinic."

"Again, I'm sorry, that doesn't matter. Those are the rules."

"But, he doesn't have a referral. This is a free walk-in clinic. Walk-in. That's why I came here."

"Yes, this is a walk-in clinic, except mental health services at this facility are not walk-in. We have counselors and therapists, but those services require a referral and a scheduled appointment."

"I'm making an appointment for right now."

"And a referral… He needs a referral for an appointment."

"Look at him. *Escúchame*! He doesn't need help someday next week. He needs help right now! I don't think he's going to make it!"

"Then I strongly suggest you take him to County USC. They're equipped to handle emergency services."

"What if he walked in from the street and he didn't have me to take him there, huh? Then what?"

"I'm sorry. Those are the rules."

We leave the clinic and walk the block up the cross street and past the school towards Amanda's car.

"Where is County USC? Is it by USC?"

"No. Farther. Other side of Downtown."

We reach her car. We get in.

"Look up the directions on your phone."

"It's okay. Just take me home, baby… I'm tired."

NE PLUS ULTRA

*NE PLUS ULTRA \NĀ-PLƏS-ƏL-TRƏ\ noun. [Latin] Literally "not further beyond"

1: the highest possible level of achievement or perfection

2: the absolute limit of which one can go

3: a warning to ships inscribed upon the Pillars of Hercules demarcating the end of the known world; the point crossed by Ulysses in Dante's *Inferno* before he encounters Purgatory.

My hands brace against the fiberglass walls as I retch into the space between my knees and down the cesspit. Somewhere outside the port-a-john, Pharrell croons "Happy" from a boom box. Astringent disinfectant tears my eyes and seizes at my throat, which makes puking while standing upright inside a box the dimensions of a garment bag a joy. Stomach acids fizz up my throat and burn sour on the back of my tongue.

The action I'm tasked with is running a footrace the equivalent length of 1,760 football fields—four back-to-back marathons—in a single push. During my run, I'll feel the warmth of dawn break upon my face and then watch the ocean extinguish the sun as the terminator, the shadowy line which separates day from night, sweep west across the globe to reclaim the ground I run upon into darkness. Then I'll continue through the night and emerge on the other side of the penumbra burnt away by a second sunrise.

I wipe my mouth on the hem of my T-shirt and exit the port-a-john and into the fog. It's dark and the scent of Pacific brine hangs in the still air. A volunteer jogs up to me exclaiming the race is about to start. The race director finishes his pre-race address to the gathering pack of runners. He warns us to stay on top of our nutrition, the possibility of hallucinations due to sleep deprivation, and that headlamps are mandatory on the course between twilight and dawn. The runners flick on their headlamps and line up between two orange cones straddling the bike path. The course is an out-and-back along the eight-mile-long concrete bike path traced along the shoreline. Twelve and a half laps from now the race staff will stretch the finish line tape across the path. The farthest I've ever run up to this point is a 50k race (about thirty-two miles) which took everything I had to finish within the eight-hour cutoff time…so, naturally, I signed up for a race three times that distance. The race director reminds us of the strict thirty-hour cutoff time: finish 30:00:01 and you get a DNF (Did Not Finish) for your efforts, and all those miles were for naught. I power up my headlamp and toe the line among the other ultrarunners right as the race director counts down from ten to zero. It's on, time to get down! I press "Record Activity" on my GPS watch and run into the gloom.

⇨ ⇨ ⇨

O-SIX HUNDRED.

Headlamps strapped to athletes' heads wash over concrete sprinkled with sand as waves slap against the shore. Sneakers slap against cement and crunch atop granules of sand. The field of runners thins. A glance at my watch shows my running pace within the lead pack is faster than I what trained for. The excitement of the race can make you run outside of your abilities, which you'll pay for later on. I temper my excitement and allow my natural pace to slip me into the rear of the pack. An ocean breeze blows away the fog and moonlight illuminates the path as a line of silver. The remaining back of the pack runners blow past me, and now I'm DFL. Dead Fucking Last.

I run alone, chasing headlamps in front of me that wink as the runners turn their heads to the side to chat with the person next to them. I ignore them and maintain my gaze a few paces ahead. While running by headlamp (as opposed to a flashlight) keeps your hands free, it poses a unique challenge. It distorts your depth perception rendering the world around you flat and two-dimensional like a cheap cartoon. If your attention lapses and you look away from where you're going, when you return your gaze forward, objects spring to life before you as you approach like cardboard cut-outs in a life sized pop-up book. Those roots across the trail you judged to be a few strides away are already grabbing at your feet.

I glide along the bike path landing on my toe shoes. My forefeet land in hushed taps in quick succession. Unencumbered by thick cushioning underfoot, I am one with the concrete.

⇨ ⇨ ⇨

FIFTEEN-O-FOUR.

Forty-three miles

What the fuck was I thinking? This is stupid! Am I out of my goddamn mind? What kind of idiot signs up to run a hundred miles on fucking cement in toe shoes with no cushioning? FUCK!

The soles of my feet make scraping sounds as I shuffle my feet along the bike path. Lifting my legs takes too much effort, and the impact of even a single step sends pain knifing up my legs and through my body. It's as though someone took a meat tenderizer to my soles for nine hours.

Back when my GPS watch chirped signifying that I've passed the fifty-kilometer distance and the farthest I have run in my entire life, a wave of euphoria washed over me. That feels like a lifetime ago. Since then, the concrete has exacted its toll, and the enormity of the task ahead of me, repeating what I've just done twice more on legs half as fresh, is mind-fucking me.

I'm sitting on jennifer dragon's sofa after wrapping a nuru massage scene for Barney Blaze, my first scene after a three-year break from the business.

Barney, Erin Masters, and I are discussing the bombing that just happened at the Boston Marathon today. My twitter feed is full of imagery of blood and suffering. I feel helpless. On the way home from set, I stop by a discount store to buy some running shoes. The only athletic shoes I have are some wrestling shoes and a dry rotted pair of Mark Gonzales skateboarding sneakers. This will be my first pair of running shoes since back when the Berlin Wall still stood.

Scanning the rack, I pick up the first pair of name brand shoes I find in my size and try them on... Not sure what I'm looking for, but they're cheap, so what the hell. As I'm leaving, I spot a shoe on the rack with individual compartments for each toe. What sport is that for? I pick it up and read its brand...then I Google it on my phone...

Right on the first page of hits are all kinds of websites with running gurus both damning the shoe or extoling its virtues in a minimalist running revolution. Heh. Running shoes?

A forum discussing the merits of minimalist running for ultramarathons...

What the fuck is an "ultramarathon"?

I Wikipedia it:

"An ultramarathon, also called ultra distance, is any footrace longer than the traditional marathon length of 42.195 kilometers (26.219 mi). There are two types of ultramarathon events: those that cover a specified distance, and events that take place during specified time (with the winner covering the most distance in that time). The most common distances are 50 kilometres (31.069 mi), 100 kilometres (62.137 mi), 50 miles (80.4672 km), and 100 miles—"

I stop reading. Holy. Shit! One hundred miles! This is for real? People do this? I've never run farther than five miles at a time in my life, and even that sucked. What would running that distance do to the human body? How have I never heard of this madness until now?

I drop the name brand shoes and, clutching the one toe shoe, I scour the racks for its mate. I find it.

Back to my phone...blogs with post-race reports from emaciated yet grinning men and women showing belt buckles won as prizes for finishing a hundred miles in one day. Those smiles...

I bookmark a few blogs, and before I leave the store I'm on Ultrasignup.com signing up for a 50k in the fall with my eyes on a hundred miler in January.

I call Amanda and mouth-diarrhea into the phone about what I've discovered, and I read some of the race reports aloud to her.

"...and the suffering these runners go through. Doesn't matter if you're first to finish or last, they all suffer... And this common experience bonds them! The races are usually in the mountains where the air is thin, or...dude, there's this race, Badwater one hundred thirty-five, in the desert that goes through Death fucking Valley? In July! They cross the desert and then they climb some fucking mountain before they finish. You believe that shit?"

"Erik—"

"There's this dude named Dean Karnazes who ran that race, and then he ran this race called Western States... I'm gonna buy his book...

"Erik, cálmese! Tell me about the people."

"Sorry... It's tradition for the first place winner to wait until the last runner crosses the finish line, even if it's a half a day later. It's a community of runners, really small, and runners who volunteer whenever they're not racing to put on races. No real big corporate sponsors, everybody is fucking broke. But everybody looks so happy!"

Amanda says, "Honestly, that doesn't sound fun to me, but I'm really glad you might have found something that excites you."

Then she laughs.

"What?"

"You're what, two hundred twenty pounds? We'll see how you feel about running a hundred miles after you try that fifty-k."

"Ha-ha, yeah, I got some work to do, but how hard can it be?"

A woman in a short running skirt says, "Good job!" as she runs past me. I pull myself out of my malaise, pick up the pace and play Chase the Skirt. Hey, whatever works…left-right-left-right…

⇨ ⇨ ⇨

SEVENTEEN-O-NINE: CIVIL TWILIGHT

The sun has set, stealing all the day's warmth with it. I'm not gonna give a poetic description full of purple prose about what the sun looks like setting over the sea. Fuck the sun. I'm not in the mood…you know what a goddamn sunset looks like. If not, Google "JMW Turner," motherfucker.

Before I turn on my headlamp, I run off the bike path a few yards into the sand and retch. Because I've not eaten anything besides Red Vines all day, this means scarlet slobber and drool on the front of my hoodie, but nothing solid. When I'm done, I look around to be sure I'm unseen before I pull my dick out to pee… It takes a long time for urine to pass…and when it does, it's the color of a dark lager. A'ight…gotta hydrate better from here on out.

I pop a handful of Ibuprofen. Water bottle is empty…I swallow them dry. Whenever I feel my morale sink, I open Twitter on my phone and tweet my progress in real time. Keeps me focused.

Tweet: "In the motherfucking pain cave. Getting my mail there… I am the King of Pain."

I need to steel myself for the probability of this mental siege worsening, because this time of year I'll run through fourteen hours of darkness. Ah, Darkness… You can't wait to trebuchet flaming balls of doubt and self-loathing over my mental walls, can you? I death march while I wait for the pain killers to kick in.

Left foot, right foot…left foot, right foot… *Hello Darkness, my old friend…*

⇨⇨⇨

TWENTY-TWO-THIRTY-TWO

Sixty-two-point-eleven miles

Because the course is a multi-lap out-and-back along the same path, you get to see the entire field of runners several times. Since the sun has set, I see others with decreasing frequency. Most times, the only human contact I have for long stretches of time are Amanda and the volunteers at the aid station which I pass every lap. At the aid station, a volunteer fills my water bottle with Mountain Dew as I swap out my shoes for a pair with cushioning, and take a few steps to the food table… Oh my God, it feels like I've got pillows strapped to my feet! I grab Red Vines and Ibuprofen at the table, kiss Amanda, and go.

Tweet: "Going on my 3rd marathon of the day. Left foot, right foot!"

⇨⇨⇨

DAY TWO

O-two-thirty

Eighty-four miles

Tweet: "Downhill from here. The last 22 miles were rough… stomach issues. Tweaked ankle."

Running on concrete isn't an option so I walk in the sand. When I get to the aid station, I'm greeted by cheers and encouragement from the volunteers. Amanda is there. She kisses my cheek and hands me an extended battery for my Magellan GPS watch, and I stick it into place.

A new volunteer takes my water bottle. She says, "Great job, I'll refill this for you! What do want to drink?"

"Hemlock."

The volunteers laugh. I wasn't trying to be funny.

I say, "Mountain Dew."

The volunteer hurries off to fill my water bottle with Mountain Dew while I shuffle over to the food table. There are pizzas on the table...sandwiches...varieties of fruits, as well as potatoes next to a bowl of salt for dipping them in to replace depleted salt levels. I ignore them all and grab a fistful of Red Vines.

Amanda says, "You haven't eaten anything but licorice and Mountain Dew all day. You should eat some pizza."

"I'm fine! I don't want fucking pizza!"

Conventional wisdom says you cannot digest more than 250–300 calories per hour. The challenge is, a man my weight burns about three times that sum per hour of running. It's an impossible deficit to bridge. Marathoners feel its effects manifest in "hitting the wall" about fourteen miles into their 26.2-mile race. During an ultra, after hitting the wall and smashing through it enough times, you "bonk." The only defense you have for this is accepting that it will happen, staying on top of your caloric intake, and keeping your emotions in check. Bonking has been known to turn ultra runners into jerks.

"I'm sorry about that, mujercita...I can't hold anything down in my stomach. Dew and licorice are the only things I can keep down. They give me the calories and caffeine I need."

Amanda points at a lawn chair. "Sit down a minute and I'll bring you a cup of soup. It'll warm up."

I look over to the series of lawn chair she's pointing to. On one of them sits a runner getting blisters on her feet lanced by a member of her crew. Next to it is an empty chair with a blanket piled upon it. The chair has gravity…I feel it pulling me toward it…a whispered suggestion building into a command. My eyelids begin a reflexive droop… My weight shifts in the beginnings of a step toward the chair. Sitting down, even if my intention is just for a moment, would be the end of my race. I just don't trust myself to get back to up to my feet if I sit. Even if I did manage to get going again, the endorphins would have long worn off and the first few miles would be a living hell until they kicked in again.

The volunteer returns with my bottle and goes off to attend to another runner. A pair of runners blow through the aid station together without stopping, all long strides. My watch says I've lingered here for too long.

"Can't. Gotta keep moving. I'm on the clock." I kiss her cheek and set off. "Te amo."

"Te amo… You can do it!"

It'll be a couple hours until I see them again. When I'm far enough away from the aid station, I take out my phone.

Tweet: "Going to be alone with my thoughts for a while…"

⇨ ⇨ ⇨

O-three-thirty-eight

Calories burned: 18,231

I'm staring at a slice of pizza lying in the sand between my feet. It's perfect… The very cliché of what a slice of pizza should look like. I nudge it with my toe. The race director warned us of our minds playing tricks on us…hallucinations…not entirely convinced that it's real, I take its picture and tweet it.

Tweet: "Am I hallucinating or is God fucking with me?"

The consensus from my followers say that it is in fact a pizza, and not a notorious ultra marathon hallucination. I pick it up, brush the sand off and take a bite as I return to the bike path. Heh...I think of Dean Karnazes and his stories of running while eating pizza.

A headlamp approaches from behind me. This is a race after all, so I run as hard as I can to put distance between us. My heart rate spikes and lactic acid snakes through my legs, so I slow to a walk. When I turn around, the light is closer. I walk off the path and make for a lifeguard tower. Just down the shoreline from the tower, a flame licks at the rim of an unattended steel drum. The tower reaches up, silhouetted against the stars like a hand of a buried giant left behind during the Great Ascension. At the base of its stairs, a plastic top hat, upside down and half-full of seawater, with "Happy New Year!" and "2014!" printed on it. Inside of the hat, a bee suspended in water by surface tension churns its legs to right itself and reach a side, but only manages to spin in circles. I collapse onto the bottom step, waiting for the runner to pass me. The night is clear and smells of salt. I turn off my headlamp. As my eyes adjust, stars burst from the sky. I scoop up a handful of sand. Moonlight glints off of the crystals. When I tilt my hand, a constellation of microstars cascades between my fingers.

Amanda holds a solitaire diamond mounted in white gold. Light glints off half its facets in an explosion of colors. The other half, an Event Horizon—black, and sucking in all light from the bedroom. Amanda closes her fist around the ring.

"In all this time I've never met a single relative of yours. No friends come over, ever. Do you have friends?

"I share your bed every night for twelve years, but I don't know you... What do you know about me? What am I to you

besides a two-dimensional anecdote in conversations with other people? Tell me, Erik…what are my dreams?"

"I can change. I love you."

"No. No, you can't, and you don't. You think you do, but you're incapable of truly loving anyone.

"You've fooled everyone into believing you're such a sweet man, but you're really a Rorschach inkblot. People see in you what they want to see. I deserve more than being used as a prop to make you seem normal. I love you, but the woman who marries you is doomed to be the second loneliest person in the world."

She opens her fist. The diamond has dug an impression into the flesh of her palm. She holds the ring up and, giving it a quarter turn, looks at it for the first time. Fire and ice. She gazes into the diamond and her thoughts take her to another time and place which I will never know.

She says, "I can't be alone again. You're all I have… Our relationship is a Gordian Knot, but if I had sense I'd cut it and run."

Amanda hands the ring back to me. The metal is warm from absorbing her body heat.

She says, "Get on your knees. Ask me again, properly. Give me that much at least."

I do. Then I tell her I love her, and I swear to her that I will never leave her. Never.

I cough, and when I do my bladder releases. I pee myself, soaking my tights and shorts through. My dignity runs down my leg, and I weep. An offshore gust buffets the lifeguard tower. Because I'm sitting still, my body cools. Soon it feels like my rib cage is made of icicles surrounding my organs, radiating coldness and chilling my heart from within. My legs won't obey my pleads to stand… It's all I can do just to keep my eyes open. There's a lulling sound as waves *shussssh* against the shoreline…

The runner approaches. Instead of continuing straight, the runner veers off the path and toward me. I wipe my eyes dry with the heels of my palms. When he gets close, he turns his headlamp off. He is a she…no bib.

She greets me with a "Hey," the way only someone familiar with you would as she steps over the top hat and sits next to me on the bottom step without asking. If she saw the piss puddling in the sand between my feet, she doesn't let on.

"Hi," I say.

I steal a glimpse of her face… There is a familiarity, but… placing how I know her eludes me. Although the night is chill enough for my breath to mist the air, enough for me to wear a hoodie and tights, she's in shorts and a T-shirt. Horizontal scars line up in ranks on the insides of her forearms…she's a cutter. I look away.

I say, "Are you the sweep?"

"Yes."

In ultras, the sweep is a designated runner who pulls runners from course who fall behind the slowest pace possible to finish the race within its time limit. On top of this, your progress is tracked at each aid station, which may have its own designated maximum allowable time to pass through it corresponding with the overall race cutoff time. The reasoning is: Being chased by the cutoff times for thirty hours with no hope of finishing the race is cruel, so late in the race if your progress at each aid station along the way is not tracking within the finishing time limit, you get pulled early. Sometimes the distance between aid stations can be vast. That's where the sweep comes in. The sweep is the physical embodiment of time, reaping straggling runners from the course between aid stations and culling the field as she goes. If the sweep catches you, you're done.

She says, "Don't worry, I'm early. You have a bit of time. A bit."

I pop a handful of Vitamin "I" (Ibuprofen).

"How many have you had?"

"All of them."

"During the pre-race address, you were warned of what of what could happen to a runner's body over the course of a hundred miles. You also were warned of the potential dangers of overdosing on Ibuprofen during an ultra."

"Yep."

"Rhabdomyolysis. Possibly even renal failure. All those toxins building up as you run that are no longer filtered by your kidneys. The toxins will begin to seep into your blood."

"Then what?"

"Roll the credits."

The bee floats in the hat. It does not move.

⇨ ⇨ ⇨

The sweeps begins her story: *There was a boy who saw bumblebees in his backyard garden. His mom gives him a jar with holes she punched into the lid with a screwdriver, and the boy catches a bee in a jar. Later, his mom puts some flower buds from the garden into the jar with the bee. He names the bee Bee. That night, the boy places Bee's jar onto his nightstand and falls asleep watching Bee, a yellow and black puff of fuzz, crawl upon the flowers. Bee is his first pet.*

The next morning when his mom takes him to day camp in the city while she works, he takes Bee with him. He avoids the other kids whenever he can at day camp because they are always pushing him and taking things from him and laughing. He sits in a patch of grass. Bee will keep him company.

"What's up, little man?"

Two older kids stand before him. The boy stands.

"Hello."

"What's in the jar?"

"It's my pet bee… His name is Bee."

"Gimmie the jar. Lemme see 'em."

"No."

"I'm not gonna do anything. I just wanna see 'em, that's all."

"But—"

The older kid snatches the jar from the boy. His hands cover most of the jar, so the boy can't see Bee inside. "Hey, it's got holes in the lid for air!"

He tosses the jar to his friend, who makes a show of almost dropping it.

"May I have my jar back, please?"

Both of the older kids laugh. "Damn, you country boys sure talk funny."

"I'm sorry."

The older kid with the jar turns the jar upside down, then rights it. The flowers tumble inside. The boy still can't see Bee.

"Please. You're going to hurt Bee. Can I have him back, please?"

"Why don't I open the lid and let 'em go?"

"No! Don't!"

The kids toss the jar back and forth like a football, until it ends up with the older kid who first snatched it from the boy.

"We're gonna play a game. I gonna shake this jar for a minute, then I'll give it back."

"What's a minute?"

"This is a minute."

He clutches the jar with both hands in front of him and shakes.

"No. Please, stop!"

The boy reaches for the jar, but the second kid intercepts the boy's stomach with a fist. The boy falls to the grass. He fights for air as the older boys laugh.

From the ground, the boy watches a jet plane streak across the sky stretching a long cloud tail behind it. He touches each fingertip to his thumb on one hand, repeats the task on then the other hand. His lips move in silence as Bee's jar shakes.

The jar falls into view onto the grass in front of the boy's face. Bored, the older kids have dropped it and walked away. Still laying on the grass, the boy reaches for the jar and unscrews the lid and lays it on its side. Bee staggers from his jar and collapses. The boy gives him a gentle nudge with his finger, but Bee doesn't fly away. Bee doesn't do anything anymore.

One minute.

You count to ten on your fingers, then you do it again six times. The instant the boy grasped the concept of time was the moment he understood death.

That night, while his dad is drawing him a bath, he tells his dad what happened. Dad lifts the boy's chin with a finger and looks into his son's face. Then Dad slaps his son with enough force to send the boy's head cracking off the tile behind him. The boy slides down into the cold porcelain to cover himself as Dad chases him around the tub with his fists.

Dad says, "You let a white boy kick your ass, and you didn't fight back? Get out of the tub. Put your hands up."

⇨ ⇨ ⇨

It's the end of another day at camp and the boy sits in the rec room with the other remaining children who wait for their parents to pick them up. Children play in groups, but the boy stays in a corner to himself. A boy his age walks over to him and tells him that a CIT, counselor-in-training, told them both to come over to her. He lets the other boy lead him across the room and toward the closet. None of the other children look up or are paying attention. A Camaro passing by the windows plays Hall & Oates "Sara Smile"; the verse, "It's you and me foreveerrrr" stretched out as the car travels farther down the street. A woman, waiting inside the closet, pulls both boys in and shuts the door. The closet smells of Play-Doh.

She says, "If either of you makes any noise, I'll kill you."

The woman says, "Pull down his pants," to the other boy. "Then pull yours down, too."

The boy is confused. The other boy, however, does what he's told and does not seem to care.

Then woman orders the other boy to touch himself and put his hands on him, too. The other child obeys, as if this wasn't his first time.

Voices pass by the other side of the door. He expects the door to burst open and Mom to pick him up. She doesn't.

"Hurry up."

He knows this isn't right... He should say something... Yell. The door is right there! But the woman is very tall. Much taller than the older kids even, and her face looks mean.

"If you tell anyone, ever, I'll kill you."

The boy remembers Bee. How he was moving one moment, and then he stopped and never moved again.

Then the woman pulls her shorts down to her sneakers... She has the same pieces as Mom.

"Come here...both of you. Open our mouths... Stick out your tongues."

He does what the grown up tells him to, sticks out his tongue. The other boy goes first. Could he tell this to his dad?

He remembers the bathtub, and the last time he told Dad. What would his dad do if he told him about this? He decides keep it to himself. To never tells anyone. Stuff it way down. Way down where it will fester inside for forty years. The boy wonders, What did I do wrong?

⇨ ⇨ ⇨

The next afternoon, instead of waiting in the rec room for his mom, he stands at the edge of the pool. The reek of chlorine burns at his nose. The surface is smooth and calm. On the tiles beneath him, the number six, and black lines that run the pool's length to the other side.

The boy steps off the lip and falls into the pool, but the instant his face goes under the water he changes his mind. He's made a mistake! He flails in place, reaching for the edge but it's just beyond his grasp. His head drops below the surface. The chlorine stings his eyes and everything he sees is a blue blur. He thrashes his way back up, and for the moments when his head's above the surface and he gasps for air, he takes in almost as much water as he does air. Coughing, he reaches for the edge but touches the side wall instead of the coping, pushing himself a bit farther away. His arms feel so heavy...so tired...

Soon it is all he can do to keep his lips and chin above the surface. Thoughts run to his mom. He so wants to live...

Kicking with his legs, he reaches for the edge of the pool...and gets fingers on the top of the coping. Not trusting his strength to pull himself out, he edges his way along the lip until he reaches the ladder. At the top, shaking and coughing out water, he promises he'll never try to hurt himself again.

⇨ ⇨ ⇨

THE SWEEP STARES AT me. No mist vapors rise from her breath. Her eyes don't reflect the steel drum's firelight. They drink it.

I say, "Is this the part where I buy time by playing you in a game of chess by the sea?"

"This is not an Ingmar Bergman film, and despite your nom de guerre, you're no knight."

"No…I suppose I'm not."

"Are you ready to come with me?"

"Can I change my mind if I feel better later?"

"All sales are final."

"I'm not ready."

"You're not here to discover how far you can run. You're here so that you can finally stop." She looks down toward the sea. Fog has rolled in, hiding the violence of crashing waves behind it, and there is no horizon to delineate the blackest depths of sea from the heavens above. I follow her gaze out to where world ends and the infinite begins.

I try to work out the math of distance remaining in the race and required pace per mile to finish… Each thought feels as though it's wrapped in individual tufts of cotton. With effort, the numbers reconcile.

"No. I still have time. What do I do now?"

She smiles. "Take a step."

The reaper powers up her headlamp, then runs onto the course back toward the direction we came from.

I watch her light. It fades and then it is gone. Dawn breaks. Down the shoreline, the burning trash can is gone.

When I stand, my bloated stomach strains against the inside of my hoodie as though I'm a Biafra refugee… In part, the effects of the Ibuprofen. There's a chill on my legs as though my piss has frozen to my leggings… Can piss freeze? Is piss ice a thing?

I power up my headlamp, and stand on legs with ankle, knee, and hip joints that feel welded in place.

Take a step…

I take a moment to brace myself against the lifeguard tower. I set off toward the bike path.

Tweet: "I've lost control of my bladder. I burst into tears for no reason. Seeing things…I've no grasp of what is real."

⇨ ⇨ ⇨

DAY TWO. DAWN

The long night challenged every one of us moment to moment to reaffirm why we are subjecting ourselves to this suffering. Regardless if you're leading the race or are DFL, we all suffer. It is a battle far more mental than physical. During this battle you will ask yourself, is this worth it? All it takes is once to not have a strong enough answer for the question…a moment of weakness, and you will find a reason to quit. The night has whittled the field of athletes away to single digits.

⇨ ⇨ ⇨

DAY TWO. O-NINE-O-FIVE

The aid station materializes through the fog yet again like a recurring lucid dream where the more I struggle toward it, the more I'm Zeno's fucking arrow. I pass through it and swipe Red Vines from the table without breaking stride.

The race director calls after me with concern. "How are you feeling?"

"Don't pull me. I can do this! Don't pull me no matter fucking what!"

I've less than a half marathon left. With a noon cutoff I should be able to walk it in the rest of the way, but this does not give me comfort. You can read all over endurance forums about the tragedy of athletes getting pulled from races, or runners' bodies just quitting on them and refusing to take their owners one step farther after running ninety-five miles. Ironman triathlete Julie Moss comes to mind. After fighting physical and mental battles for 140 miles, she was within the length of a driveway from the finish line and victory when she collapsed, crawling on her hands and knees toward the tape, only to get passed by another racer.

⇨ ⇨ ⇨

DAY TWO. ELEVEN-O-ONE

I've death marched for the past two hours. I don't even bother to pick my feet up from the concrete to step. I kinda shuffle along by shifting my weight side to side and leaning forward. My bladder has released again, and my gut is so distended, my belly button threatens to pop out like a turkey timer. I need to puke, but I manage to hold it in.

The race director's wife pedals next to me on a bike.

She says, "Great job. Two miles left!"

"Thanks."

"I need you to start running."

"No way. Impossible. Besides, I don't have to run. Plenty of time."

"How you finish matters. How do you want to remember the end?"

She smiles, then pedals away.

Take a step…

I pick up my pace, but my feet scream in pain and I return to shuffling.

There's a signpost aside the path a bit farther down… What if I ran to that? I can do that.

After I pass the signpost I slow down, but not to the death march pace of before. Instead, I pick a couple sitting on a beach towel. When I pass them, I keep running until I cross the finish line to a cheering Amanda and a group of volunteers. I do burpees, but stop at two. The race director hands me my finisher's belt buckle. It has the Buddha engraved on it. Below the godhead the words, "Enlightened 100."

Amanda hugs me and I kiss her cheek.

The race director says, "Congratulations! You've accomplished something only point-zero-zero-zero-zero-one percent of the world's population has ever done."

A volunteer says, "Fourth place among men, fifth place finisher overall!"

"Ha-ha!" Amanda says. "You know what that means?"

"What?"

"A girl beat you… You got chicked!"

A volunteer takes my photo holding my buckle with Amanda. We walk toward the aid station table. To be accurate, she walks and I shuffle.

She says, "Are you sure you're going to be able to handle going to Vegas in a couple days? You never cared about winning ATM awards."

"I don't. I'm in no danger of winning anything I'm nominated for, but it's my first year back in the business so I have to be seen pretending to care."

At the aid station, smiling volunteers load up a plate of food for me. I thank them and work on a cinnamon roll as we walk to the car.

"Really good people, Erik."

"Heh, yeah…I'm gonna do this again. I'll volunteer at a race for sure. The people here are special."

"Maybe then you'll see what I've known all along."

"What's that?"

"The human race…it's worth participating in."

End.

"Dedicated to all human beings." —Radiohead

For the OG Forum

ACKNOWLEDGMENTS

THANK YOU, YUVAL TAYLOR, the first publishing professional to believe in my talent (huge for a writer's confidence during the nascent stages of his career), and for introducing me to my literary agent; Tucker Max, for reading my work early on and creating a thread on The Rudius Media forums to develop my storytelling craft. I printed and carried your first email of encouragement in my wallet for years until it disintegrated. My literary agents, Peter McGuigan and (Mr.) Matt Wise, at Foundry Literary + Media for the postgrad level refinement of my craft, the countless editing hours, for fighting for me, and your friendships. John August and Craig Mazin for the *Scriptnotes Podcast*, a great educational tool for all storytellers regardless of the medium. Thank you, Tyson and the Rare Bird staff, you're the new incarnation of Grove Press from its mid-century heyday, and I'm proud to be on your list. Jerry Stahl, for *Permanent Midnight*, which showed me what is possible in a memoir. Joe Rogan, for always telling the truth. The Cult writing workshop. My beta readers. Axel

Braun, for providing a safe space to fail while I learned how to perform. Without that talk back in '02, I would have quit and this tome wouldn't exist. "Amanda," my greatest advocate in life. And to my detractors who said I couldn't: your vitriol is a napalm-soaked log tossed into my furnace of desire (Thanks, cocksuckers!).